THE ICSA COMPANY LAW HANDBOOK

THE ICSA
COMPANY LAW HANDBOOK

Nigel Banerjee

icsa
Trust through governance

Published by
ICSA Publishing
Saffron House
6–10 Kirby Street
London EC1N 8TS

© ICSA Publishing Ltd, 2015

All rights reserved. No part of this publication may be reproduced, stored in a retrieval system, or transmitted, in any form, or by any means, electronic, mechanical, photocopying, recording or otherwise, without prior permission, in writing, from the publisher.

The right of Nigel Banerjee to be identified as author of this Work has been asserted by him in accordance with sections 77 and 78 of the Copyright, Designs and Patents Act 1988.

Designed and typeset by Paul Barrett Book Production, Cambridge

Printed in Great Britain by Hobbs the Printers Ltd, Totton, Hampshire

British Library Cataloguing in Publication Data A catalogue record for this book is available from the British Library

ISBN 9781860726118

AN INTRODUCTION TO COMPANY LAW

1.2.2.3 This background is important for three reasons.

- First, the sheer size of the Act means that it covers an enormous amount of ground, and that in turn means that it contains answers to many of the company law questions one encounters in practice. For example, if the question concerns the means by which a company may change its name, the starting point is s. 77(1), which states that a company may change its name by special resolution or by any other means specified in its articles of association. Similarly, if a director wants to know what duties he owes to the company, he will find them set out in Part 10 of the Act, and if a company secretary wants to know what information needs to be included in the company's register of members, he will find the answer in s. 113.

  Given that the Act is so wide in scope, it will be obvious that anyone who works with companies regularly needs to gain some idea as to what topics it addresses. This is no easy task, and the only really effective way to familiarise oneself with the Act's contents is actually to make use of it over a period of years. However, Figure 1.1 below provides an indication of the main areas dealt with in the Act which are likely to be of interest in relation to a private company's day-to-day activities.

Figure 1.1 Breakdown of CA2006

Area of law	Main provisions in the Act
Company formation	ss. 7–16
Articles of association	ss. 17–28, 31–36
General filing requirement	ss. 29–30
Execution of documents	ss. 43–52
Choice/change of name (including business names)	ss. 53–81, ss. 1192–1208 (business names)
Registered office	ss. 86–88
Register of members	ss. 112–128
Appointment/removal of directors (including register of directors)	ss. 154–169
Directors' duties	ss. 170–187
Transactions with directors (including long-term service contracts)	ss. 188–231
Directors' indemnities	ss. 232–238
Ratification of directors' breach of duty	s. 239
Company secretaries	ss. 270–280

Shareholder decisions (including written resolutions, decisions by a sole member and general meetings)	ss. 281–361
Accounts (including small companies regime, directors' report, deadline for filing accounts)	ss. 380–474
Audit and the auditor (including appointment/removal of auditor, auditors' liability)	ss. 475–539
Shares (including allotment, pre-emption right, alteration, class rights, reduction of capital, purchase of own shares, redeemable shares, dividends)	ss. 540–737, 829–853
Share certificates and transfer of shares	ss. 768–790
Annual return	ss. 854–858
Charges (including company's register of charges)	ss. 859A–894
Unfair prejudice remedy	ss. 994–999
Striking off (including voluntary striking off)	ss. 1000–1011
Service of documents on company, directors, etc.	ss. 1139–1142
Communications by/to company	ss. 1143–1148, Schedules 4 and 5
Definitions of terms used in the Act	ss. 1158–1174, Schedule 8

- Second, the fact that the Act was preceded by a lengthy consultation process and subsequent debates in Parliament means that anyone seeking to comply with its provisions can draw upon a considerable amount of background material by way of guidance.

    As with any piece of legislation, the best source of guidance on the meaning of the Act is case law. Another source of information is the detailed explanatory notes which accompany the Act. Although the notes are not endorsed by Parliament, they provide useful commentary on many of the Act's more opaque provisions; for instance, while it may not be immediately obvious that the common law unanimous consent rule (see paragraphs 8.3.8.1 to 8.3.8.6) is preserved by s. 281(4), which does not expressly refer to the rule, the relevant explanatory note states clearly that that is, indeed, the effect of the sub-section.

The reports of the parliamentary debates in Hansard, and the numerous consultation papers and reports produced in the course of the development of the legislation, provide a further source of guidance as to what the Act was seeking to achieve. The best example of this may be in relation to the directors' duties. The statutory provisions in this area are already being fleshed out by court decisions, but the process is a slow one, and the text of the parliamentary debates provides indicative answers to at least some of the questions which arise when one comes to consider how the duties are to be applied in practice. In fact, some years ago the government went so far as to publish what it felt were key excerpts from the debates in an effort to provide interested parties with a starting point for their analysis of the newly codified duties ('Companies Act 2006 – Duties of company directors – Ministerial statements' (DTI, June 2007)). Even today, these excerpts contain valuable guidance as to the scope of the duties.

- Third, it is helpful to be aware that the English company law regime has recently been subject to an extremely wide-ranging review, because the lesson one can draw from that fact is that the regime is unlikely to undergo further large-scale remodelling in the foreseeable future. In other words, the broad outline of company law as it is currently set out in CA2006 is unlikely to change in the short to medium term, and those who are charged with ensuring compliance with the regime should find this relative stability reassuring.

That is not to say that specific areas of the law will not be amended. The aftermath of the introduction of the Act has seen a number of consultations on proposed changes, some of them fairly significant. In the summer of 2013, for example, BIS sought views as to whether the core loyalty duty of a director should be amended in respect of bank directors, such that they should be obliged to give the financial soundness of the bank priority over shareholders' interests (a proposal which, as it happens, was subsequently rejected). Company law needs to adapt to the world around it, and is therefore never static, but while there will always be a need to consider changes in specific areas, a further review on a scale which might affect the big picture of the legal framework is certainly not on the horizon.

1.2.2.4 As substantial as CA2006 is, it is supplemented by numerous pieces of secondary legislation. Detailed rules on the form and content of company accounts, for example, are contained in the Small Companies and Groups (Accounts and Directors' Report) Regulations 2008 and the Large and Medium-sized Companies and Groups (Accounts and Reports) Regulations 2008, while trading disclosure rules, which require companies to disclose certain corporate details on letters, emails and websites, are contained in the Company, Limited Liability Partnership and Business (Names and Trading Disclosures) Regulations 2015, and model forms of articles of association are set out in the Companies (Model Articles) Regulations 2008.

1.2.2.5 Although the Act received Royal Assent on 8 November 2006, most of its provisions came into force in tranches over the following three years, the final tranche taking effect on 1 October 2009. This staggered implementation was achieved by means of eight commencement orders which not only brought particular sections of the Act into force on a particular date, but also contained provisions addressing the transition from CA1985 to the new regime. Some of those transitional provisions remain relevant today, so it is important to remember that the commencement orders are not merely part of the history of CA2006, but, in part at least, form a source of current law. By way of an example, consider paragraph 19 of Schedule 3 to the third commencement order (SI 2007/2194), which states that the obligation under CA2006 s. 248 to keep board minutes for at least ten years applies to board meetings held on or after 1 October 2007, and that CA1985 s.382, which does not specify any minimum period for retaining board minutes, continues to apply to board meetings held before that date. The effect of this provision is that older companies need to be aware that they are in the curious position of being obliged to keep their pre-October 2007 minutes forever, but being permitted to discard their more recent board minutes after ten years (although best practice is, of course, to keep all board minutes indefinitely).

1.2.2.6 Finally, on the matter of CA2006, it is important to note that the Act is not the only piece of primary legislation in the company law sphere. As far as private companies limited by shares are concerned, the two most important statutes other than CA2006 are the Insolvency Act 1986 and the Company Directors Disqualification Act 1986. It will be apparent from their names that these Acts are of only peripheral relevance to the day-to-day activities of a well-run company, but they contain provisions which are of considerable importance to companies which are encountering financial difficulties or are not being managed properly. The former not only deals with the process by which a company goes into administration or is wound up, but supplements a director's core duties under CA2006 by requiring him, in effect, to seek to minimise the damage to creditors in the event that the company is about to fail. The latter gives the court the power to disqualify a person from acting as a director in certain circumstances; for example, the court is obliged to disqualify a director of a failed company whom it adjudges to be unfit to be involved in the management of a company.

1.2.3 Case law

1.2.3.1 From a compliance perspective, the main source of the law governing companies is undoubtedly CA2006. However, it is important to avoid falling into the trap of assuming that case law has no role to play.

1.2.3.2 Naturally, court decisions are of interest inasmuch as they consider the meaning of statutory provisions. On the whole, CA2006 is well drafted, but inevitably some of its provisions contain words and phrases which are susceptible of different interpretations. Take, for instance, the unfair prejudice remedy in s. 994, which refers to the conducting of a company's affairs 'in a manner that is unfairly prejudicial' to the members' interests. The concept of unfairness is potentially extremely elastic, but the large body of case law on this point has restricted its scope in this context, making it clear that the courts will not apply their own notions of fairness, but will be guided by the need to give effect to any agreement between the parties (*O'Neill v Phillips* [1999] BCC 600). Another example concerns s. 51, which provides that if a person enters into a contract purportedly on behalf of a company, but before the company has actually been formed, the contract has effect as if it is made by him personally 'subject to any agreement to the contrary'. The courts have considered the meaning of 'agreement' in this context, and have taken the view that an express agreement is required (*Phonogram Ltd v Lane* [1982] 1 QB 938).

1.2.3.3 The courts also create company law.

- In some instances, it will be apparent to anyone seeking to ensure compliance with the law that he needs to see what the courts have to say on a particular point. For example, while the duties owed by directors to their company are set out in the Act, the legislation does not specify the consequences of a breach of the duties, expressly leaving the question of remedies to be determined by the courts (s. 178). Similarly, s. 168 gives shareholders the power to remove a director from his office by means of an ordinary resolution, but does not address the question as to whether weighted voting rights can be used to, in effect, entrench a particular director; the courts have stepped in to answer that question in the affirmative (*Bushell v Faith* [1970] AC 1099).
- In some instances, however, it may not be quite so obvious that judge-made law exists. The best example of this concerns s. 21, which gives shareholders the power to alter the company's articles by means of a special resolution. There is nothing in the wording of the section to suggest that the courts have imposed any restrictions on the use of this power, but in fact they have: if the power is not exercised bona fide for the benefit of the company as a whole, it will be struck down (*Allen v Gold Reefs of West Africa, Ltd* [1900] 1 Ch 656). Another example is the common law unanimous consent rule, which provides that a unanimous decision of the shareholders is effective even if the Act's formal decision-making procedures are not complied with (*Re Duomatic Ltd* [1969] 2 Ch 365). Although, as noted in paragraph 1.2.2.4, the Act preserves the rule, it refers to it in such opaque terms (see s. 281(4)) that anyone who is not already aware of the rule would be unlikely thereby to be alerted to its existence.

1.2.3.4 Given the various alerting services which are available in the market, legal advisers should find it easy to keep up to date with case law developments.

1.2.3.5 Company secretaries and, especially, directors, are in a slightly different position. Not only might they not have ready access to such facilities, but they may in any case feel that they are not justified in taking the time to pore over reports of the latest cases. The fact is, though, that case law forms part of the company law regime, and so the temptation to assume that it may safely be ignored must be resisted. Just as anyone involved in running a company needs to have an understanding of his (and his company's) obligations under CA2006 and other relevant legislation, so too he needs to ensure that – one way or another – he is familiar with those aspects of the company law regime which happen to be set out in court decisions.

1.2.4 Articles of association

1.2.4.1 In practice, a company's articles of association are every bit as important, in relation to its day-to-day activities, as CA2006, and in fact the two often need to be read together, for the articles normally contain extensive provisions modifying or supplementing the requirements of the Act.

1.2.4.2 From the perspective of someone who is relatively new to company law, the problem with articles of association is that it is difficult to define their scope. While the Act requires a company to have articles (s. 18), it does not impose any requirements as to their contents.

1.2.4.3 Some guidance as to the areas which might be dealt with in a company's articles may be derived from those provisions of the Act which are explicitly stated to be default provisions, subject to modification in the company's articles. Section 550, for example, gives directors of private companies with only one class of shares authority to allot further shares of that class 'except to the extent that they are prohibited from doing so by the company's articles'. Consider also s. 284, which states that shareholders voting on a written resolution have one vote for each share they hold, but goes on to provide that this rule is 'subject to any provision of the company's articles'.

1.2.4.4 Further guidance may be derived from an examination of matters upon which the Act is silent, since one would expect the articles to fill in many of those gaps. Take, for instance, the means by which directors take decisions. The Act does not tell us whether directors may take decisions by way of a written resolution, what the quorum is for a board meeting or whether directors may attend a board meeting by telephone. Another area on which the Act is silent is the procedure for declaring dividends. The Act has a good deal to say about the funds from which dividends may be paid, and the accounts by reference to which the necessary calculations must be made, but does not tell us whether it is for the shareholders or the directors to declare a dividend, whether a dividend may be paid otherwise than in cash or whether an interim dividend may be paid.

1.2.4.5 In practical terms, however, the best guide to the usual contents of a company's articles are the model articles of association, which apply by default if a company chooses not to adopt a set of bespoke articles (see s. 20 and, for the model articles themselves, the Companies (Model Articles) Regulations 2008). The key areas covered in the model articles for private companies limited by shares are as follows:

- the shareholders' limited liability;
- the basic division of powers between the shareholders and the directors;
- the appointment of directors;
- the means by which directors take decisions;
- shares, including the procedure for declaring dividends;
- general meetings of shareholders; and
- directors' indemnity and insurance.

Whether or not a private company chooses to adopt the model articles, its articles will almost certainly deal with these core topics.

1.2.4.6 As a source of rules affecting a company's activities, then, the articles are of great importance, and anyone who is responsible for ensuring compliance with the company law regime needs to get into the habit of consulting them regularly.

1.2.4.7 Consider the case of a company secretary who is asked to set the wheels in motion for the removal of one director and the appointment of two new directors. CA2006 will tell him, among other things, that a board must have at least one director who is a 'natural person' (as opposed to a company), that there is a statutory procedure for removing a director by means of an ordinary resolution and that shareholders of private companies may pass resolutions by means of a written resolution. Only the articles, however, will tell him, among other things, whether there is any upper limit on the number of directors who may be appointed, the means by which a director is appointed and whether any of the shareholders have weighted voting rights on a resolution to alter the board's composition.

1.3 Company law as a balancing act

1.3.1 While most company law experts would agree that there is nothing in CA2006 that comes close to the impenetrability of, say, the tax regime, there seems to be a view that company law is inherently difficult, and certainly newcomers to the field sometimes struggle to get to grips with it.

1.3.2 One reason for this is simply that company law covers a great deal of ground and imposes many detailed prescriptive requirements on companies. Unfortunately, there are no short-cuts to acquiring a familiarity with the regime's myriad technical rules. As one works in this area over a period of time, one slowly starts to absorb the Act's key provisions, the main lessons to be drawn from the case law and the interaction between individual companies' articles and the rest of the governing framework.

1.3.3 Another reason is that company law does not consist of neat building blocks which a newcomer can study in turn, gradually building up an understanding of the regime in a series of logical steps. This is one of those areas of the law which makes sense only once one has at least a basic understanding of *all* of its component parts. As a result, someone who has just started to work with companies may not feel that he is beginning to appreciate how the various elements of the regime fit together for quite some time. Fortunately, there is a solution to this problem. If one takes the time at an early stage to think about the big picture – what the regime is trying to achieve, and how it goes about its task – one begins to see how the different aspects of the regime fit together, and the broad scheme of the law starts to make sense.

1.3.4 The aim of the regime

1.3.4.1 What, then, is the regime trying to achieve? In simple terms, it is seeking to provide an efficient and attractive vehicle for carrying on a business. When the initial consultation document which launched the review of company law in March 1998 (see paragraph 1.2.2) set out proposed terms of reference for the review, the first item read as follows:

> 'To consider how core company law can be modernised in order to provide a simple, efficient and cost-effective framework for carrying out business activity which: a. permits the maximum amount of freedom and flexibility to those organising and directing the enterprise; b. at the same time protects, through regulation where necessary, the interests of those involved with the enterprise, including shareholders, creditors and employees; and c. is drafted in clear, concise and unambiguous language which can be readily understood by those involved in business enterprise.'

1.3.5 Achieving the aim

1.3.5.1 Contained in the passage above is a hint as to the means by which the regime seeks to achieve its aim of providing an attractive business vehicle. Paragraph b refers to the protection of the interests of shareholders, creditors and employees, and this is the key: if the vehicle is to be truly fit for purpose, it needs to address the interests not only of those who wish to carry on the business in the first place, namely the shareholders, but also of those who are affected by the company.

1.3.5.2 This point can be illustrated by reference to the essential features of a company, which are as follows:

- It is, in law, a legal entity in its own right, a 'person' distinct from those involved in forming, funding and running it – as a result, it is able to enter into contracts in its own name, hold property in its own name, hire employees in its own name and bring legal proceedings in its own name.
- Those who take a stake in it (the shareholders) can choose to enjoy the benefit of limited liability, which means that whereas the company itself is fully liable for its debts in the normal way, they can opt to limit their liability for those debts.
- It incorporates a ready-made governance structure in which shareholders (the owners) play a largely supervisory role in running its affairs, while directors (the managers) are responsible for carrying on its day-to-day business – this gives the participants the option of acting primarily as investors, with no obligation to play a full role in managing the business.
- It issues shares, which can be used to take profits out of the company on an ongoing basis in the form of dividends, and which can be sold if the owners wish to end their association with the company.

1.3.5.3 It will be apparent that these features exist in order to make the corporate vehicle attractive to those who wish to start a business, namely the shareholders. Take the option of limited liability, for instance. Naturally, an entrepreneur will be more inclined to invest his money in a business venture if he knows that he will not face personal liability for the company's debts should it fail. Similarly, he will be more inclined to invest if he feels that he will be able to realise his investment relatively easily, and the share is a mechanism which allows him to do just that, whether by drawing profits from the venture in the form of dividends or by selling his shares to a third party.

1.3.5.4 The regime recognises, however, that a vehicle which caters only for the interests of shareholders will run into problems. Again, consider the option of limited liability. While this aspect of company law is very attractive to shareholders, it has a decidedly negative impact on creditors, since it severely restricts their ability to pursue the shareholders in the event that the company fails. If the law did not offer some protection to creditors, they would be reluctant to extend credit to companies, and the company would therefore lose its effectiveness as a vehicle for carrying on a business. It is for this reason that companies are required to publish accounts, make public information about their directors and comply with trading disclosure rules. These obligations, and many others like them, serve a real purpose: they are part of a deliberate exercise to ensure that creditors are able to make an informed decision about whether they want to do business with the company.

1.3.5.5 As to the identity of the parties whose interests the company law regime takes into account, it will be obvious that the main parties are the shareholders, the directors and the company's creditors. To that list one might also add the company itself and society at large, a nebulous concept, admittedly, but one which catches the likes of employees, the environment, the local community and the wider economy.

1.3.6 Making sense of company law

1.3.6.1 Company law, then, aims to provide a vehicle for carrying on a business which is efficient and attractive, and which strikes a fair balance between the interests of those who are involved in, or affected by, the vehicle's activities.

1.3.6.2 Looked at in this way, the regime's intricacies begin to seem less mysterious. Thus:

- directors' duties exist primarily in order to protect the shareholders, who have entrusted the management of their company (and, therefore, their money) to the board;
- restrictions on a company's freedom to pay dividends are designed to protect creditors, for their aim is to ensure that companies retain their capital as a source of funds out of which to pay their debts in the event that they eventually become insolvent;
- the common law rule requiring any amendment to the company's articles to be made for the benefit of the company seeks to protect minority shareholders from oppression by majority shareholders;
- the statutory pre-emption right is designed to protect shareholders' interests by ensuring that the board cannot dilute their stake in the company against their will;
- the restrictions on a public company's freedom to allot shares otherwise than for cash seek to protect creditors and existing shareholders by ensuring that shares are not issued for less than their true value;
- the written resolution procedure is made available to shareholders of private companies in order to assist smaller companies by minimising the administrative burden to which they are subject; and
- the success duty seeks to address the interests of society at large by requiring directors to take into account such matters as the impact of the company's activities on employees and the environment during their decision-making process.

1.3.6.3 Company law may be complex and, in places, cumbersome, but it is not composed of random rules and requirements. Once it is appreciated that the underlying logic of the regime is to be found in its attempt to ensure that the company is a suitable vehicle for commercial activity by balancing the interests of the relevant parties, and once the purpose of individual provisions becomes clear, the pieces of the jigsaw start to fall into place, and the regime as a whole starts to make sense.

2

Forming a company

> ### Summary
> - In order to form a company, three documents must be delivered to Companies House: a memorandum of association, a set of articles of association and Companies House Form IN01 (Application to register a company).
> - In many cases, it will be easy to complete Companies House Form IN01. However, one of the areas which can cause difficulties in practice is the obligation to state the proposed name of the company, for the rules governing the choice of a company's name are extremely complex.
> - Once a company has been formed, the directors will need to hold a board meeting to attend to various administrative matters.

2.1 Introduction

2.1.1 This chapter discusses the procedure for forming a private company and the company law issues which it raises. It comprises the following sections:

- The incorporation process – this section details the information and documentation requirements which anyone seeking to form a company must comply with, and in particular considers various potential difficulties which might be encountered in connection with Companies House Form IN01 (Application to register a company).
- Incorporation – this section notes the key consequences which flow from the fact that the company has been incorporated.
- Post-incorporation – this section contains a list of the main matters which will normally be addressed at a newly formed company's first board meeting.

2.1.2 The implications of the company's formation, including its existence as a distinct legal entity and the acquisition on the part of its shareholders of the benefit of limited liability, are considered in detail in Chapter 3, The company as a separate entity.

2.2 The incorporation process

2.2.1 It is remarkably easy to form a private company in the United Kingdom. The costs involved are modest, primarily because CA2006 does not impose a minimum capital requirement on private companies, and the information and documentation requirements are minimal.

2.2.2 The incorporation process can be undertaken electronically (subscribers wishing to form a company electronically can use either a formation agent or (provided the company is to adopt the model articles in their entirety) the Companies House Web Incorporation Service – details of these options are available on the Companies House website) or by submitting hard copies of certain documents to Companies House. By way of an indication of the fees involved, Companies House charges the following fees for hard copy applications: £40 for a standard incorporation service and £100 for a same-day service (Companies House Guidance Booklet GP1 – 'Incorporation and names' according to the booklet, straightforward applications in hard copy using the standard incorporation service are normally processed within five days).

2.2.3 In order to form a company, the following documents must be submitted to Companies House:

- a memorandum of association (s. 9(1));
- a set of articles of association (unless the company is adopting the model articles under the Act in their entirety) (s. 9(5)(b)); and
- a completed Companies House Form IN01 (Application to register a company).

2.2.4 Memorandum of association

2.2.4.1 The memorandum of association is a very simple document in which the subscribers (i.e. the prospective shareholders) record their desire to form a company. The content requirements for a memorandum are set out in s. 8(1) of the Act, which specifies that the documents must state that the subscribers wish to form a company, that they agree to become members of the company and (in the case of a company limited by shares) that they agree to take at least one share each in the company.

2.2.4.2 Section 8(2) goes on to specify that a memorandum must be in the prescribed form and that it must be 'authenticated' by each subscriber.

2.2.4.3 The prescribed form is contained in Schedule 1 to the Companies (Registration) Regulations 2008 (SI 2008/3014), a copy of which is set out in Appendix 1 (SI 2008/3014). Schedule 1 sets out the prescribed form for use where the company is to have a share capital. Schedule 2 sets out the prescribed form for use where the company will not have a share capital). Perhaps the only possible difficulty that can arise in connection with the memorandum concerns compliance with the prescribed form, for Companies House has made it clear that any deviations from the form, whether by way of the inclusion of extra information or the omission of specified information, will result in the application to form a company being rejected. According to the Companies House Guidance Booklet GP1 – 'Incorporation and names': 'Please note, the wording of the memorandum is prescribed and it cannot be amended in any way. If you add or change the wording, your application will not be accepted.' In other words, the prescribed form is to be followed strictly. There should not be any difficulty about ensuring that none of the wording in Schedule 1 is omitted, but there may be a temptation to add in extra information, such as the addresses of the subscribers or the total number of shares which each of them will take in the company. That temptation must be resisted.

2.2.4.4 In the case of a hard copy application, the 'authentication' requirement amounts to nothing more than a requirement that each subscriber signs the memorandum (Rule 23(3), Volume 2, Registrar's Rules 2009 (available on the Companies House website)).

2.2.4.5 Although the language adopted in the paragraphs above assumes that there will be more than one subscriber to the memorandum, a private company (or, for that matter, a public company) can, in fact, be formed under the Act by a single subscriber (s. 7(1)).

2.2.4.6 The memorandum plays a vital role in the formation of a company, in that it confirms the subscribers' wish to form a company, but it contains no provisions of continuing significance. It cannot be amended, and there should be no reason to want to amend it. It is, in short, merely an historical document, which has no bearing on the life of a company once it has been duly incorporated. (Prior to the introduction of the Act, by contrast, the memorandum was an important constitutional document which had a very significant impact on a company's activities. The impact of the Act on the memoranda of companies incorporated under earlier companies legislation is discussed in section 3.6.7, in the context of an analysis of the law governing objects clauses.)

2.2.5 Articles of association

2.2.5.1 The Act requires an application to register a company to be accompanied by a set of articles of association 'to the extent that these are not supplied by the default application of model articles' (s. 9(5)(b)).

2.2.5.2 'Model articles' are standard articles of association, prescribed by statutory instrument, which apply to a company which has chosen not to adopt tailored articles (s. 20). There are three sets of model articles, all contained in the Companies (Model Articles) Regulations 2008 (SI 2008/3229): a set for private companies limited by shares, a set for private companies limited by guarantee and a set for public companies.

2.2.5.3 If the subscribers are content to adopt the relevant model articles in their entirety, they will simply need to tick a box to that effect on Companies House Form IN01 (Application to register a company) (section A7, Companies House Form IN01), and will not be required to send a copy of the model articles to Companies House.

2.2.5.4 In many cases, however, the subscribers will want to amend the model articles to suit their needs, or indeed to prepare an entirely bespoke set of articles which are not based on the model articles. If the model articles are not adopted in their entirety, the drafting of the articles is likely to be the most time-consuming and difficult part of the formation process, and certainly the scope of many bespoke articles is such that they can raise numerous difficult points of law. The contents of articles are discussed in Chapter 4 (Articles of association), but it is worth noting here that there are two types of tailored articles: short form articles and long form articles.

- Short form articles state that the model articles apply to the company 'save as follows' (or words to that effect), and then proceed to set out provisions amending or supplementing the wording of the model articles. Thus, they incorporate some or all of the provisions of the model articles by reference.
- Long form articles exclude the model articles altogether, and so do not incorporate any of their provisions by reference. In theory, long form articles may be entirely bespoke, in the sense that none of their provisions replicate those in the model articles. In practice, however, it is far more common for long form articles to adopt some of the provisions of the model articles wholesale, building bespoke provisions around that core of standard wording.

2.2.5.5 The advantage of the short form approach is that the bespoke articles themselves are often quite short. The disadvantage, plainly, is that the company's internal rules are set out in two places: anyone seeking to ensure compliance with them needs to have access to both the short form articles and the relevant model articles. Ultimately, it is a matter of personal preference whether to opt for the short form approach or the long form approach. The key point, for present purposes, is that, whichever approach is adopted, the bespoke articles will need to be filed at Companies House as part of the process of applying to register the company.

2.2.6 Companies House Form IN01

2.2.6.1 The main provisions of CA2006 which concern the formation process are ss. 7 to 16. In addition to requiring the subscribers to send a memorandum of association and a set of articles of association to Companies House, these provisions detail certain information which they must provide. Specifically, the following information, confirmations and consents must be provided in respect of a company limited by shares:

- the company's proposed name (s. 9(2)(a);
- the part of the United Kingdom in which the company's registered office is to be situated (s. 9(2)(b) (i.e. England and Wales, Scotland or Northern Ireland);
- the intended address of the company's registered office (s. 9(5));
- confirmation that the shareholders' liability is to be limited by shares (s. 9(2)(c));
- a statement as to whether the company is to be a private company or a public company (s. 9(2)(d));
- a statement of capital and initial shareholdings (which must contain prescribed information concerning the subscribers and the company's shares) (ss. 9(4)(a) and 10);
- details of the company's director(s) and, if it is to have one, its secretary (ss. 9(4)(c) and 12);
- consent from each director and any secretary to act as such (s. 12); and
- confirmation that the Act's provisions on formation have been complied with (ss.9(1) and 13).

The Small Business, Enterprise and Employment Act 2015 will make minor changes in this area. In particular, it will amend CA2006 s. 12 so as to require the subscribers to state that the director(s) and any secretary have consented to act as such (this change is expected to be introduced in October 2015), and insert a requirement to state the company's proposed business activities (this change is expected to be introduced in April 2016).

2.2.6.2 The details are not to be sent to Companies House piecemeal, but in the shape of Companies House Form IN01 – Application to register a company. A copy of the current version of Form IN01 is set out in Appendix 2.

2.2.6.3 In many cases, the information requirements will pose no difficulties. Some of the requirements can, however, give rise to problems in certain situations, and the discussion below highlights the main areas in which difficulties may be encountered.

2.2.7 Sections A1, A2 and A3: the company's name

2.2.7.1 The choice of the company's name is potentially a far more complicated matter than it may sound, for the rules governing company names are complex and can be difficult to apply in practice.

2.2.7.2 The rules are set out primarily in the Act itself (ss. 53 to 76, as far as the specific question of the choice of a name is concerned) and in supplementary regulations (principally the Company, Limited Liability Partnership and Business (Names and Trading Disclosures) Regulations 2015 (SI 2015/17) and the Company, Limited Liability Partnership and Business Names (Sensitive Words and Expressions) Regulations 2014 (SI 2014/3140)). The core rules, which are listed in Figure 2.1, are discussed in turn below.

Figure 2.1 The core rules affecting a company's choice of name

- The name must be made up of 'permitted characters' and must contain no more than 160 characters.
- If the company is a private company limited by shares, the name must end with the word 'limited' or the abbreviation 'ltd'.
- The name must not contain certain specified sensitive words or expressions unless the Secretary of State for Business, Innovation & Skills has approved their use.
- The name must comply with restrictions on the use of certain words which are contained in legislation other than CA2006.
- The name must not be such that the Secretary of State would consider that its use by the company would constitute a criminal offence or that it is offensive.
- The name must not be the same as a name which is already on the index of company names.
- The name must not be 'too like' a name which is already on the index of company names.
- If the company's name 'gives so misleading an indication of the nature of its activities as to be likely to cause harm to the public', the Secretary of State might order the company to change it.
- If the name is similar to a name in which a third party has goodwill, the third party is entitled to object to the Company Names Tribunal, which has the power to direct the company to change its name.
- Other matters to consider in this connection include the tort of passing off, the Trade Marks Act 1994 and restrictions in the Insolvency Act 1986 on the use of the name of a failed company.

2.2.7.3 The name must be made up of 'permitted characters' and must contain no more than 160 characters (CA2006 s.57; section 2 and Schedule 1, Company, Limited Liability Partnership and Business (Names and Trading Disclosures) Regulations 2015 (SI 2015/17)). The permitted characters comprise the letters of the English alphabet, the numbers 0 to 9, certain forms of punctuation and a selection of signs and symbols (such as '&', '£' and '#'). A name which includes characters from one of the Japanese alphabets, for example, would not be acceptable.

2.2.7.4 If the company is a private company limited by shares, the name must end with the word 'limited' or the abbreviation 'ltd' (s. 59. Sections 60 to 64 detail a number of exceptions to the rule, including in relation to charities (s. 60). Public companies are subject to a similar requirement, section 58 stating that the name of a public company must end with the words 'public limited company' or the abbreviation 'p.l.c.'). This requirement is part of the regime's attempts to ensure that third parties dealing with companies are properly protected. Its purpose is to alert them to the fact that the shareholders of the company have opted to limit their liability for its debts.

2.2.7.5 The name must not contain certain specified sensitive words or expressions unless the Secretary of State for Business, Innovation & Skills has approved their use (for these purposes, references to the Secretary of State are to be treated as references to Companies House, which deals with the name approval process on the Secretary of State's behalf). The key provisions are ss. 54 and 55. Under s. 54, approval is required for a name which would be likely to give the impression that the company is connected with the government, a local authority or any public authority specified in regulations (the regulations in question are the Company, Limited Liability Partnership and Business (Names and Trading Disclosures) Regulations 2015 (SI 2015/17)). Under s. 55, approval is required for a name which includes a word or expression which is specified in Schedule 1 to the Company, Limited Liability Partnership and Business Names (Sensitive Words and Expressions) Regulations 2014 (SI 2014/3140). The rules on sensitive words are designed to protect the public by ensuring that companies do not operate under names which give a misleading impression of their purpose or status, and the words and expressions specified in Schedule 1 include 'charity', 'institute', 'licensing', 'royal' and 'trust'.

2.2.7.6 In many cases, approval will not be granted unless the subscribers have obtained the views of a particular government department or other body and have included a copy of any response received from that department or body with the application to register the company. For example, if the subscribers wish to include the word 'bank' in the company's name, they will need to seek the views of the Financial Conduct Authority, while they will need to get in touch with the Department for Business, Innovation & Skills if they want the name to use the word 'accreditation'. If they are required to obtain the views of a government department or other body in this way, they will need to tick the box in section A2 of Form IN01 and attach the response of the department or body to the form.

2.2.7.7 A good starting point for anyone who is trying to make sense of the law in this area is the Companies House guidance booklet entitled 'Incorporation and names' (GP1, February 2015), which discusses the regime and contains lists of the sensitive words and expressions, including details, where appropriate, of the department or other body whose views need to be obtained. It is always wise, though, to double-check the position by referring directly to the statutory provisions.

2.2.7.8 The name must comply with restrictions on the use of certain words which are contained in legislation other than CA2006. Annex C to the Companies House Guidance Booklet GP1 lists words whose use is prohibited or restricted by legislation other than CA2006. For example, the list notes that the word 'pharmaceutical' is controlled by the Medicines Act 1968 and cannot be used without the approval of the General Pharmaceutical Council or the Pharmaceutical Society of Northern Ireland, and that the use of the expression 'Red Cross' is controlled by the Geneva Conventions Act 1957 and cannot be used. If the name can be used with the approval of a third party, the box in section A2 of Form IN01 will need to be ticked and the response of the third party will need to be attached to the form.

2.2.7.9 The list in Annex C is not exhaustive, which means that subscribers should give careful thought to the name which they wish to adopt, and carry out their own research or seek legal advice if they think there is any chance that the name may contain words whose use is restricted. This is a matter worthy of serious attention, because breach of a restriction may constitute a criminal offence.

2.2.7.10 The name must not be such that the Secretary of State would consider that its use by the company would constitute a criminal offence or that it is offensive (s. 53). As noted in paragraph 2.2.7.9, a breach of a restriction imposed by legislation other than CA2006 might constitute an offence.

2.2.7.11 When the government consulted on reforming the law on company names in 2013, it addressed the question of names which might constitute an offence or be offensive in passing, suggesting that the prohibition would catch the likes of swear words and words which are blasphemous or racially offensive ('Company and Business Names Consultation – Red Tape Challenge' (BIS, February 2013)).

2.2.7.12 The name must not be the same as a name which is already on the index of company names (s. 66). The Act requires the registrar to maintain an index containing the name of every UK company (s. 1099), and, as one might expect, provides that a company cannot adopt as its name a name which is already on the index.

2.2.7.13 More surprisingly, perhaps, the prohibition prevents a company not only from using a name which is identical to an existing name, but also from using a name which is *treated* for these purposes as being the same as an existing name. For example, 'Animaginaryco Plus UK plc' is treated for these purposes as being the same as Animaginaryco + Ltd'. The procedure for determining whether a proposed name is treated as being the same as an existing name is set out in the Company, Limited Liability Partnership and Business (Names and Trading Disclosures) Regulations 2015, and can be rather difficult to apply in practice. However, the Company, Limited Liability Partnership and Business (Names and Trading Disclosures) Regulations 2015 have, in fact, reduced the scope of the prohibition, such that many names which were previously treated as being the same as an existing name no longer fall foul of it, so in most cases the prohibition will not significantly restrict a company's freedom to adopt a name of its choice. What is more, the Company, Limited Liability Partnership and Business (Names and Trading Disclosures) Regulations 2015 provide a limited exemption from the prohibition in relation to companies which are part of the same group; essentially, if the new company wishes to adopt a name which is treated as being the same as the name of an existing company within the same group, the latter can consent to the former's use of the name in question (Regulation 8, Company, Limited Liability Partnership and Business (Names and Trading Disclosures) Regulations 2015). Any such consent will need to be included with Form IN01.

2.2.7.14 As to the practicalities of searching the index, the WebCHeck service on the Companies House website includes a free Company Name Availability Search feature, which identifies any names on the index which are identical to, or treated for these purposes as being the same as, a proposed name. The search feature is no doubt very reliable, but in cases where the new company is required as a matter of urgency, such that a rejection of the proposed name by Companies House and the consequent delay in incorporating the company would cause serious problems, it would be prudent to double-check the results of the online search by working through the rules in the Company, Limited Liability Partnership and Business (Names and Trading Disclosures) Regulations 2015 step by step, in order to ensure that the proposed name will not be treated as being the same as an existing name.

2.2.7.15 The name must not be 'too like' a name which is already on the index of company names (s. 67). If a company registers a name which is, in the Secretary of State's opinion, too like a name which is already on the register, the Secretary of State can direct the company to change its name. Neither the Act, nor any of the regulations concerning company names, provides guidance on the circumstances in which a name might be found to be 'too like' an existing name, but some assistance is to be found in the Companies House Guidance Booklet GP1. According to the guidance booklet: 'A name may be "too like" an existing name if it differs from another name on the index by only a few characters, signs symbols or punctuation or if it looks and sounds the same.'

2.2.7.16 It will be apparent that this rule acts as a substantial supplement to the 'same as' provisions discussed immediately above, and as such must be given serious consideration when choosing a new company's name. There are, however, two points to note in this connection. First, it would appear that the Secretary of State (acting through Companies House) will normally take action under s. 67 only if there is a formal objection to the name by a third party. Second, any direction to change the name must be made within 12 months of the company's registration under the name in question (s. 68).

2.2.7.17 If the company's name 'gives so misleading an indication of the nature of its activities as to be likely to cause harm to the public', the Secretary of State might order the company to change it (s. 76). As to the sorts of situation in which this rule might be engaged, an earlier version of Companies House Guidance Booklet GP1 (Companies House Guidance Booklet GPI – 'Incorporation and names' (June 2013) gave the example of a name which suggests that training courses offered by the company lead to a recognised qualification.

2.2.7.18 If the name is similar to a name in which a third party has goodwill, the third party is entitled to object to the Company Names Tribunal, which has the power to direct the company to change its name. This aspect of the rules governing company names is dealt with in CA2006 ss. 69 to 74, and in the Company Names Adjudicator Rules 2008 (SI 2008/1738). A useful source of information on the practicalities involved in making an objection or establishing a defence to an objection is the Company Names Tribunal's website. Section 69 seeks to ensure that a company does not improperly take advantage of a name in respect of which a third party has accumulated goodwill. Specifically, it is designed to address the problem of opportunistic registration, where a company adopts a particular name with the intention of obtaining money from a third party or preventing him from using the name. Thus, if a company is formed with a name which is very similar to that of a well-known multinational in the hope that the multinational will be willing to pay the company to stop using the name, the multinational will be able to object to the company's use of the name under s. 69.

2.2.7.19 The detailed workings of s. 69 are not unduly complicated. Essentially, the section sets out a two-stage test for determining whether the company will have to change its name. At the first stage, the third party (referred to in the section as 'the applicant') must show that the name is either 'the same as a name associated with the applicant in which he has goodwill' or 'sufficiently similar to such a name that its use in the United Kingdom would be likely to mislead by suggesting a connection between the company and the applicant'. If one of these grounds has been established, the company will be directed to change its name unless it has a defence, as follows:

(i) if the company can show that it adopted the name in good faith or that the interests of the applicant are not significantly affected, it will be allowed to keep the name

(ii) if the company can show that the name was registered before the applicant began the activities which generated the goodwill which he is seeking to protect, that it is using the name, that it is planning to use the name and has incurred substantial start-up costs, that it previously used the name and is now dormant or that it adopted the name in the course of a company formation business, it will be allowed to keep the name *unless* the applicant can demonstrate that the name was in fact adopted in order to obtain money from him or to prevent him from using the name.

2.2.7.20 Although s. 69(7) gives the term 'goodwill' a broad definition by stating that it 'includes reputation of any description', it will be apparent from the above discussion that its scope is not unduly wide, in that, for example, it will not affect a company which innocently adopts a name which happens to be similar to a name in which someone else has goodwill. It is also worthy of note, finally, that as of February 2015 a fee of £400 is payable by a third party who wishes to object to a company's name.

2.2.7.21 Although the Act is the main source of rules governing company names, other areas of the law may have an impact on a company's freedom to adopt a name of its choice. It was noted in paragraph 2.2.7.8 that various other pieces of legislation impose restrictions on the use of particular words. In addition, the following aspects of the wider law will in some cases need to be considered when choosing a name.

- **The tort of passing off.** A tort is a class of civil wrong which involves a breach of a general rule of law (as opposed, for example, to a breach of a provision of a contract). The tort of passing off has been described as follows: 'The law of passing off can be summarised in one short general proposition – no man may pass off his goods as those of another' (*Reckitt & Colman Products Ltd v Borden Inc* [1990] 1 WLR 491, per Lord Oliver). More specifically, the tort involves a misrepresentation made by a person which leads the public to believe that his goods or services are the goods or services of a third party, and which damages the third party's goodwill. Crucially, the misrepresentation does not have to be made intentionally, so whereas the procedure under s. 69 seeks to protect a third party's goodwill against deliberate attack, a company which, quite innocently, uses a name which happens to cause the public to believe that its goods are those of a third party may find itself liable to pay damages for the tort of passing off.

- **The Trade Marks Act 1994.** Depending upon the nature of the company's activities, its name may contribute to an infringement by it of a third party's registered trade mark. The Trade Marks Act 1994 provides for the registration of trade marks, which it defines as follows: 'any sign capable of being represented graphically which is capable of distinguishing goods or services of one undertaking from those of other undertakings. A trade mark may, in particular, consist of words (including personal names), designs, letters, numerals or the shape of goods or their packaging' (s. 1(1), Trade Marks Act 1994). A company's name may form an element of an infringement of a registered trade mark in various ways. For example, if a company's name contains words which are a registered trade mark, and its business involves goods which are identical to those in respect of which the trade mark has been registered, it will be exposing itself to the risk of legal action by the owner of the trade mark (ss. 10 and 14, Trade Marks Act 1994. Note that the Act also creates criminal offences in relation to the use of a third party's registered trade mark (s. 92)).

    The law governing trade marks is complex, and in some cases specialist advice from an intellectual property lawyer will be required. In most cases, however, it should suffice for those who are choosing the company name to check that the proposed name does not contain any words which are the same as, or similar to, any words which appear on the trade marks database which is available for inspection on the Intellectual Property Office's website.

- **Restrictions on the use of the name of a failed company.** Under the Insolvency Act 1986, a director of a failed company may be prohibited from forming or managing a company whose name is the same as, or similar to, the company name or business name of the failed company (Insolvency Act 1986 s.216).

    The prohibition addresses the problem of 'phoenix trading', where a director of a failed company forms a new company which acquires the failed company's business at an undervalue and carries it on under a similar name to that of the failed company. Although the directors are thus able to use the medium of the new company to carry on trading as before, the use of a similar name allowing them to take advantage of the failed company's goodwill, the creditors of the failed company are left with debts which they have no prospect of recovering. In the words of the Company Law Review Steering Group: 'At the worst, phoenix trading represents a dishonest exploitation of limited liability by unscrupulous individuals whose commercially unsustainable operations survive only at the expense of their creditors' (Paragraph 15.56, 'Modern Company Law: Final Report', Company Law Review Steering Group, July 2001).

However, the prohibition is not confined to cases where directors have behaved unscrupulously. Its effect is simply that, in general, no one who was a director of a failed company is permitted to exploit any goodwill remaining in that company through the use of another company with a similar or identical name.

Although there are several situations in which the prohibition will not apply, Insolvency Act 1986 s.216(3) and Rules 4.228 to 4.230, Insolvency Rules 1986), and in any case it has effect only for a period of five years after the company's failure, directors who have been involved with a company which has gone into insolvent liquidation need to consider carefully whether, if they wish to become involved with another company with a similar or identical name, they might fall foul of the prohibition. The consequences of breaching the prohibition are potentially serious. Not only does a breach constitute a criminal offence (Insolvency Act 1986 s. 216(4)), but the director in question is personally liable for any debts of the second company incurred during his period of involvement with it (Insolvency Act 1986 s. 217).

In many cases, the choice of a name for the company will present no difficulties at all. However, there is no escaping the fact that the rules governing the choice of a name are extremely complex, and in some instances the most difficult part of Form IN01 to complete will be the opening sections. The key point to bear in mind is just how wide-ranging the rules are. It is vital, of course, to check that the proposed name does not already appear on the index of company names, but equally it is vital to ensure that none of the other rules discussed above are contravened. A search using the Company Name Availability Search feature on the Companies House WebCHeck service should be just the start of a wider process of considering whether a particular name should be adopted.

Sections A7 and A8: articles of association

2.2.7.22 As discussed in paragraphs 2.2.5.3 and 2.2.5.4, a company can choose either to adopt a set of model articles (e.g. the model articles for private companies limited by shares) in their entirety or to prepare articles which are tailored to its particular needs. If it decides to prepare tailored articles, it has a choice between preparing short form articles (which incorporate elements of the model articles by reference) or long form articles (which contain the full text of the company's articles and do not incorporate any elements of the model articles by reference).

2.2.7.23 As far as Form IN01 is concerned, the appropriate box in section A7 will need to be ticked, and if the company is adopting tailored articles they will need to be attached when the form is submitted to Companies House.

2.2.7.24 Section A8 concerns 'restricted company articles', which the explanatory note explains are 'those containing provision for entrenchment'.

2.2.7.25 Under CA2006, the articles can be amended by means of a special resolution. (A special resolution is, broadly, a resolution agreed to by 75% or more of the shareholders.) The articles may, however, specify that specific provisions can be amended only if some additional condition is met (s. 22(1)). If the articles so specify, they are said to contain 'provision for entrenchment'. An example of an additional condition is a requirement that 90% of the shareholders must vote in favour of any amendment to the provision in question. Another example is a requirement that a named shareholder must vote in favour of any such amendment.

2.2.7.26 Take the case of the following provision in a company's articles: 'Alan Brook is entitled to be a director of the company for as long as he is a shareholder of the company.' If the articles go on to specify that this provision can only be amended if Mr Brook himself votes in favour of the amendment (in other words, that a special resolution against which Mr Brook voted would not suffice), the provision is described as entrenched, which means that the articles are restricted and the box in section A8 will need to be ticked. The law on entrenched provisions is discussed in paragraph 4.4.1.2.

Sections C3 and C4: corporate secretaries

2.2.7.27 A private company is not required to appoint a secretary (unless its articles require it to do so) (s. 270(1)). If it nevertheless chooses to appoint one, certain information about the individual or company concerned will need to be included on Form IN01. Specifically, the details which, in due course, will have to be included in the company's register of secretaries pursuant to ss. 277 and 288 will need to be disclosed (s. 12).

2.2.7.28 The disclosure requirements present few difficulties. The only matters which may cause some confusion are two of the obligations which apply only in respect of corporate secretaries.

- Section C3 requires the disclosure, in respect of a corporate secretary which is an EEA company, of details of where the company is registered and its registration number. (The law underpinning section C3 is to be found in CA2006 ss. 12, 278(1)(c) and 1170. Section 278(1)(c) refers, more specifically, to 'an EEA company to which the First Company Law Directive (68/151/EEC) applies', and the effect of s. 1170 is that for these purposes an 'EEA company' is defined as a company which is governed by the law of a state which is a member of the European Economic Area.) The explanatory note adds that the former requirement is a reference to details of 'the register mentioned in

Article 3 of the First Company Law Directive (68/151/EEC)'. This explanatory note is not particularly illuminating, for the First Company Law Directive (a core piece of EU company legislation) has now been repealed and replaced by Directive 2009/101/EC, but the requirement is simply to provide details of the name of the register in which the company is registered, and the state in which it is registered. If the company is a UK company, for example, it would seem to be sufficient to state: 'Register of companies, UK.'

- Section C4 requires the disclosure, in respect of a corporate secretary which is not an EEA company, not only of details of where the company is registered and its registration number (if indeed it is registered), but also details of its 'legal form' and 'governing law'. (The law underpinning section C4 is to be found in ss. 12 and 278(1)(d)). The reference to 'legal form' would seem to be to the nature of the company: the equivalent, for example, of a UK private company limited by shares. The reference to 'governing law' is presumably to the specific piece of legislation governing such companies: the equivalent, for example, of CA2006.

Sections D2 and D4: directors' addresses

2.2.7.29 Details of a director's service address are to be included in section D2, and details of his residential address are to be included in section D4. Section D4 also deals with s. 243 exemptions, which concern the use which the registrar may make of details of the director's residential address.

2.2.7.30 Under the Act, a company must, in respect of each of its directors, notify the registrar of details of both a 'service address' (i.e. an address at which documents can be served on the director) (ss. 167 and 1141). As is apparent from the explanatory note to section D2, it is acceptable for the service address to be the address of the company's registered office) and the director's home address, but the registrar is prohibited from making details of the home address public (ss. 240 and 242). The rationale for this two-tier approach is that although it is important for the public to be able to contact the people who run companies, it is felt that it would be unfair to expose directors whose companies operate in controversial business sectors to the risk of harm from activists and the like by making their home address publicly available.

2.2.7.31 Although the registrar must not, then, place details of home addresses on the public register, in certain circumstances he is permitted to pass the details on to specified public authorities (such as the police) or to credit reference agencies (ss. 242 and 243, and the Companies (Disclosure of Address) Regulations 2009 (SI 2009/214)). A director cannot prevent the disclosure of his home address to a public authority, but he is entitled to apply to the registrar to refrain from disclosing the address to a credit reference agency on the ground that he faces a serious risk of intimidation or violence as a result of the company's activities (s. 243(4) and the Companies (Disclosure of Address) Regulations 2009 (SI 2009/214)).

2.2.7.32 If a proposed director of the new company is in the process of making an application to the registrar to refrain from disclosing his address, or if such an application has been successful, the box under the 'Section 243 exemption' heading in section D4 will need to be ticked and the form will have to be delivered not to the usual address to which applications to register a company must be sent, but to the address specified in section D4.

Sections E3 and E4: corporate directors

2.2.7.33 A private company is required to have at least one director (s. 154), although its articles may impose a higher minimum number. Certain information about each of the proposed directors will need to be included on Form IN01. Specifically, the details which, in due course, will have to be included in the company's register of directors and register of directors' residential addresses pursuant to ss. 163, 164 and 165 will need to be disclosed (s. 12).

2.2.7.34 The disclosure requirements present few difficulties. The only matters which may cause some confusion are two of the obligations which apply only in respect of corporate directors.

- Section E3 requires the disclosure, in respect of a corporate director which is an EEA company, of details of where the company is registered and its registration number. (The law underpinning section E3 is to be found in CA2006 ss. 12, 164(c) and 1170. Section 164(c) refers, more specifically, to 'an EEA company to which the First Company Law Directive (68/151/EEC) applies', and the effect of s. 1170 is that for these purposes an 'EEA company' is defined as a company which is governed by the law of a state which is a member of the European Economic Area.) The explanatory note adds that the former requirement is a reference to details of 'the register mentioned in Article 3 of the First Company Law Directive (68/151/EEC)'. This explanatory note is not particularly illuminating, for the First Company Law Directive (a core piece of EU company legislation) has now been repealed and replaced by Directive 2009/101/EC, but the requirement is simply to provide details of the name of the register in which the company is registered, and the state in which it is registered. If the company is a UK company, for example, it would seem to be sufficient to state: 'Register of companies, UK.'
- Section E4 requires the disclosure, in respect of a corporate director which is not an EEA company, not only of details of where the company is registered and its registration number (if indeed it is registered), but also details of its 'legal form' and 'governing law' (the law underpinning section E4 is to be found in ss. 12 and 164(d)). The reference to 'legal form' would seem to be

to the nature of the company: the equivalent, for example, of a UK private company limited by shares. The reference to 'governing law' is presumably to the specific piece of legislation governing such companies: the equivalent, for example, of CA2006.

Sections F1 to F3: details of share capital

2.2.7.35 The opening sections of the statement of capital in Part 3 of Form IN01 look complicated, but in practice should not cause difficulties for anyone who is familiar with the law governing shares and capital. Those who do not have much experience in that area might, however, find some of the terminology in sections F1 to F3 confusing, in which case the following brief comments may be of some assistance (the law governing shares and capital is explored in more detail in Chapter 9).

- A company can issue shares to which different rights are attached. For example, it might want to issue shares with extra voting rights or preferential rights in respect of dividends. Shares which carry the same rights are said to form a 'class'.
- Every share must have a fixed 'nominal value'. The nominal value is an arbitrary value chosen by the company. A company may choose, for example, to assign a nominal value of £1 to its ordinary shares, in which case the shares would be described as 'ordinary shares of £1 each'. A share's nominal value is also known as its 'par value'.
- If a person agrees to pay the company more than the nominal value of a new share, the additional sum constitutes 'share premium'. For example, if the company issues an ordinary share of £1 to a subscriber, and the subscriber pays the company £10 in exchange, he is paying the company £1 in respect of the share's nominal value and £9 by way of premium.
- When a company issues a share, the subscriber does not necessarily have to pay the company the full amount owed on the share immediately (unless the company's articles say otherwise). (Article 21 of the model articles for private companies limited by shares, for instance, requires shares, other than those which are taken on the company's formation, to be fully paid up.) In other words, some or all of the amount owed on the share can remain 'unpaid' for the time being. If, for example, a subscriber pays the company £8 in respect of an ordinary share of £1 which is issued at a premium of £9 (i.e. where the total amount payable for the share is £10), the share is described as 'partly paid', since £2 remains unpaid for the time being.
- Unless a company's articles say otherwise, its shares need not be 'denominated' in pounds sterling (s. 542(3)). For example, it may choose to issue shares denominated in dollars (e.g. 'ordinary shares of $1 each') or euros (e.g. 'ordinary shares of €10 each').

Section F4: prescribed particulars of rights attached to shares

2.2.7.36 The part of the statement of capital which is most likely to cause difficulties is s. F4, which requires the disclosure of details of what are known as the 'prescribed particulars' of the rights attached to the company's shares. (The particulars are prescribed in article 2, Companies (Shares and Share Capital) Order 2009 (SI 2009/388).) The information required is detailed in the explanatory note to the section, and must be provided in relation to each class of the company's shares. The question arises as to where the required information is to be found and how it should be set out.

2.2.7.37 In many cases, the company will have only one class of shares, and although its articles will provide for dividends to be paid in accordance with each shareholder's holding (see, for example, article 30 of the model articles for private companies), they will be silent on voting rights and rights on a distribution of capital, leaving those matters to be determined by the general law. In such cases, the position is that each share carries one vote (s. 284) and confers equal rights with the other shares to a dividend and to any distribution of capital. As to how this information should be set out in section F4, the Companies House website contains sample wording for use where the company has adopted the model articles for private companies: 'Ordinary shares have full rights in the company with respect to voting, dividends and distributions' (it is not clear whether this wording strictly complies with the statutory obligation to disclose prescribed particulars, but given the fact that it is contained in Companies House guidance no doubt the registrar will accept it). The sample wording is not easy to find. It is contained in a set of Frequently Asked Questions concerning the Companies House Web Incorporation Service. From the Companies House website's front page, click on 'Starting a company', then on 'Register a private limited company online', then on 'Start now' and then on the 'Help' button on the right-hand side of the screen. The sample wording is included in the answer to question 6.6: 'How do I complete the prescribed particulars section of the statement of capital?'

2.2.7.38 Where the company will issue shares of different classes, and its articles contain detailed provisions concerning the rights attached to each class, there will be no difficulty in identifying the required information. It may be less clear how the information should be set out in section F4. Clearly, bespoke wording will be needed, but the best approach to adopt will depend upon the nature of the rights. If the rights are fairly straightforward, it should be possible to summarise them in a few lines. If, however, they are more complicated – for example, if they run to several paragraphs or pages and/or cross-refer to other parts of the articles – it may be difficult to summarise them accurately, in which case the temptation will be simply to refer the reader to the articles. Unfortunately, Companies House has made it clear that this approach is not acceptable (see question 6.6 of the

Frequently Asked Questions concerning the Companies House Web Incorporation Service, referred to in paragraph 2.2.7.37), so the only alternative to providing a summary is to copy over the relevant provisions of the articles word for word. (If the provisions are very lengthy, it may be worth contacting Companies House to enquire if limited references to the articles may be permitted on the facts, for example where the provisions contain numerous cross-references to other parts of the articles, but if the company is required as a matter of urgency the safest option is to copy over all of the relevant provisions, however long they are.)

Section F5: initial shareholdings

2.2.7.39 The requirement to include details of the company's initial shareholders and their respective holdings should not cause any significant difficulties. Perhaps the only issue which may arise concerns the heading 'Amount (if any) unpaid', for it is not clear from Form IN01 whether this refers to any amount unpaid as respects the shares' nominal value or to any amount unpaid as to the total consideration for the shares, comprising not only their nominal value but also any premium. The Act makes it clear that the reference is to any amount unpaid as to the total consideration, including any premium (s. 10(4)(b)). Take the case of a company with ordinary shares of £1 each which will issue one share to a subscriber at a premium of £9 (i.e. for a total consideration of £10). If the subscriber will pay the company £7 for the share immediately, leaving the remaining £3 of the premium unpaid for the time being, the entry in the 'Amount (if any) unpaid' column in Section F5 will need to be '£3'.

Sections H1 and H2: statement of compliance

2.2.7.40 The statement of compliance required as part of Form IN01 is a statement that the requirements of CA2006 as to registration have been complied with (s. 13(1)). The statement may be made either by the subscribers to the memorandum (in which case each of them must sign their name in section H1) or by an agent for them (in which case the agent must sign his name in section H2). There are no restrictions as to the identity of the agent. The subscribers may wish to appoint their legal adviser, for example, or, indeed, one of their own number.

Ancillary matters

2.2.7.41 The last page of Form IN01 contains useful information, including a reminder to enclose the fee payable in respect of the application and a list of the addresses to which the form may be sent. The last page also contains a useful checklist of key points concerning the application process; this should be reviewed carefully before submitting the form in order to reduce the chances that it might be rejected.

2.3 Incorporation

2.3.1 If the registrar is satisfied that the requirements for registration have been complied with, he will register the documents (s. 14) and issue a certificate of incorporation (s. 15).

2.3.2 The certificate of incorporation will state the company's name, its registered number, the date of its incorporation, the fact that it is a private company limited by shares and the part of the United Kingdom in which its registered office is situated. All of this information is, of course, important, but the registered number and the date of incorporation are worthy of particular note.

- **Registered number.** Whereas a company may well change its name several times over the course of its life, its registered number will remain the same. The registered number therefore plays a crucial role in helping those charged with managing the company's internal affairs to keep track of its documentation. In the group context, for example, a company secretary of a subsidiary who remembers to include the subsidiary's registered number on all board minutes, shareholder written resolutions and other such documentation will be in no danger of mixing its records up with those of another group company should the two companies subsequently switch names.
- **Date of incorporation.** The date of the company's incorporation is of great significance, for that is the date on which the company comes into existence as a legal person, the subscribers become shareholders and the directors and any company secretary take office (s. 16). The notion of the company as a legal person, distinct from its shareholders and directors, is one of the foundations of English company law, and is examined in detail in Chapter 3, The company as a separate entity. For the moment, it suffices to highlight one of the topics which is covered in Chapter 3, namely 'pre-incorporation contracts' (see section 3.8). These are contracts entered into by someone (one of the subscribers, for example), purportedly on behalf of a company, but before the company has actually been incorporated. Such contracts should generally be avoided, because they will not bind the company once it has been formed, and will instead bind the person in question in his personal capacity.

2.4 Post incorporation

2.4.1 First board meeting

2.4.1.1 Once the company has come into existence, the directors will, naturally, want to focus their attention on the business for which it has been formed. They must not, however, neglect to hold an initial board meeting to attend to a number of administrative matters.

2.4.1.2 Directors are ultimately responsible for overseeing the administrative aspects of a company's operations, and should not fall into the trap of feeling that they do not need to take such 'formalities' seriously. The rules governing the company's internal affairs are, after all, part of the wider efforts of the company law regime to ensure that the company is an efficient vehicle for doing business. For example, the requirement that companies keep their books up to date is not the result of a whim on the part of Parliament, but an attempt to ensure that prospective shareholders and creditors can make an informed decision as to whether they wish to do business with the company. It may serve to focus directors' minds on this aspect of their role to note that in many instances a breach of the Act's provisions concerning the administration of companies may constitute a criminal offence on the part of the directors. By way of an example, a failure to keep a register of members constitutes an offence on the part of the company and of every officer who is in default (s. 113(7)). Although a director who takes reasonable steps to ensure that a register is maintained will not be liable (s. 1121(3)), the mere fact that the section provides for a criminal sanction should alert directors to the importance which the company law regime attaches to compliance with this administrative requirement.

2.4.1.3 The company's first board meeting should, then, be regarded as an opportunity to put the company's internal affairs on a sound footing at the start of its life. Among other things, the directors will normally use their first meeting to:

- note, for the record, the documents which were submitted to the registrar of companies in connection with the application to register the company;
- note, for the record, the fact of the company's incorporation, the identity of its subscribers, the identity of its first directors (and, if there is one, its first secretary) and the address of its registered office;
- adopt a set of company books, which will comprise a minute book and various registers, such as the register of members and the register of directors;
- (in the event that the company does not have a secretary) allocate responsibility for ensuring that the company books are updated on an ongoing basis to one of their number;
- issue share certificates to the subscribers in respect of the shares for which they subscribed. These shares will not be allotted to the subscribers in the usual way, because the subscribers will have become shareholders automatically upon the company's incorporation (ss. 16(5), 112 and 559);
- approve any service contracts for executive directors, such as a managing director;
- note the company's accounting reference date (by reference to which its financial year is determined) and, if appropriate, alter it (ss. 390–392);
- consider whether the company is required to have its accounts audited and, if it is, appoint auditors. Although the appointment of an auditor is normally

a matter for the shareholders, the directors have the power to appoint the company's first auditor (s. 485(3)(a)). Note, however, that Although the Act provides for the deemed re-appointment of the auditor of a private company in certain circumstances, the scope of this provision does not extend to an auditor who was appointed by the directors (s. 487(2)(a)); and
- appoint bankers.

3

The company as a separate entity

> **Summary**
> - The company law regime is based on the related principles that a company is a legal entity in its own right and that shareholders can limit their liability for the company's debts.
> - In exceptional cases, the courts will 'lift the corporate veil' so as to, in effect, treat a company and its shareholders as a single entity.
> - Fraudulent and wrongful trading provisions in the Insolvency Act 1986 mitigate the harm caused to creditors by the principle of shareholders' limited liability by giving the courts the power, in some situations, to require directors (or shareholders) of companies which are being wound up to contribute to their assets.
> - A company is, clearly, an artificial entity, so it has to act through human beings. Complex rules govern the circumstances in which a person acting on behalf of a company can commit the company to a contract with a third party.

3.1 Introduction

3.1.1 The notion that a company is a legal entity, distinct from its shareholders and directors, lies at the heart of the company law regime.

3.1.2 Much of the material which is contained in this handbook will make sense only if this essential feature of the corporate vehicle is properly understood. It is, for example, the reason why directors' duties are owed to the company itself, and not to the shareholders, and it helps to explain why a company may only pay a dividend out of profits, not out of capital.

3.1.3 This chapter begins by establishing the basis in law for the company's separate personality. It then turns to some of the consequences which flow directly or indirectly from that separate identity and from the fact that, plainly, the company is by nature an *artificial* creature. Specifically, the chapter examines the following topics:

- the legal basis for the company's separate identity;
- the option available to shareholders to limit their liability for the company's debts;
- the circumstances in which the courts may be prepared to 'lift the corporate veil' and so in effect disregard the company's separate identity – for example, in order to hold to account a shareholder who is using a corporate vehicle for an improper purpose;
- the law on wrongful trading and fraudulent trading, which in certain circumstances provides for those behind a company to be forced to contribute to its assets when it is wound up – in effect, the law in this area erodes the notion of the company's separate identity and, in some cases, the protection afforded to shareholders who have limited their liability for the company's debts;
- the law on objects clauses, which historically were used to place limits on a company's capacity to act;
- the means by which a company enters into contracts – for example, do all contracts signed by a director on behalf of his company constitute contracts entered into by the company, such that it is bound by their terms; and
- the law on pre-incorporation contracts (i.e. contracts signed on behalf of the company before it has been formed).

3.2 The company's separate identity

3.2.1 Legal basis

3.2.1.1 It is, perhaps, typical of the company law regime that it is not entirely clear whether the principle that lies at its heart is derived from statute or case law. In a landmark decision on the circumstances in which the company's identity might be disregarded, Lord Neuberger commented as follows on the basis of the notion that a company is a person in its own right: 'Whether that is characterised as a common law rule or a consequence of the companies legislation (or an amalgam of both), it is a very well established principle of long standing and high authority' (*Prest v Petrodel Resources Ltd* [2013] UKSC 34, at para 66). The best view, perhaps, is that the notion is technically founded in statute, the relevant case law serving to confirm that the correct interpretation of the legislation is, indeed, to the effect that a company is an entity distinct from its shareholders, directors and anyone else.

3.2.1.2 As far as the legislative component of this analysis is concerned, the starting point is CA2006 s. 16 sub-sections (2) and (3) of which provide that, as from the date of a company's incorporation:

'(2) The subscribers to the memorandum, together with such other persons as may from time to time become members of the company, are a body corporate by the name stated in the certificate of incorporation.
(3) That body corporate is capable of exercising all the functions of an incorporated company.'

3.2.1.3 Two other statutory provisions are worth noting. First, under the Interpretation Act 1978, where the word 'person' is used in an Act of Parliament, it is taken to include 'a body of persons corporate' unless the contrary intention is shown Interpretation Act 1978 s. 5 and Schedule 1). Similarly, the Law of Property Act 1925 provides that where the word 'person' is used in a contract, it is taken to include 'a corporation' unless the context otherwise requires (Law of Property Act 1925 s. 61).

3.2.1.4 As far as the judicial contribution to the notion of corporate personality is concerned, the key decision is that of the House of Lords in *Salomon v A Salomon & Co Ltd* [1897] AC 22. The case, which is generally considered to be the most important in English company law, involved a Mr Aron Salomon, who transferred his business as a boot manufacturer into a newly formed company in which he and his family held all the shares. When the company was subsequently wound up, it could not pay off all its creditors, and the question for the court was whether Mr Salomon was required to indemnify the company in respect of its debts. The judgments deal with the related topics of separate corporate personality and shareholders' limited liability, and as far as the former is concerned the judges were in no doubt that Mr Salomon and his company were, in legal terms, two distinct entities. The following extracts illustrate the judges' view:

> 'once the company is legally incorporated it must be treated like any other independent person with its rights and liabilities appropriate to itself.' (per Lord Halsbury LC)

> 'The company is at law a different person altogether from the subscribers to the memorandum...' (per Lord Macnaghten)

3.2.2 Practical implications

3.2.2.1 Since a company has an identity of its own, it is able to act very much as a human being. It can, for example, enter into contracts, hire and fire employees, purchase assets, own property, bring legal proceedings, buy shares in another company and even commit criminal offences.

3.2.2.2 By way of an illustration of the importance of its ability to act in its own right, consider the case of a group of friends who decide to open a grocery shop on the high street. If they did not have the option of forming a company which could sign supply contracts with local farmers in its own name, who would sign such contracts? Certainly, they could be signed by any one of the friends, but in that case the individual in question would be personally liable on them. No doubt, too, it would be possible to construct a web of contracts between the friends such that the burden of the signatory's liabilities under the contract was shared among them, but this would be a cumbersome and expensive enterprise. A corporate vehicle which possesses the advantage of having its own identity, such that it can sign contracts in its own name, is a much more efficient solution.

3.2.2.3 It is important to recognise that the company's separate corporate personality cannot be discarded at the will of its shareholders or directors. If a business is owned by a company, it is by definition not owned by its shareholders. This is the case even if the company has just one shareholder who also happens to be its only director. In *Macaura v Northern Assurance Company Ltd [1925] AC 619*, an individual sold timber on his estate to a company in which, effectively, he was the sole shareholder. He subsequently insured the timber against the risk of fire, and when a fire did in fact destroy much of the timber duly claimed under the insurance policies. The House of Lords noted that the timber was owned by the company, and held that the shareholder had no insurable interest in it. As Lord Wrenbury put it: 'the corporator even if he holds all the shares is not the corporation, and … neither he nor any creditor of the company has any property legal or equitable in the assets of the corporation.'

3.2.2.4 It is easy to fall into the habit of thinking that since a company is owned by its shareholders, logically the company's business too must, in effect, be owned by its shareholders. As a matter of company law, however, this analysis is quite wrong. The notion that a company is a separate entity can sometimes seem artificial, but it is no less robust for that.

3.3 Shareholders' limited liability

3.3.1 Legal basis

3.3.1.1 Of the various attributes of the corporate vehicle, the most attractive from a shareholder's perspective is the option which it affords him of limiting his liability for its debts.

3.3.1.2 It is important to recognise at the outset that when limited liability is being discussed in the corporate context, reference is being made to the liability of the shareholders rather than the company. A company is liable for any debts which it incurs in just the same way as a 'natural person', that is to say a human being, is. If a company enters into a supply contract under which it is to pay the supplier a certain sum, it is liable for the full amount of that sum. Its liability, in other words, is not limited.

3.3.1.3 If a company is wound up in circumstances in which its debts outweigh its assets, the unpaid creditors will naturally wonder if they can recover the sums due to them from the shareholders. After all, when a company prospers, the shareholders benefit through dividends and an increase in the value of their shares; would it not be fair for them to bear the burden in the event of the company's failure?

3.3.1.4 As a matter of fact, the default position is that shareholders *do* bear the burden of the company's failure. Under the Insolvency Act 1986 s. 74(1):

> 'When a company is wound up, every present and past member is liable to contribute to its assets to any amount sufficient for payment of its debts and liabilities, and the expenses of the winding up, and for the adjustment of the rights of the contributories among themselves.'

3.3.1.5 However, this broad rule is subject to exceptions. The scope of past members' liability is restricted Insolvency Act 1986 s. 74(2)(a), (b) and (c)) and, more importantly for present purposes, there is an exception in relation to 'a company limited by shares'. Where such companies are concerned, 'no contribution is required from any member exceeding the amount (if any) unpaid on the shares in respect of which he is liable as a present or past member' Insolvency Act 1986 s. 74(2)(d)).

3.3.1.6 The meaning of 'company limited by shares' is to be found in CA2006 ss. 3(1) and (2):

> '(1) A company is a "limited company" if the liability of its members is limited by its constitution. It may be limited by shares or limited by guarantee.
> (2) If their liability is limited to the amount, if any, unpaid on the shares held by them, the company is "limited by shares".'

3.3.1.7 In order to opt in to limited liability, then, shareholders must insert appropriate limitation wording into their company's constitution. The standard wording adopted is that set out in article 2 of the model articles for private companies limited by shares: 'The liability of the members is limited to the amount, if any, unpaid on the shares held by them.' In the absence of this wording, the shareholders are obliged under the Insolvency Act 1986 s. 74(1) to stand behind the company so as to ensure that its debts are paid. If the wording is included, the shareholders enjoy limited liability: their liability for the company's debts, in the event that upon its demise it is unable to pay them, is limited.

3.3.2 Scope of the limitation

3.3.2.1 If a company's articles limit its shareholders' liability, a shareholder who has paid the full amount due on his shares is not required to contribute any further sum to the company's assets in the event that, when it is wound up, it is unable to pay its debts. Consider the case of an individual who subscribes for one ordinary share of £10 in Animaginaryco Ltd, and duly pays the company £10 for the share. If the company subsequently fails, owing £100,000 to various creditors, the shareholder will not have to contribute a penny towards those debts.

3.3.2.2 It is normal practice nowadays for shareholders to pay their shares up in full, and in fact the model articles for private companies are drafted on the basis that all shares save those taken upon the company's formation are fully paid (article 21). In those relatively rare cases where shares are unpaid or partly paid, however, the effect of including wording in the articles limiting the shareholders' liability is that their liability is confined to the unpaid sum. The point can be illustrated by adjusting the example in the paragraph above slightly, such that the individual has paid Animaginaryco Ltd only £5 for the £10 share. If the company subsequently fails, he is obliged to contribute only the amount unpaid on the share, namely £5. Once he has paid that sum, his obligation towards the company is extinguished, no matter how much money its creditors are still owed.

3.3.2.2 From a shareholder's perspective, the company's failure raises not only the question of what he may have to contribute towards its debts, but also the question of whether he is entitled to recover the value of his share. Having paid £10 for a £10 share, for example, a shareholder of a company limited by shares will not have to contribute any further sum towards the company's debts, but will he be able to recover the £10 which he has already paid?

3.3.2.3 The answer is that he will not be able to do so. This is because the principle underlying the complex rules governing the order in which a liquidator applies the company's assets upon its winding up is that creditors are paid in priority to shareholders (Insolvency Act 1986 ss. 107 (in relation to a voluntary winding up) and 143 (in relation to a winding up by the court)). Thus, if a company cannot pay its debts in full at the end of its life, all its assets will be deployed in favour of its creditors, and there will be nothing left over for the shareholders.

3.3.2.4 This may seem a harsh rule, but the logic behind it is that if creditors are barred from calling on the shareholders' personal assets upon the company's demise, they should at least have first call on the company's assets. It is also the case that if the company had ever enjoyed success during its life, its shareholders may well have received a healthy return on their investment in the form of dividends, and so will not necessarily be walking away from the company with nothing.

3.3.3 Impact on the company law regime

3.3.3.1 The company law regime offers shareholders the option of limiting their liability in order to encourage them to invest in businesses. An IT graduate is more likely to launch a business to try to exploit a piece of software which he developed at university if he knows that the failure of the venture will not result in creditors seizing his personal assets. Similarly, albeit at the other end of the spectrum, a multinational retail company is more likely to try to break into a hostile but potentially lucrative new market if it can do so by forming a subsidiary whose debts, in the event of its failure, will be entirely its own.

3.3.3.2 The use of a vehicle which allows its backers to limit their liability does not eliminate the risk of failure, however. It merely shifts the risk from the shareholders to the creditors. If the venture fails, the shareholders may be able to walk away relatively unscathed, but the burden of the company's losses are left to be borne by those who have lent it money.

3.3.3.3 Having taken the view, as a matter of policy, that creditors are better placed to bear the risk of business failures than shareholders, the company law regime is at great pains to ensure that creditors are not left completely unprotected. As noted in paragraph 1.3.5.4, if the regime placed too heavy a burden on creditors, they would be reluctant to deal with companies, and the effectiveness of the company as a vehicle for doing business would be compromised. The impact of shareholders' limited liability on the company law regime, therefore, is that large swathes of the regime exist at least in part in order to protect creditors' interests.

3.3.3.4 In some instances, the protection afforded is direct in nature. For example, the wrongful trading provisions of the Insolvency Act 1986 require a director who realises that his company has no reasonable prospect of surviving to seek to minimise the loss to the company's creditors (Insolvency Act 1986 s. 214). If he fails to do so, the court may require him to contribute to the company's assets.

3.3.3.5 In other instances, the protection is more subtle, taking the form of transparency measures which seek to ensure that creditors have the information they need in order to decide whether or not to do business with a particular company. For example, creditors have access through Companies House not only to companies' accounts, but also to other internal information, such as the identity of companies' shareholders and directors.

3.3.3.6 The role played by transparency measures in counterbalancing the burden placed on creditors by the availability of limited liability for shareholders was highlighted in *Salomon v A Salomon & Co Ltd* [1897] AC 22 (the facts of the case are outlined in paragraph 3.2.1.4). In that case, the lower courts were concerned that Mr Salomon was using the option of limiting his liability to, in effect, defraud creditors. Not only was the company essentially a one-man company (at the time, companies were required to have at least seven shareholders, but the only shareholders in A Salomon & Co Ltd besides Mr Salomon himself were members of his family, and they only held one share each), but Mr Salomon took a charge over the company's assets which, if valid, would entitle him to priority over the company's unsecured creditors in the event of its liquidation. The House of Lords had less sympathy for the creditors, holding that the transparency requirements of the company law regime of the time were such that a creditor who took the trouble to look into a company's affairs would know precisely what sort of an entity he was dealing with. Lord Watson observed as follows:

> 'The unpaid creditors of the company, whose unfortunate position has been attributed to the fraud of the appellant, if they had thought fit to avail themselves of the means of protecting their interests which the [Companies] Act [1862] provides, could have informed themselves of the terms of purchase by the company, of the issue of debentures to the appellant, and of the amount of shares held by each member. In my opinion, the statute casts upon them the duty of making inquiry in regard to these matters. ... But the apathy of a creditor cannot justify an imputation of fraud against a limited company or its members, who have provided all the means of information which the Act of 1862 requires; and, in my opinion, a creditor who will not take the trouble to use the means which the statute provides for enabling him to protect himself must bear the consequences of his own negligence.' ([1897] AC 22, at 40).

3.4 Lifting the corporate veil

3.4.1 Overview

3.4.1.1 The notion that a company is a separate legal entity is central to company law, but it is not an absolute rule. A company and its shareholders or directors may, in exceptional circumstances, be treated, in effect, as a single entity. A well-known example of this is to be found in CA2006 s. 399, which requires parent companies to produce group accounts. Although it is true that companies within a group are technically separate entities, the Act recognises the fact that a third party dealing with a group company will not be able to form a true picture of its financial health unless he has access to information about the performance of the group as a whole. In effect, the law is recognising that in this context, at least, the notion of the company's separate identity has its limits.

3.4.1.2 When a company is identified with its shareholders, it is usually said that the 'corporate veil' is being lifted. In fact, there are two expressions in common use: 'lifting the corporate veil' and 'piercing the corporate veil'. Although they have long been used interchangeably, the Supreme Court has recently sought to end this practice by defining 'piercing' in very narrow terms (*Prest v Petrodel Resources Ltd* [2013] UKSC 34. See, in particular, Lord Sumption's judgment at paragraph 16 and Lord Neuberger's judgment at paragraphs 60 and 61). It seems unlikely, however, that in casual conversation at least the technical distinction between the two will be strictly adhered to, and for the sake of simplicity this handbook will refer to the 'lifting' of the veil as an umbrella term to encompass all means by which a company's separate legal identity may be compromised.

3.4.1.3 The law on veil lifting is extremely confused, and it is no exaggeration to say that this is one of the most difficult areas in the whole of company law. The following paragraphs do not attempt an exhaustive consideration of the circumstances in which the veil may be lifted, but rather seek to impose a degree of order on a chaotic body of case law by identifying the basic principles which form the framework of the law.

3.4.1.4 In seeking to assess the impact of the rules on veil lifting from a practical perspective, there are two points to note at the outset. First, the separate identity of the company is normally guarded very jealously. In other words, the veil of incorporation is only rarely cast aside or otherwise compromised. Second, although the core function of the rules on lifting the veil is, as might be expected, the prevention of misuse of the corporate vehicle, there are, in fact, situations in which a company and its shareholders may be treated as one despite the fact that neither was behaving improperly.

3.4.1.5 The two most important decisions on lifting the veil are the Supreme Court's decision in *Prest v Petrodel Resources Ltd* [2013] UKSC 34 and the Court of Appeal's decision in *Adams v Cape Industries plc* [1990] 1 Ch 433. The former is more recent and, being a decision of the highest court in the land, more authoritative, but the latter played an important role in the development of the law in this area and certain elements of it remain highly relevant today.

3.4.1.6 So important are these two cases that it is worth pausing for a moment to outline their facts and the courts' decisions.

- **Prest v Petrodel Resources Ltd (2013).** This was a matrimonial case, and the background was that Mr Prest had been ordered to pay a lump sum to Mrs Prest in connection with their divorce. The question for the Supreme Court was whether it could order seven properties which were legally owned by two companies to be transferred to Mrs Prest in partial satisfaction of that lump sum.

    Although the two companies in question were part of a group which was owned and controlled by Mr Prest, it will be apparent from the discussion above (see section 3.2.2 on the practical implications of the notion that a company is a separate person) that the starting point for the court's analysis of this question was that the properties were owned not by Mr Prest, but by the companies, and so could not in the normal course of events be called upon to satisfy Mr Prest's obligation to pay his wife the lump sum. The issue which confronted the Supreme Court, then, was whether there was any ground on which the fundamental notion of a company's separate personality could, on the particular facts of the case, be challenged.

The judges were unanimous in their conclusion that the properties were held on trust for Mr Prest, and so had to be transferred to Mrs Prest. Thus, the fact that the properties were held by companies, and that companies are generally regarded as separate legal persons, did not prevent the court from deciding that their assets could be used to satisfy a debt of their ultimate owner.

In the course of reaching its decision, the court engaged in an in-depth analysis of the law on veil lifting, and sought to rationalise the substantial body of case law in this area. There are points of difference in the various judgments, and it remains to be seen whether, in the coming years, the courts will feel that we now have a workable set of principles. For the time being, however, the Supreme Court's decision represents the law, and the discussion in the following paragraph of the circumstances in which the veil might be lifted reflects the essence of the court's analysis. Readers who are particularly interested in the question of lifting the veil may wish to read the decision in *Prest v Petrodel Resources Ltd* in full, for the case provides a useful insight into the complexities of the law in this area. The judgments of Lord Sumption and Lord Neuberger contain the bulk of the analysis, but those of the other judges are equally important in that they cast some doubt on the framework which Lord Sumption, in particular, attempted to formulate.

- *Adams v Cape Industries plc (1990).* The background to this case was that a US court had ordered Cape Industries plc (a UK company) to pay damages to approximately 200 individuals who had been exposed to asbestos emitted from a factory in the US. Cape did not own the factory, but the corporate group of which it formed a part had marketed asbestos in the US and it was allegedly responsible for supplying asbestos to the factory's operators without warning them of its dangers.

    Cape did not have any assets in the US, so the individuals in favour of whom the US judgment had been made sought to enforce it in England. In order to succeed in their claim, they had to show that the US court had jurisdiction over Cape, and they sought to establish jurisdiction on the basis that Cape was present in the US at the relevant time. Specifically, they argued that Cape should be regarded as having been present in the US because one of its subsidiaries and a company with which it was closely associated were present in that country.

    As was the case in *Prest v Petrodel Resources Ltd*, the starting point for the court's analysis was the principle that companies are separate legal entities. If, then, it was to conclude that Cape was present in the US through the presence of the subsidiary and the associated company, it would be compromising this fundamental rule by, in effect, treating each of the subsidiary and the associated company as one with Cape.

In a lengthy judgment, the Court of Appeal held that there were no grounds, on the facts, upon which to lift the corporate veil, and therefore refused to enforce the US judgment. In reaching its decision, it examined the law in this area in some detail, and its observations were regarded as the authoritative statement of the law for more than two decades. Although *Prest v Petrodel Resources Ltd* must now be regarded as the most important case in this area, the underlying principles set out by the Supreme Court in that case do not represent a significant departure from those set out by the Court of Appeal in *Adams v Cape Industries plc*. What is more, the Court of Appeal dealt in detail with certain matters which were barely touched upon in the later case, and so its comments in those areas in particular remain highly relevant today.

3.4.2 Grounds for lifting the veil

3.4.2.1 As complex as the decisions in *Prest v Petrodel Resources Ltd* and *Adams v Cape Industries plc* were, and as substantial as the body of other cases in this area is, it is possible to distil from them a number of general principles.

3.4.2.2 First, the courts will not lift the veil simply because a company has been used in order to insulate the shareholder from the risk of liability in respect of future activities. If, for example, a retail company wishes to open a shop in a new market, and is conscious that the venture is risky and might well fail, it is perfectly entitled to form a subsidiary to undertake the expansion, and can do so safe in the knowledge that should the venture fail, creditors of the subsidiary will not be able to call upon it (the parent company) to meet their claims. As was noted both in *Prest v Petrodel Resources Ltd* [2013] UKSC 34, at [34] and *Adams v Cape Industries plc* [1990] 1 Ch 433, at 544 the use of companies to allocate future risk is entirely unobjectionable from a company law perspective.

3.4.2.3 Second, the courts will not lift the veil simply because justice demands that they do so. This point was made unequivocally in *Adams v Cape Industries plc*, where the Court of Appeal commented that 'save in cases which turn on the wording of particular statutes or contracts, the court is not free to disregard the principle of *Salomon v A Salomon & Co Ltd* [1897] AC 22 merely because it considers that justice so requires' [1990] 1 Ch 433, at 536. Take, for instance, the case of a long-established and highly profitable company which, due to an unexpected change in the business climate, suddenly fails, leaving dozens of loyal employees unpaid and owing substantial sums to many small local businesses. If the courts are asked to require the shareholders to make up the shortfall in the amount owed by the company, they will reject any argument to the effect that, since the shareholders enjoyed profits from the company's past successes, it is only fair that they should now contribute towards the payment of its debts.

3.4.2.4 Third, there are various grounds on which the courts might be prepared to lift the veil. Some of the grounds listed below are relatively clearly defined in the case law and therefore easy to understand. Others are less so. In particular, the precise scope of the evasion and concealment principles which were introduced by the Supreme Court in *Prest v Petrodel Resources Ltd* is as yet somewhat unclear. The list should, then, be treated not so much as a definitive statement of the precise circumstances in which the veil will be lifted, but as a broad guide to the approach which the courts are likely to adopt to this difficult question.

Interpretation of a statute

3.4.2.5 When considering statutory provisions, the courts sometimes feel that they have latitude to interpret them in such a way as to blur the line between a company and its shareholders (*Adams v Cape Industries plc* [1990] 1 Ch 433, at 532–536). In *Gross v Rackind, Re City Branch Group Ltd* [2004] EWCA Civ 815, the Court of Appeal considered CA1985 s. 459, which allowed a shareholder to seek relief from the court if 'the company's affairs are being or have been conducted' in an unfairly prejudicial manner (the corresponding provision in CA2006 is s. 994, which is discussed in 8.4.7). The question for the court was whether the conduct of the affairs of a subsidiary company could constitute conduct of the affairs of its parent company, and the judges had no hesitation in concluding that it could. On the facts, and for the purposes of s. 459, the two companies were, in effect, treated as one.

3.4.2.6 Another case which may be cited as an application of this ground is *DHN Food Distributors Ltd v Tower Hamlets London Borough Council* [1976] 1 WLR 852. This well-known case can, on one reading, be read as introducing a much wider ground for lifting the veil, namely that the court will lift the veil in the context of a group of companies if the companies form a single economic unit. However, in *Adams v Cape Industries plc*, the Court of Appeal rationalised the decision in the case as an example of the court being prepared, in appropriate circumstances, to compromise the notion of a company's separate identity when interpreting a statute, in that case the Land Compensation Act 1961 ([1990] 1 Ch 433, at 533–534, 536).

Interpretation of a contract

3.4.2.7 Similarly, the courts may be prepared in appropriate cases to interpret wording in contracts in such a way as to compromise the notion that a company is a distinct legal entity (*Adams v Cape Industries plc* [1990] 1 Ch 433, at

532–536). In *Beckett Investment Management Group Ltd v Hall* [2007] EWCA Civ 613, an individual had entered into an employment contract under which his freedom to provide services 'of a type provided by the Company' would be restricted once his employment came to an end. In fact, the company in question did not provide any services; it was a holding company, and services to clients were provided through a subsidiary. In construing the scope of the wording in the employment contract, Kay LJ, who delivered the main judgment in the Court of Appeal, took the view that the restriction extended to services of a type provided by the subsidiary. In reaching this conclusion, he noted as follows: 'I do not feel inhibited by a purist approach to corporate personality.'

Prevention of the misuse of a company in connection with wrongdoing

3.4.2.8 Although, as noted above, the courts will not lift the veil simply in order to see justice done, they will be prepared to compromise a company's separate personality if it has been used specifically to further an improper act. This proposition encompasses two distinct principles. Under the evasion principle, the court will lift the veil if a person uses a company to evade an existing legal obligation or restriction. Under the concealment principle, the court will lift the veil if a person uses a company to try to disguise his role in an improper act.

3.4.2.9 An illustration of the evasion principle is to be found in *Gilford Motor Company Ltd v Horne* [1933] Ch 935. In that case, a managing director (Mr Horne), had entered into an agreement with his company (Gilford Motor) to the effect that he would not compete with it for a period after his employment ended. When his employment ended, he carried on a competing business through the medium of a company in which his wife and an associate were the shareholders and directors. The Court of Appeal was unanimous in its view that Mr Horne should not be allowed to use a corporate vehicle to evade his obligations under the agreement with the company, and granted Gilford Motor an order restraining both Mr Horne and his company from breaching the non-compete clause.

3.4.2.10 An illustration of the concealment principle is to be found in *Gencor ACP Ltd v Dalby* [2000] 2 BCLC 734, in which Mr Dalby breached his duty as a director of Gencor ACP by arranging for a third party to pay commission which was properly due to Gencor ACP to a company in the British Virgin Islands (Burnstead) which he controlled. Counsel for Burnstead suggested that it was not liable to account to Gencor ACP for the commission, basing his argument on the notion that it was an entity quite distinct from Mr Dalby: Burnstead, he argued, had not breached any duty to Gencor ACP, but had merely received a sum of money. Rimer J gave this analysis short shrift and had no qualms about identifying Burnstead with Mr Dalby, holding it liable to account for the commission. As he put it: 'In my view this is the type of case in which the court ought to have no hesitation in regarding Burnstead simply as the alter ego through which Mr Dalby enjoyed the profit which he earned in breach of his fiduciary duty to [Gencor] ACP.'

3.4.2.11 The evasion and concealment principles formed the cornerstone of Lord Sumption's comments on lifting the veil in *Prest v Petrodel Resources Ltd*, and some readers may feel that the distinction between the two is clear. Others will be less convinced, and will take comfort from the fact that, in the same case, Lord Neuberger appeared to disagree with Lord Sumption's view that *Gilford Motor Company Ltd v Horne* was an example of the operation of the evasion principle [2013] (UKSC 34, at [69]–[72]). They will also note the judgment of Lady Hale, who harboured doubts as to where the dividing line between the two lies. As she put it: 'I am not sure whether it is possible to classify all of the cases in which the courts have been or should be prepared to disregard the separate legal personality of a company neatly into cases of either concealment or evasion. They may simply be examples of the principle that the individuals who operate limited companies should not be allowed to take unconscionable advantage of the people with whom they do business' ([2013] UKSC 34, at [92]). In any case, for the purposes of this handbook it suffices to conclude that the courts will, one way or another, prevent the corporate form from being misused in connection with wrongdoing.

Existence of an agency relationship

3.4.2.12 If a company is found to be its shareholder's agent, its acts may be treated as the acts of the shareholder. Thus, although technically the two remain separate entities (after all, an agency relationship cannot exist without two separate entities: a principal and an agent), in practical terms the effect of a finding of agency is to identify the company with its shareholder.

3.4.2.13 In what circumstances, then, will an agency relationship exist? The mere fact that the shareholder owns all the shares in the company will not, in itself, suffice (*The Gramophone and Typewriter Ltd v Stanley* [1908] 2 KB 89). The question is as to whether the company is carrying on its own business or that of the shareholder, and in answering this question the courts will take into account all the facts of the case. There is no exhaustive list of the factors which the courts will consider, and no one factor which will always determine whether or not an agency relationship exists. However, the Court of Appeal in *Adams v Cape Industries plc* felt that the most important factor is likely to be whether the company had authority to commit the shareholder to binding contracts with third parties ([1990] 1 Ch 433, at 530–531 and 545–549). A shareholder who gives his company authority to subject him to binding contractual obligations to third parties may well, therefore, find that the courts will conclude that the company is his agent.

3.4.2.14 The courts will not readily infer the existence of an agency relationship (indeed, even the existence of an agency agreement may not be enough to establish an agency relationship for these purposes) (*Adams v Cape Industries plc* [1990] 1 Ch 433, at 547–549). However, where they do find that a company is its shareholder's agent, the consequences for the shareholder may be serious. In *Adams v Cape Industries plc*, for example, the finding of an agency relationship between Cape Industries plc and either its US subsidiary or another associated US company would have sufficed to establish that Cape Industries plc was present in the US through the presence there of the company in question, and so would have exposed it to the jurisdiction of the US courts (see paragraph 3.4.1.6 for the background facts in *Adams v Cape Industries plc*).

Existence of a trust relationship

3.4.2.15 In exceptional cases, the courts may find that assets owned by a company are beneficially owned by its shareholder. In *Prest v Petrodel Resources Ltd*, properties were owned by companies which were part of a group which was in turn controlled by Mr Prest. The question for the court was whether it could order the properties to be transferred to Mrs Prest in connection with the couple's divorce (see paragraph 3.4.1.6 for further background to this case). The principle that a company is a separate entity would suggest that since the properties were owned not by Mr Prest, but by his companies, they were not available for use in satisfying his personal obligations to his wife. The court concluded, however, that it could order the properties to be transferred to Mrs Prest, on the basis that the companies held them on trust for Mr Prest.

3.4.2.16 In reaching his decision on this point, Lord Sumption noted that the question as to whether a trust relationship exists is 'a highly fact-specific issue' ([2013] UKSC 34, at [52]) and declined to provide guidance on the circumstances in which such a relationship might arise. Crucial to his conclusion in the case before him, however, was his finding that Mr Prest had funded the companies' acquisition of the properties.

3.4.2.17 So, when might a trust relationship arise? The fact that a shareholder owns all the shares in a company does not, in itself, give him any interest in the company's assets. Nor will a shareholder who provides his company with a loan be likely to be found to have any interest in assets purchased by the company with those funds. Take the case, however, where the sole shareholder of a company which operates a high street bakery gives the company £40,000 with which to purchase a sports car for his personal use. The car serves no purpose as far as the company's activities are concerned, and clearly the shareholder's intention on these facts is to retain full control over it. It is in circumstances such as these that the courts might find a trust relationship, such that although the asset is legally the property of the company, it is beneficially owned by the shareholder.

Assumption by shareholder of responsibility for the welfare of the company's employees

3.4.2.18 In certain situations, the courts may find that a shareholder owes the company's employees a duty to ensure their health and safety. If that duty is breached, the shareholder will be liable in negligence to the employees.

3.4.2.19 The authoritative statement of the law in this area is to be found in Arden LJ's judgment in *Chandler v Cape plc*:

> 'In summary, this case demonstrates that in appropriate circumstances the law may impose on a parent company responsibility for the health and safety of its subsidiary's employees. Those circumstances include a situation where, as in the present case, (1) the businesses of the parent and subsidiary are in a relevant respect the same; (2) the parent has, or ought to have, superior knowledge on some relevant aspect of health and safety in the particular industry; (3) the subsidiary's system of work is unsafe as the parent company knew, or ought to have known; and (4) the parent knew or ought to have foreseen that the subsidiary or its employees would rely on its using that superior knowledge for the employees' protection. For the purposes of (4) it is not necessary to show that the parent is in the practice of intervening in the health and safety policies of the subsidiary. The court will look at the relationship between the companies more widely. The court may find that element (4) is established where the evidence shows that the parent has a practice of intervening in the trading operations of the subsidiary, for example production and funding issues.' (*Chandler v Cape plc* [2012] EWCA Civ 525, at [80])

3.4.2.20 In other words (and staying with the example of a parent company), a duty may arise where the parent company is in the same line of business as the subsidiary, has superior knowledge of relevant health and safety issues and involves itself in the subsidiary's affairs.

3.4.2.21 This is very much still a developing area of the law, and Arden LJ's statement does not purport to define exhaustively the circumstances in which a shareholder might owe a duty of care to the company's employees. It does seem safe, however, to draw some tentative conclusions. On the one hand, a duty will not arise simply by virtue of the fact that the shareholder happens to own all of the company's shares (*Chandler v Cape plc* [2012] EWCA Civ 525, at [69]), or even by virtue of the fact that the shareholder has appointed to the company's board a director who is responsible for health and safety matters (*Thompson v The Renwick Group plc* [2014] EWCA Civ 635, at [24]–[25]). On the other hand, a duty may arise even if the shareholder does not have complete control over all of the subsidiary's affairs (*Chandler v Cape plc* [2012] EWCA Civ 525, at [66]).

3.4.2.22 On the facts before her in *Chandler v Cape plc*, Arden LJ concluded that a parent company was liable in respect of asbestosis contracted by an employee of its subsidiary as a result of his working conditions. She insisted, however, that she was not lifting the corporate veil ([2012] EWCA Civ 525 at [69]). Technically, that may be so, but the application of normal principles of the law of negligence in this way undoubtedly has the effect of blurring the line between a company and its shareholders. After all, an analysis based purely on company law principles would suggest that since a parent company and its subsidiary are separate entities, the former should be immune from claims by employees of the latter.

3.4.3 Practical implications of the law for shareholders

3.4.3.1 It is important to maintain a sense of perspective in relation to the rules on lifting the corporate veil. It is true that the rules are complex and confusing, and can be exceedingly difficult to apply to any given set of facts. However, the notion that a company is a separate entity is one of the founding principles of English company law, and on the whole the courts are very reluctant to set it aside. Not only do they recognise that shareholders who use a company to shift the risk of future business activities away from themselves are doing nothing wrong, but they will not identify shareholders with their company simply on the basis of vague notions of the demands of justice.

3.4.3.2 That is not to say that the law in this area has no practical implications for shareholders. On the contrary, shareholders should, at the very least, bear in mind when they are arranging their affairs that the separate identity of a company *can*, in exceptional circumstances, be compromised, and ideally should consider whether to take steps to try to minimise the chances of ever being identified with their company. For example, if they wish to reduce the risk of triggering the agency ground for lifting the veil, they should ensure that the company is not carrying on their business. Similarly, a parent company which is in the same line of business as its subsidiary, but does not want to be exposed to liability in negligence for injuries suffered by the latter's employees, should refrain from involving itself in the subsidiary's affairs.

3.5 Wrongful trading and fraudulent trading

3.5.1 Overview

3.5.1.1 When a third party enters into a contract with a company, the effect of the company's separate personality is that neither its shareholders nor its directors are parties to the contract. If the third party is owed money under the contract, it will be for the company alone to satisfy the debt.

3.5.1.2 When a company is trading profitably and can pay its debts as they fall due, its creditors will be content with this arrangement. What is the position, though, when a company fails, and is unable to pay its debts? Naturally, its creditors will want to look beyond the company to those who own or run it.

3.5.1.3 As far as the former are concerned, assuming the company is a company limited by shares, its shareholders' liability for its debts in the event of its failure is limited to any amount unpaid on their shares. Unpaid creditors might hope that the courts will lift the corporate veil and attach the company's liabilities to the shareholders, but, as was noted in the previous section of this chapter, this is not a road down which the courts are easily persuaded to go.

3.5.1.4 As far as the latter are concerned, it might be thought that the rule that the company is a separate person affords directors complete protection against attempts by creditors to pursue them in relation to debts incurred by the company. As part of the company law regime's efforts to mitigate the adverse effects on creditors of the limited liability principle, however, it provides certain mechanisms which seek to hold directors to account for behaviour which prejudices creditors' interests.

3.5.1.5 One of those mechanisms is built into the general duties owed by a director to his company. CA2006 s. 172(3) preserves the common law rule that, when a company is approaching insolvency, the duty imposed on directors to run the company in the interests of its shareholders is displaced by a duty to act in the interests of its creditors (s. 172(3) is discussed in paragraph 7.3.10.2).

3.5.1.6 This common law rule is supplemented by the provisions in the Insolvency Act 1986 concerning wrongful trading and fraudulent trading.

- Under the Insolvency Act 1986 s. 214, a director must not continue to trade once the company has reached the point at which it has no reasonable prospect of avoiding insolvent liquidation.
- Under the Insolvency Act 1986 s. 213, a director (or anyone else, for that matter) must not be party to the carrying on of the company's business with the intention of defrauding creditors.

3.5.1.7 If a director is found liable under either section, he can be ordered to contribute to the company's assets. Since this increases the pool of funds available to the company's creditors, ss. 213 and 214 can be regarded as means of allowing the courts to look behind the corporate veil so as to, in effect, force some of those behind the company to satisfy its debts.

3.5.2 Wrongful trading

3.5.2.1 The essential feature of the Insolvency Act 1986 s. 214 – the feature which should give comfort to creditors and concern directors – is that it potentially imposes liability not only on directors who have deliberately misbehaved in their management of the company's affairs, but also on directors who have merely been incompetent.

3.5.2.2 Unfortunately, the section is not drafted as clearly as it might have been, and so in order to understand how it works it is necessary to dissect it with some care. The text of the section is set out in full in Figure 3.1.

Figure 3.1 Text of Insolvency Act 1986 s. 214

Section 214 – Wrongful trading

'(1) Subject to subsection (3) below, if in the course of the winding up of a company it appears that subsection (2) of this section applies in relation to a person who is or has been a director of the company, the court, on the application of the liquidator, may declare that that person is to be liable to make such contribution (if any) to the company's assets as the court thinks proper.

(2) This subsection applies in relation to a person if –
    (a) the company has gone into insolvent liquidation,
    (b) at some time before the commencement of the winding up of the company, that person knew or ought to have concluded that there was no reasonable prospect that the company would avoid going into insolvent liquidation, and
    (c) that person was a director of the company at that time;
    but the court shall not make a declaration under this section in any case where the time mentioned in paragraph (b) above was before 28 April 1986.

(3) The court shall not make a declaration under this section with respect to any person if it is satisfied that after the condition specified in subsection (2)(b) was first satisfied in relation to him that person took every step with a view to minimising the potential loss to the company's creditors as (assuming him to have known that there was no reasonable prospect that the company would avoid going into insolvent liquidation) he ought to have taken.

(4) For the purposes of subsections (2) and (3), the facts which a director of a company ought to know or ascertain, the conclusions which he ought

to reach and the steps which he ought to take are those which would be known or ascertained, or reached or taken, by a reasonably diligent person having both –
   (a) the general knowledge, skill and experience that may reasonably be expected of a person carrying out the same functions as are carried out by that director in relation to the company, and
   (b) the general knowledge, skill and experience that that director has.
(5) The reference in subsection (4) to the functions carried out in relation to a company by a director of the company includes any functions which he does not carry out but which have been entrusted to him.
(6) For the purposes of this section a company goes into insolvent liquidation if it goes into liquidation at a time when its assets are insufficient for the payment of its debts and other liabilities and the expenses of the winding up.
(7) In this section 'director' includes a shadow director.
(8) This section is without prejudice to section 213.'

3.5.2.3 The main features of the provision are as follows.

- Proceedings for wrongful trading may be brought only when an insolvent company is being wound up (s. 214(1) and (2)(a) – the effect of the latter subsection is that the company must be in 'insolvent liquidation'. That expression is defined for these purposes in s. 214(6)).
- They may be brought only on the application of the liquidator. Section 214 cannot, therefore, be used by individual creditors (s. 214(1)). According to the Insolvency Act 1986 s. 251, as amended by the Small Business, Enterprise and Employment Act 2015 as from 26 May 2015, a shadow director is 'a person in accordance with whose directions or instructions the directors of the company are accustomed to act, but so that a person is not deemed a shadow director by reason only that the directors act – (a) on advice given by that person in a professional capacity …'.
- A claim may only be brought against a director (s. 214(1)). The term 'director' is interpreted widely. It will catch not only anyone who has been properly appointed as a director (a 'de jure director') (de jure directors are discussed in section 5.6.2), but also 'de facto directors' (*Re Hydrodam (Corby) Ltd* [1994] 2 BCLC 180 at 182) and 'shadow directors' (s. 214(7)). A 'de facto director' is someone who has not been properly appointed as a director, but who nevertheless acts as a director (de facto directors are discussed in section 5.6.3).

   This definition, in turn, will be widely interpreted, so as to encompass not only someone who 'lurks in the shadows' and controls every facet of the company's business, but also someone who quite openly gives the de jure directors instructions in relation to certain aspects of the business (*Secretary of *State for Trade and Industry v Deverell* [2001] Ch 340. The case concerned the meaning of 'shadow director' in the context of the Company Directors Disqualification Act 1986, but the court's analysis, and in particular Morritt LJ's summary of the law at [36] and [37], applies equally to the definition of the expression set out in the Insolvency Act 1986 s. 251. The case, and the law on shadow directors generally, is discussed in section 5.6.4). In theory, a parent company which plays an active role in its subsidiary's affairs could be found to be a shadow director and, as such, liable under the wrongful trading provision.

- Liability arises where a director who knows, or ought to know, that the company is not going to survive nevertheless does not do all he can to minimise creditors' losses.

More specifically, a claim will succeed only if, before the winding up of the company began, the director 'knew or ought to have concluded that there was no reasonable prospect that the company would avoid going into insolvent liquidation' (s. 214(2)(b)), *and* failed to take 'every step with a view to minimising the potential loss to the company's creditors as (assuming him to have known that there was no reasonable prospect that the company would avoid going into insolvent liquidation) he ought to have taken' (s. 214(3)).

Each of these conditions raises a question. First, how strictly do the courts interpret the 'no reasonable prospect' test? Second, what steps is a director expected to take in order to minimise creditors' losses?

Before answering these questions, it is important to note the objective nature of the two conditions. Not only do they refer to a conclusion which a director 'ought' to have reached, and steps which he 'ought' to have taken, but s. 214(4) specifies that the conclusion which he ought to have reached and the steps which he ought to have taken are those which would have been reached and taken by a reasonably diligent person with the level of skill expected of a director of such a company or, if greater, the level of skill of the particular director in question. This injection of an objective standard has the effect of imposing on directors an obligation to be competent: a director who does his best for his company may nevertheless be liable for wrongful trading if he did not act as a reasonably diligent and capable director would have done. Loyalty and good intentions are no defence, in other words, in s. 214 proceedings.

As far as the first question is concerned, the courts have adopted a sensible approach to the 'no reasonable prospect test'. They will certainly take a dim view of a director who, although his company is plainly in serious financial difficulties, turns a blind eye to its predicament, hoping despite all the evidence that its fortunes will, as if by magic, somehow improve (*Roberts v Frohlich* [2011] EWHC 257 (Ch), at [112]) but they will not punish rational business decisions. Their view was summed up neatly by the deputy judge in *Earp v Stevenson, Re Kudos Business Solutions (in liquidation)*: 'the answer to the question of whether a director knew (or ought to have concluded) that there was no reasonable prospect that the company would avoid an insolvent liquidation depends on rational expectations of what the future might hold. Directors are not required to be clairvoyant' (*Earp v Stevenson, Re Kudos Business Solutions Ltd (in liquidation)* [2011] EWHC 1436 (Ch), at [61]). A competent director who weighs up the evidence and takes a considered view that his company, though in financial difficulties, can trade its way out of trouble, is unlikely to be held liable under s. 214 simply because the company's subsequent failure proves that his judgment was wrong.

As far as the second question is concerned, a director who has concluded that his company has no reasonable prospect of surviving should normally seek the advice of an insolvency expert and then (depending, of course, on the nature of that advice) cause the company to cease trading and set in motion the winding-up process. That is not to say, though, that he may (or, indeed, must) not take other steps. For example, if the company is in possession of valuable perishable stock, it might well make sense to continue trading in a limited fashion until that stock, at least, has been disposed of (*Re Produce Marketing Consortium Ltd* (1989) 5 BCC 569, at 596F).

3.5.3 Fraudulent trading

3.5.3.1 Fraudulent trading is potentially both a criminal matter and a civil matter. CA2006 s. 993 contains a criminal sanction, while civil liability is imposed by the Insolvency Act 1986 s. 213 (ss. 993 and 213 adopt very similar wording, although the former deals with fraudulent trading at any time in a company's life, while the latter is available only on the application of the company's liquidator). For the purposes of this chapter, s. 213 is of particular interest, because it gives the court the power to order someone other than the company to contribute to the pool of assets out of which the company's creditors are to be paid, and as such provides, in effect, for the company's separate identity to be compromised. The text of s. 213 is set out in full in Figure 3.2.

Figure 3.2 Text of Insolvency Act 1986 s. 213

Section 213 – Fraudulent trading

'(1) If in the course of the winding up of a company it appears that any business of the company has been carried on with intent to defraud creditors of the company or creditors of any other person, or for any fraudulent purpose, the following has effect.

(2) The court, on the application of the liquidator may declare that any persons who were knowingly parties to the carrying on of the business in the manner above-mentioned are to be liable to make such contributions (if any) to the company's assets as the court thinks proper.'

3.5.3.2 Section 213 is a much simpler provision than s. 214. It is readily apparent from its wording that fraudulent trading requires the following: (a) the company's business to have been carried on with intent to defraud creditors or for any fraudulent purpose; and (b) the person in question to have been knowingly party to the carrying on of the company's business in that way.

3.5.3.3 The scope of s. 213 is at once narrower and wider than that of s. 214. It is narrower because it is available only if there has been deliberate wrongdoing. In *Re Patrick and Lyon Ltd*, the judge held, in relation to a predecessor of s. 213, that 'the words "defraud" and "fraudulent purpose," where they appear in the section in question, are words which connote actual dishonesty involving, according to current notions of fair trading among commercial men, real moral blame' ([1933] Ch 786, at 790). It is wider because whereas wrongful trading proceedings may be brought only against a director of one kind or another (see paragraph 3.5.2.3), a fraudulent trading claim may be brought against 'any persons' who were knowingly party to the company's misconduct. This expression encompasses directors, certainly, but equally it can in theory catch shareholders, managers and even creditors.

3.5.4 Planned reform of the law

3.5.4.1 In theory, the liquidator's power to bring proceedings against a director for wrongful trading or fraudulent trading should act as a powerful counterbalance to the risks faced by creditors when doing business with a company. The company's debts may be its own and no one else's, and the shareholders' liability for its debts may be limited to any amount unpaid on their shares, but at least the directors can, if their behaviour falls below an acceptable standard, be ordered to contribute to the pool of assets available for distribution to creditors in the event of the company's failure.

3.5.4.2 In practice, however, claims under ss. 213 and 214 are relatively rare (see paragraphs 260, 263 and 270, 'Transparency & Trust: Enhancing the Transparency of UK Company Ownership and Increasing Trust in UK Business – Government Response' (BIS, April 2014); it is noted at paragraph 260 that there had been only 'around 30' reported cases brought under s. 214 since 1986), and so the Small Business, Enterprise and Employment Act 2015 will reform the law in order to seek to increase the number of claims being brought. One element of the reform will be the extension of the power to bring fraudulent and wrongful trading proceedings to administrators, but the principal reform will be the introduction of a power on the part of a liquidator (or an administrator) to assign the right to bring such proceedings. Take, for example, the case of a liquidator whose considered view is that a wrongful trading claim is, on the facts, unlikely to succeed. At present, that would be the end of the matter. Once the reforms take effect, however, the liquidator would be allowed to assign the right to bring the claim to a third party. Thus, a large creditor who disagrees with the liquidator's assessment of the merits of the claim would be able to buy the claim, pursue it himself and, if it succeeded, keep any payment which the court ordered the director to make.

3.5.4.3 The implementation date for the reforms has yet to be announced, but in any case it is important to understand the changes as part of the wider efforts of the company law regime to ensure that creditors receive sufficient protection. This is an issue which has exercised Parliament and the courts from the earliest days of the regime, and the balance between the protection of creditors on the one hand, and the protection of directors and shareholders on the other, is constantly being adjusted. Indeed, these reforms will sit alongside changes to the rules governing the disqualification of directors, which are contained in the Company Directors Disqualification Act 1986. The changes relating to the disqualification regime (which are also contained in the Small Business, Enterprise and Employment Act 2015) are quite substantial; of particular relevance to the topic at hand is a new power on the part of the courts to order a director whom they are disqualifying to pay compensation to the company or to creditors who suffered loss as a result of his misconduct.

3.5.4.4 None of the reforms will substantially alter the balance of power, in that creditors will still bear a considerable risk when doing business with a company whose shareholders enjoy the benefits of limited liability. They will, however, give creditors a little more protection than they had previously, primarily by exposing directors to a greater risk of personal liability.

3.6 Objects clauses and a company's capacity

3.6.1 Since a company is a legal entity, it acts in its own name, whether it is buying property, entering into contracts with employees or dealing with customers. The question arises, therefore, as to whether there are any restrictions on its freedom to act.

3.6.2 Historically, the answer to this question was emphatically that there were, indeed, such restrictions. A company was required to set out in its memorandum of association a statement of the purposes – or 'objects' – for which it was formed, and this so-called 'objects clause' acted as a limit on its capacity. If, say, a company's object was stated to be to manufacture cars, an attempt to diversify into shipbuilding was regarded as being beyond its capacity, and any contracts which it purported to enter into as part of the diversification were ultra vires (i.e. beyond its powers) and void (i.e. entirely invalid).

3.6.3 The objects clause was designed to protect shareholders and creditors, in that it enabled them to invest in, or otherwise deal with, a company safe in the knowledge that it could not subsequently move into a new, and possibly more risky, line of business. To the extent that it sought to safeguard creditors' interests, the objects clause was part of the wider scheme of creditor protection which endeavoured to mitigate the adverse impact on creditors of the principle of shareholders' limited liability. An illuminating discussion of the rationale for the objects clause can be found in *Ashbury Railway Carriage and Iron Company (Ltd) v Riche* (1875) LR 7 HL 653. See, in particular, the passage of Lord Hatherley's judgment at 684.

3.6.4 Objects clauses were not, however, without their drawbacks. Not only did they restrict the ability of companies to respond to changing market conditions by entering new areas of business, but the fact that a contract entered into between a creditor and a company which was acting outside its stated objects was void meant that objects clauses could, in practice, also operate to the detriment of creditors. In relation to the former point, a one stage, the objects clause could not be altered Joint Stock Companies Act 1862 s. 12), which meant that if the directors wanted the company to enter into a line of business which was not catered for in its objects clause, there was no option but to wind the company up and form a new company with a fresh set of objects. This strict rule was gradually eased, but even as the law stood immediately before CA2006 overhauled the regime, the objects clause could be amended only by the shareholders, and then only by means of a special resolution (CA 1985 s. 4).

3.6.5 The impact of these drawbacks was minimised by two developments. First, companies adopted the practice of drawing their objects clauses so widely that they could, by and large, undertake any business their board saw fit. Second, statute intervened latterly to provide that an act of a company was valid even if it was not covered by its objects, and was thus beyond its capacity.

3.6.6 The current law

3.6.6.1 Prior to the introduction of CA2006, the law and practice as far as objects clauses were concerned were in a curious state. On the one hand, companies were obliged to state their objects in their memorandum. On the other hand, companies habitually adopted objects clauses which were so broad in scope that the company could undertake any type of business it pleased, and, in any case, an act which was outside a company's objects was nevertheless valid.

CA2006 rationalised the position by abolishing the requirement for companies to state their objects, thus allowing companies to have unlimited capacity without the administrative burden of having to adopt a lengthy objects clause.

3.6.6.2 The Act's main provisions on objects clauses and a company's capacity are ss. 31(1) and 39(1).

THE COMPANY AS A SEPARATE ENTITY

- **Section 31(1):** *'Unless a company's articles specifically restrict the objects of the company, its objects are unrestricted.'* The effect of this provision is that a company is not required to have an objects clause, but is free to have one if it wishes. If it chooses to restrict its objects, an objects clause will need to be inserted into its articles of association. An objects clause cannot be inserted into the company's memorandum. Under the Act the memorandum has been reduced to a simple document which essentially just records the fact that the subscribers wish to form a company (see section 2.2.4).
- **Section 39(1):** *'The validity of an act done by a company shall not be called into question on the ground of lack of capacity by reason of anything in the company's constitution.'* This provision is relevant only in relation to companies which have chosen to restrict their objects. It retains the pre-CA2006 statutory protection for creditors by providing that an act by a company (for example, the entry by it into a contract with a creditor) is valid even if it is outside the company's objects.

3.6.7 Practical implications of the law

3.6.7.1 When considering the practical implications of the law in this area, it is helpful to divide companies into two categories: those formed under CA2006 and those formed under earlier companies legislation.

CA2006 companies

3.6.7.2 Many commercial companies will be content to have unrestricted objects. As long as they do not include wording in their articles to restrict their objects, their capacity will be free from restrictions and they will be able to act as they please.

3.6.7.3 Companies which want to restrict their objects will need to insert wording to that effect into their articles (the insertion of an objects clause into the articles is effected in the same way as any other alteration to the articles, namely by means of a special resolution (CA2006 s. 21). However, the insertion is not effective until it has been notified to Companies House and the notification has been duly registered (s. 31(2))). The option of having restricted objects will be of particular interest to companies in the not-for-profit sector (for example, charitable companies are required to restrict their objects to charitable objects. Note, in this connection, that the Act's provisions on objects clauses and a company's capacity are modified in their application to charitable companies: see ss. 31(4), 39(2) and 42). It may also be of interest to shareholders of commercial companies who want to try to rein in the board's power. The value of an objects clause in this context can be illustrated by reference to the example of a company which has the object of operating restaurants. If the directors were to move the company into the field of financial services, say, any contract to which they committed the company in connection with its new business would be protected by virtue of s. 39(1), but in breaching the objects clause the directors would be acting in breach of their statutory duty to abide by the articles CA2006 s. 171(a); this duty is discussed in section 7.3.8), and so would potentially be liable to compensate the company should the venture fail. The risk of being held liable in this way is likely to weigh on the directors' minds sufficiently to persuade them to confine the company's activities to the restaurant trade.

Companies formed under earlier companies legislation

3.6.7.4 Companies formed before CA2006 was introduced were required to include an objects clause in their memorandum. As a result of CA2006 s. 28, these objects clauses were carried over into the companies' articles with effect from 1 October 2009 (CA2006 Paragraph 7(3), Schedule 2, (Commencement No 8, Transitional Provisions and Savings) Order 2008 (SI 2008/2860)), where (subject to s. 39) they continued to act as a restriction on their capacity.

3.6.7.5 Such companies are, however, perfectly entitled to avail themselves of the option under CA2006 s. 31(1) of having unrestricted objects. If they wish to do so, they simply need to remove the objects clause from their articles. The removal of an objects clause from the articles is effected in the same way as any other alteration to the articles, namely by means of a special resolution (CA2006 s. 21). However, the removal is not effective until it has been notified to Companies House and the notification has been duly registered (s. 31(2)).

3.7 Entering into contracts

3.7.1 The paragraphs immediately above address the question of the extent to which a company has capacity to act. Logically, the next question which arises is as to *how* a company acts or, to put it another way, through *whom* a company acts.

3.7.2 A company's actions in relation to internal matters are of interest primarily to its directors and shareholders. When a company decides to launch a new product or enter a new jurisdiction, for example, its internal rules will determine who is responsible for taking that decision, and the validity or otherwise of the decision will not affect third parties.

3.7.3 By contrast, a company's actions in relation to the outside world are clearly of interest to third parties. In particular, third parties who transact business with companies have a very real interest in knowing whether a contract purportedly entered into by a company has, in fact, been entered into properly (i.e. does, in fact, constitute an act of the company), such that it is enforceable against the company. This section of the chapter deals, therefore, with the specific matter of the means by which a company enters into contracts. The question under consideration may be phrased as follows: in what circumstances will a company be said to have entered into a contract with a third party?

3.7.4 The answer to this question is not as straightforward as one might assume. Since a company, though a person, is artificial in nature, the company law regime has had to devise some rather complex rules governing the situations in which a company will be regarded as having entered into a contract.

3.7.5 As is often the case, the potential difficulties are easier to describe than to resolve. Consider the example of a large retail company, with a turnover of billions of pounds, a workforce numbering in the tens of thousands and dozens of shops across the length and breadth of the country. In what circumstances does such a company enter into a contract with a third party?

- If its managing director signs a contract purportedly committing the company to a £10 billion acquisition, has he bound the company? In other words, has the company itself, through his actions, entered into the contract?
- What would be the situation if the contract had been signed not by the managing director, but by a middle manager in the company's head office? Would his signature suffice to commit the company to the acquisition?
- What if the document under consideration were a lease for premises for a new shop? Would the middle manager's signature on the lease constitute an act of the company?
- Consider, finally, the position of a sales assistant in one of the company's shops. Would her signature on the £10 billion acquisition agreement be regarded as an act of the company? Would her signature bind the company to the lease for the premises? What about her dealings with a customer who is buying his weekly groceries? In taking the customer's money and giving him a receipt, has she committed the company to a contractual relationship with him? Through her actions, has the company itself acted?

3.7.6 It will be apparent from these examples that the law in this area has to deal with a wide variety of situations, and the workings of the regime – which comprises a mixture of common law rules and statutory provisions – can raise genuinely difficult issues. The following points should, however, serve to lay the foundations for an understanding of its core principles.

- As in every other area of company law, the regime is designed to strike a balance between competing interests, in this case the interests of creditors and the interests of companies. On the one hand, when a third party enters into a contract which he believes imposes binding obligations on a company, he wants the law to ensure that those obligations are enforceable. On the other hand, a company does not want to find itself bound by each and every contract entered into in its name. In this instance, the law favours creditors, in that it seeks to promote the validity of contracts purportedly entered into by companies. The immediate policy objective behind this approach is the need to provide certainty to those who deal with companies, the wider aim being, as always, the promotion of business activity.

- As complicated as the detail of the law can be, the principles which underpin it are straightforward. They may be reduced to a simple proposition: a company may enter into contracts with third parties either through its organs or through an agent.

The reference to the company's 'organs' is to the shareholders (acting collectively) and the board of directors. The company's articles will normally divide up responsibility for the company's affairs between these two organs, and as long as it has responsibility for acting in relation to the matter at hand either organ can validly commit the company to a contract. If a company's articles give full management power to the board, for example, and the only two directors decide to enter into a contract to purchase goods from a third party and duly sign the supply contract, the company will be bound by its terms, since it has acted through one of its organs, namely the board of directors.

In practice, at least with larger companies, contracts are rarely entered into by the board or the shareholders. Instead, they are normally entered into by someone – be he a director, a manager, a junior employee or, indeed, someone entirely outside the company – who has authority to act on behalf of the company, and so is able to bind it to contractual obligations to third parties. Such people are described as 'agents' of the company, and the chief difficulty one encounters in this area of the law is in determining whether a purported agent really possesses the necessary authority. The different types of authority are discussed in section 3.7.9.

3.7.7 CA2006 ss. 43 and 44 set out certain formalities concerning the making of contracts by companies and the execution of documents by companies. The text of these sections is set out in full in Figure 3.3.

Figure 3.3 Text of CA2006 ss. 43 and 44

CA2006 ss. 43 and 44 Section 43 – Company contracts

'(1) Under the law of England and Wales or Northern Ireland a contract may be made –
    (a) by a company, by writing under its common seal, or
    (b) on behalf of a company, by a person acting under its authority, express or implied.

(2) Any formalities required by law in the case of a contract made by an individual also apply, unless a contrary intention appears, to a contract made by or on behalf of a company.'

Section 44 – Execution of documents
'(1) Under the law of England and Wales or Northern Ireland a document is executed by a company –
   (a) by the affixing of its common seal, or
   (b) by signature in accordance with the following provisions.
(2) A document is validly executed by a company if it is signed on behalf of the company –
   (a) by two authorised signatories, or
   (b) by a director of the company in the presence of a witness who attests the signature.
(3) The following are 'authorised signatories' for the purposes of subsection (2) –
   (a) every director of the company, and
   (b) in the case of a private company with a secretary or a public company, the secretary (or any joint secretary) of the company.
(4) A document signed in accordance with subsection (2) and expressed, in whatever words, to be executed by the company has the same effect as if executed under the common seal of the company.
(5) In favour of a purchaser a document is deemed to have been duly executed by a company if it purports to be signed in accordance with subsection (2).
   A 'purchaser' means a purchaser in good faith for valuable consideration and includes a lessee, mortgagee or other person who for valuable consideration acquires an interest in property.
(6) Where a document is to be signed by a person on behalf of more than one company, it is not duly signed by that person for the purposes of this section unless he signs it separately in each capacity.
(7) References in this section to a document being (or purporting to be) signed by a director or secretary are to be read, in a case where that office is held by a firm, as references to its being (or purporting to be) signed by an individual authorised by the firm to sign on its behalf.
(8) This section applies to a document that is (or purports to be) executed by a company in the name of or on behalf of another person whether or not that person is also a company.'

3.7.8 It is important to recognise that ss. 43 and 44 (which are often the subject of much discussion by solicitors when the practicalities of entering into a transaction are being considered) do not deal with the substantive question as to whether the person or persons through whom the company is apparently acting are in a position to bind it. (There seems to be a view that s. 44(5), which deals with the particular case of a third party who is a purchaser in good faith, creates a presumption that the signatories have ostensible authority (see the court's *obiter* comments in *LNOC Ltd v Watford Association Football Club Ltd* [2013] EWHC 3615 (Comm), at [83]–[97]), but the wording of the provision does not, on the face of it, appear to support this analysis.) This is obvious from the wording of s. 43, which provides at sub-section (1)(b) that a contract may be made 'on behalf of a company, by a person acting under its authority, express or implied'. It is less obvious from the wording of s. 44, which provides that a company executes a document by various means, including the signature of two directors (s. 44(1)–(3)). However, the fact that a means of execution provided for in s. 44 has been adopted does *not* necessarily mean that the document is binding on the company. Consider the case of two non-executive directors of a multinational company who sign a contract to purchase a larger rival for £10 billion. The signature of two directors constitutes compliance with the rules governing formalities, as set out in s. 44, but the contract will nevertheless not be binding on the company unless the directors in question had authority to enter into the contract, and so were acting as its agents.

3.7.9 An agent's authority to bind the company

3.7.9.1 As noted above, when an agent purports to enter into a contract on behalf of a company, the contract will be binding on the company only if the agent had authority to act on its behalf.

3.7.9.2 In this context, 'authority' comprises actual authority and ostensible authority (also known as apparent authority). Actual authority itself can be divided into two types: express actual authority and implied actual authority.

3.7.9.3 The position may, therefore, be stated more precisely as follows: when an agent purports to enter into a contract on behalf of a company, the contract will be binding on the company only if the agent had express actual authority, implied actual authority or ostensible authority to act on its behalf.

Actual authority

3.7.9.4 The law on actual authority was summarised by Lord Denning MR in *Hely-Hutchinson v Brayhead Ltd* in the following terms:

'... actual authority may be express or implied. It is express when it is given by express words, such as when a board of directors pass a resolution which authorises two of their number to sign cheques. It is implied when it is inferred from the conduct of the parties and the circumstances of the case, such as when the board of directors appoint one of their number to be managing director. They thereby impliedly authorise him to do all such things as fall within the usual scope of that office.' ([1968] 1 QB 549, at 583)

3.7.9.5 In order for express actual authority to exist, therefore, there will need to be express words in some form. In practice, the words will often take the form of a board resolution giving certain named directors authority to sign a particular document on the company's behalf (see further paragraph 3.7.10).

3.7.9.6 By contrast, implied actual authority arises from conduct and circumstances. The extract above notes that implied actual authority may exist by virtue of the fact that the person in question has been appointed to a particular office, but it may also exist in the absence of an official appointment. In *Hely-Hutchinson v Brayhead Ltd* itself, a company was held to be bound by a contract which had been entered into by its de facto managing director. By allowing the individual concerned to act as managing director, and to enter into contracts without first obtaining its approval, the board had impliedly given him authority to enter into the contract in question.

Ostensible authority

3.7.9.7 Ostensible authority exists where a company holds someone out as having authority to act on its behalf.

3.7.9.8 It was described by Diplock LJ in the following terms in *Freeman & Lockyer v Buckhurst Park Properties (Mangal) Ltd*:

'An "apparent" or "ostensible" authority ... is a legal relationship between the principal [eg a company] and the contractor [ie a third party] created by a representation, made by the principal to the contractor, intended to be and in fact acted upon by the contractor, that the agent has authority to enter on behalf of the principal into a contract of a kind within the scope of the "apparent" authority, so as to render the principal liable to perform any obligations imposed upon him by such contract.' ([1964] 2 QB 480, at 503)

3.7.9.9 In *Armagas Ltd v Mundogas SA*, Lord Keith confirmed this analysis in language which is perhaps more readily comprehensible:

'Ostensible authority comes about where the principal [eg a company], by words or conduct, has represented that the agent has the requisite actual authority, and the party dealing with the agent has entered into a contract with him in reliance on that representation.' ([1986] 1 AC 717, at 777)

3.7.9.10 The rationale for the rule that an agent who has ostensible authority can bind the company is that if the company holds someone out as having authority to act on its behalf, it would be unfair for a third party who relied on that representation to be left with an unenforceable contract on the ground that the agent did not, in fact, have any such authority. It is thus said that ostensible authority is based on the notion of 'estoppel by representation'.

3.7.9.11 The following points in relation to the law on ostensible authority should be noted.

- The holding out, or representation, by the company does not necessarily involve a direct communication from the company to the third party. In fact, it is in practice much more likely to involve appointing a person to a particular office (*Hely-Hutchinson v Brayhead Ltd* [1968] 1 QB 549, at 583), permitting a person to act as if he occupied a particular office (*Freeman & Lockyer v Buckhurst Park Properties (Mangal) Ltd* [1964] 2 QB 480, at 510) or honouring contracts which the agent has entered into with the third party over a period of time (*Armagas Ltd v Mundogas SA* [1986] 1 AC 717, at 777).
- The scope of an agent's ostensible authority is by no means always clear, especially where it arises through his occupation (whether through formal appointment or otherwise) of a particular office. Take the case of a board which appoints one of its members to act as the company's finance director. By doing so, the company is holding that individual out to third parties as having authority to act on its behalf in relation to such matters as a finance director would normally be expected to act. But what exactly does this mean? What, in other words, are the matters which would normally fall within a finance director's competence?

    The starting point when answering such questions is to use common sense. Thus, a managing director has ostensible authority to enter into contracts which concern the day-to-day business of the company, a finance director has ostensible authority to enter into contracts concerning the day-to-day financial affairs of the company, a company secretary has ostensible authority to enter into contracts of an administrative nature and, to return to one of the scenarios set out in paragraph 3.7.5, a sales assistant has ostensible authority to sell goods in the company's shops to customers.

    Case law, too, may provide some assistance, for the courts have, from time to time, considered the nature of certain offices within the company structure (see, for example, *Smith v Butler* [2012] EWCA Civ 314 in relation to the role of a managing director, *Hely-Hutchinson v Brayhead Ltd* [1968] 1 QB 549 in relation to the role of a chairman and *Panorama Developments (Guildford)*

Ltd v Fidelis Furnishing Fabrics Ltd [1971] 2 QB 711 in relation to the role of a company secretary).

Inevitably, though, there will be instances in which it is not clear whether an act falls within the normal scope of competence of someone who occupies the office in question, and in such cases ultimately the extent of the agent's ostensible authority will fall to be determined by the courts.

- A third party who knows (*Criterion Properties plc v Stratford UK Properties LLC* [2004] UKHL 28, at [31]) or should know (*Thanakharn Kasikorn Thai Chamkat (Mahachon) v Akai Holdings Ltd (in liquidation)* [2010] HKCFA 64, at [62]), that an agent does not have actual authority to enter into a contract cannot rely on the agent's ostensible authority. This is because in such circumstances a third party cannot be said to have relied on the company's representation that the agent had authority to act. Take the case of a managing director who enters into a small contract with one of the company's regular suppliers, but does so with the intention of securing a personal gain. In doing so, he is breaching the duties which he owes to the company, and so is acting without actual authority (*Hopkins v TL Dallas Group Ltd* [2005] 1 BCLC 543, at [88]). If the supplier is aware of the managing director's improper motive, he will not be able to argue that it is within the scope of a managing director's ostensible authority to enter into small contracts, and so he will not be able to enforce the contract.

- CA2006 s. 40 deals with the specific problem of restrictions on an agent's authority which are set out in the company's articles. Since a company's articles of association are a public document, the doctrine of constructive notice states that a third party dealing with companies is taken to have notice of their provisions. If, therefore, a company's articles contain a provision restricting an agent's authority, a third party is taken to have notice of that provision, and to know that an agent who breaches the restriction has no actual authority. In accordance with the point above, the effect of this deemed knowledge is that a third party dealing with an agent who breaches a restriction in the company's articles cannot rely on his ostensible authority.

Consider the case of a provision in a company's articles which states that the managing director may not borrow more than £5,000. A lender who is dealing with the managing director is taken to have knowledge of this provision, even if he has never seen the company's articles and has not been informed of their contents. If he proceeds to agree to lend £10,000 to the company, and the agreement is signed by the managing director on the company's behalf, the effect of the doctrine of constructive notice is that the lender is taken to know that the managing director has no actual authority to enter into the agreement, and so cannot rely on his ostensible authority to do so. The agreement will be unenforceable.

It was noted in paragraph 3.7.6 that the law in this area favours creditors. That statement was based in part upon the fact that the law takes the view that the operation of the doctrine of constructive notice in this way unfairly prejudices third parties dealing with companies, and so contains a rule which cancels out the impact of the doctrine. That rule is contained in s. 40. (The statutory response to the problem is of relatively recent vintage. Historically, the difficulties caused by the doctrine of constructive notice were addressed by what was known variously as the rule in Turquand's case (a reference to the decision in *Royal British Bank v Turquand* (1856) 6 E & B 327), the indoor management rule and the internal management rule. The rule provided that a third party dealing with an agent was entitled to assume that any internal procedures which had to be complied with in order to enable the agent to act on the company's behalf had been duly complied with. If, for example, the articles stated that a managing director could not take on a loan of more than £5,000 without first obtaining the board's approval, a third party was entitled to assume that board approval had duly been obtained. The rule is still good law today, but it has largely been superseded by s. 40 and so should now be considered only if it has been determined that s. 40 does not rescue the transaction in question.)

Section 40(1) provides as follows: 'In favour of a person dealing with a company in good faith, the power of the directors to bind the company, or authorise others to do so, is deemed to be free of any limitation under the company's constitution.'

Section 40 contains some grey areas, but for the purposes of this handbook it suffices to say that its effect, broadly, is that a third party will normally be able to rely on an agent's ostensible authority even if the agent has breached a restriction on his authority contained in the company's articles. Thus, it renders enforceable many contracts which would otherwise be unenforceable by virtue of the application of the doctrine of constructive notice.

The relationship between actual authority and ostensible authority

3.7.9.12 Those who are new to this area of company law sometimes wonder what the relationship is between actual authority and ostensible authority, but to ask this question is to misunderstand the law on an agent's authority. Aside from the fact that, as noted in paragraph 3.7.9.11, a third party who knows that an agent does not have actual authority cannot rely on his ostensible authority, the two concepts are quite distinct. As Diplock LJ put it in *Freeman & Lockyer v Buckhurst Park Properties (Mangal) Ltd*: 'Actual authority and apparent authority are quite independent of one another. Generally they co-exist and coincide, but either may exist without the other and their respective scopes may be different.' In short, the only question to ask is whether an agent has either actual authority or ostensible authority. Only if he has one or the other (or, indeed, both) will the contract be enforceable against the company. The relationship between the two is neither here nor there.

3.7.10 Practical implications of the law

3.7.10.1 As far as run-of-the-mill contracts of relatively modest value are concerned, the law's bias in favour of creditors should give third parties dealing with companies a certain amount of confidence. As long as the person with whom they are dealing is someone who would normally be capable of acting for the company in the matter at hand, the chances are good that he will have authority to bind the company, in which case the contract will be enforceable against the company.

3.7.10.2 Where, however, the contract is more significant, third parties will not want to risk being exposed to the grey areas which are built into the rules on implied actual authority and ostensible authority, and should therefore seek evidence that the person with whom they are dealing has express actual authority to enter into the contract on the company's behalf. This evidence may take the form of a minute of a board resolution conferring authority, perhaps along the following lines: 'The directors resolved that the contract would promote the success of the company for the benefit of its members as a whole, and that, accordingly, [name of director] was authorised to sign the contract on the company's behalf.'

3.8 Pre-incorporation contracts
3.8.1 CA2006 s. 51

3.8.1.1 Since a company is a legal entity in its own right, and not merely an extension of its shareholders or directors, logically contracts which are entered into purportedly on its behalf before it has been formed (a noted in section 2.3, a company comes into being not on the date when the documents connected with the application to register it were sent to the registrar of companies, but on the date of its incorporation as set out in its certificate of incorporation (CA2006 s. 16) cannot be binding upon it. After all, a company can enter into a contract only through one of its organs or through an agent who has authority to act on its behalf (see section 3.7), and a company which does not yet exist does not have any organs through which to act and is in no position to give anyone authority to act on its behalf.

3.8.1.2 That is not to say, though, that such contracts, which are known as 'pre-incorporation contracts', are void. On the contrary, by virtue of CA2006 s. 51, they will generally take effect as contracts made between the third party and the person who entered into the contract purportedly on behalf of the company. Section 51(1) reads as follows:

'A contract that purports to be made by or on behalf of a company at a time when the company has not been formed has effect, subject to any agreement to the contrary, as one made with the person purporting to act for the company or as agent for it, and he is personally liable on the contract accordingly.'

3.8.1.3 As with so much of the law in the area of company contracts, the aim of s. 51 is to protect third parties, such as creditors, by ensuring that contracts into which they enter are not worthless. True, a pre-incorporation contract does not take effect as the creditor intended – that is to say, as a contract with the company – but at least it can be enforced against the individual who purported to be acting for the company. (Equally, the individual in question can normally enforce the contract against the third party (*Braymist Ltd v Wise Finance Co Ltd* [2002] EWCA Civ 127). Indeed, the effect of the Contracts (Rights of Third Parties) Act 1999 ss. 1(1) and (3) is that the company itself, though it will not be bound by the contract, may be able to enforce some of its terms against the third party.)

3.8.1.4 The impact of s. 51 in practice may be illustrated by a simple example. Take the case of an entrepreneur who instructs his solicitor to form a company and then, a few days before the company is incorporated, enters into a contract with a third party, purportedly on the company's behalf, for the purchase of goods for use in the company's business. This is a contract which 'purports to be made by or on behalf of a company at a time when the company has not been formed', and so s. 51 operates to give effect to it as a contract between the third party and the entrepreneur in his personal capacity.

3.8.2 Residual relevance of the common law

3.8.2.1 Section 51 is widely drawn, but the courts will construe it strictly. In *Cotronic (UK) Ltd v Dezonie* [1991] BCC 200, a Mr Dezonie entered into a contract in 1986, purportedly on behalf of a company named Wendaland Builders Ltd. In fact, the company had, unbeknownst to him, been dissolved in 1981. He discovered this fact in 1987, and a new company, also named Wendaland Builders Ltd, was formed in 1988. The Court of Appeal held that a predecessor provision to s. 51 did not apply to the contract. The first Wendaland Builders Ltd, on behalf of which Mr Dezonie had purported to act, was not a company which had yet to be formed, while the second Wendaland Builders Ltd was a company which had yet to be formed, but was not the company on behalf of which Mr Dezonie had purported to act.

3.8.2.2 In the rare instances in which s. 51 does not apply, the contract may nevertheless be valid under the traditional common law approach to pre-incorporation contracts, which provides that they bind the person who signs on behalf of the yet-to-be-formed company if, in fact, he intends to be a party to the contract in his personal capacity (*Phonogram Ltd v Lane* [1982] 1 QB 938, at 945E). In practice, however, the signatory will generally be seeking to bind the company rather than himself, (in *Cotronic (UK) Ltd v Dezonie* [1991] BCC 200, for example, the Court of Appeal concluded that, on the facts, the contract was not intended to bind Mr Dezonie personally) and if that is the case the contract will be void.

4

Articles of association

Summary
- A company must have a set of articles of association. The articles act, essentially, as the company's internal rulebook.
- It is for individual companies to determine the contents of their articles. In practice, many private companies either adopt the statutory model articles in their entirety, or use them as a starting point for producing bespoke articles.
- Articles are not set in stone, but may be amended by the shareholders by means of a special resolution. The power to amend the articles is, however, subject to various restrictions.
- The law governing the enforcement of articles is unsatisfactory, in that it is not clear precisely what sort of provisions are enforceable, and by whom.

4.1 Introduction

4.1.1 A company's articles of association serve as its main constitutional document. They typically deal with such matters as the means by which the board takes decisions, the procedure for declaring dividends and the rights attached to different classes of shares, and so are often referred to as the company's 'internal rulebook'.

4.1.2 This label provides a useful shorthand description of the role of the articles, but it does not accurately describe their precise scope. On the one hand, many aspects of a company's internal affairs are, in fact, addressed by CA2006. For example, the Act contains extensive provisions dealing with the procedure for passing shareholders' written resolutions. On the other hand, although the articles certainly focus primarily on internal matters, their most important provision is the statement limiting the shareholders' liability for the company's debts in the event of its failure (this aspect of the articles of association is discussed in paragraph 3.3.1), and plainly this is a matter which goes well beyond the regulation of a company's internal affairs.

4.1.3 This chapter examines the legal framework governing articles of association in outline, before considering three of its elements in more detail:

- The contents of articles of association – this part of the chapter identifies the main matters which are normally dealt with in articles, and provides an analysis of the key provisions of the model articles of association for private companies.
- Amending articles of association – this part of the chapter notes the basic rule that articles may be amended by the shareholders by means of a special resolution, and highlights the qualifications to which the rule is subject.
- Enforcing articles of association – this part of the chapter examines the legal status of the articles, and summarises the rather confusing law concerning their enforcement.

4.2 The legal framework

4.2.1 The statutory provisions

4.2.1.1 References to the articles are scattered throughout the Act, but the provisions which establish the legal framework governing them are to be found in Part 3, which comprises ss. 17 to 38. Within Part 3, the most important provisions are ss. 18(1) to (3), 19(1) and (3), 20 and 21(1). The text of these provisions is set out in Figure 4.1.

Figure 4.1 Text of CA2006 ss. 18(1) to 3, 19(1) and (3), 20 and 21(1)

Section 18(1) to (3)
'(1) A company must have articles of association prescribing regulations for the company.
(2) Unless it is a company to which model articles apply by virtue of section 20 (default application of model articles in case of limited company), it must register articles of association.
(3) Articles of association registered by a company must –
  (a) be contained in a single document, and
  (b) be divided into paragraphs numbered consecutively.'

Section 19(1) and (3)
'(1) The Secretary of State may by regulations prescribe model articles of association for companies.
...
(3) A company may adopt all or any of the provisions of model articles.'

> **Section 20**
> '(1) On the formation of a limited company –
>   (a) if articles are not registered, or
>   (b) if articles are registered, in so far as they do not exclude or modify the relevant model articles,
>   the relevant model articles (so far as applicable) form part of the company's articles in the same manner and to the same extent as if articles in the form of those articles had been duly registered.
> (2) The "relevant model articles" means the model articles prescribed for a company of that description as in force at the date on which the company is registered.'
>
> **Section 21(1)**
> '(1) A company may amend its articles by special resolution.'

4.2.1.2 The effect of ss. 18 and 19 is that companies are required to have a set of articles of association, but may choose to adopt so-called 'model articles' rather than undertake a drafting exercise to create a bespoke set of articles (a process which can potentially be very expensive). If a company has not adopted any articles at all, whether the model articles or a bespoke set, the model articles will apply by default by virtue of s. 20. The model articles are discussed in section 4.2.2.

4.2.1.3 The effect of s. 21 is that the articles are not set in stone, but may be amended. Only the shareholders have the power to make amendments, though, and even they can do so only by means of a special resolution. The law on amendments to the articles is discussed in section 4.4.

4.2.2 The model articles

4.2.2.1 The model articles are contained in the Companies (Model Articles) Regulations 2009 (SI 2009/3229). In fact, the regulations set out three sets of model articles, one each for private companies limited by shares, private companies limited by guarantee and public companies.

4.2.2.2 The model articles serve three purposes. First, as noted in section 4.2.1, they operate as default articles which will apply if, for any reason, a company has not adopted articles. Second, they provide companies which do not have the resources to produce bespoke articles with a standard set of articles which they can adopt wholesale. Third, they provide companies which want to adopt bespoke articles with a toolbox of provisions upon which to draw.

4.2.2.3 The model articles are, on the whole, well-drafted and fairly comprehensive, and there is no reason why a small private company should not adopt them wholesale, as long as its internal affairs are uncomplicated. Take the case of a businessman who has operated as a sole trader for a few months, but who wishes to form a company in order to avail himself of the option of limiting his liability for the business's debts. If he is to be the sole shareholder and the sole director, the business to be carried on precisely as it always has been (save that it will technically be owned by the company rather than him), he might legitimately decide that the model articles adequately address the company's needs as far as internal regulation are concerned.

4.2.2.4 Companies which have more complex internal structures are likely to want to have a set of articles which are tailored to their needs, and so will not be content to adopt the model articles wholesale. Such companies are free to devise an entirely bespoke set of articles, but more often than not it will make sense to base their bespoke articles on the model articles. Instead of drafting completely new provisions on directors' decision-making, for example, it will normally be easier to use the provisions on decision-making in the model articles as a starting point for the drafting exercise.

4.2.2.5 There are two ways to base bespoke articles on the model articles. One way is to adopt short-form articles, which incorporate provisions from the model articles by reference (it might be thought that s. 18(3)(a), which requires articles to be contained in a single document, prevents provisions of the model articles from being incorporated into a set of bespoke articles by reference, but paragraph 76 of CA2006 Explanatory Notes confirms that this is not the case) and then supplement and/or amend them as appropriate. There are no requirements regarding the means by which the incorporation by reference is to be effected, but a provision along the following lines is typical: 'The model articles for private companies limited by shares in force on [date] apply to the Company, save that articles 7 to 16 are modified as follows.' The other way to use the model articles is to adopt long-form articles which exclude the model articles but then copy out some or all of their provisions, amending and/or supplementing them as appropriate. Although it is up to individual companies to decide whether short-form articles suit their needs better than long-form articles, it is worth bearing in mind that although long-form articles will normally take a little longer to prepare, they are easier to use, since they gather all the provisions in a single document.

4.3 The contents of articles

4.3.1 It is not easy to summarise the matters which fall within the province of the articles. As has been noted above, it is true that the articles deal primarily with aspects of the company's internal regulation, but it is also the case that many of the provisions of CA2006 concern internal matters. The question, then, is as to where the line is drawn between internal matters which are addressed in the Act and internal matters which are addressed in the articles, and unfortunately the line follows rather an arbitrary path. The point may be illustrated by reference to the means by which directors are appointed and removed, for the Act is silent as to the former but provides a procedure for effecting the latter.

4.3.2 In order to identify those matters which are dealt with in the articles, therefore, it is necessary to understand the precise scope of the Act. The first step towards developing such an understanding is to appreciate the following points:

- Some of the Act's provisions are of mandatory application – for example, it is not open to a company to use its articles to opt out of s. 442, which specifies the deadline by which accounts must be filed with the registrar.
- Some of the Act's provisions set out a default position, which companies are free to adjust in their articles – for example, s. 550 gives directors the power, in certain circumstances, to allot shares without first obtaining shareholder approval, but states expressly that the power is subject to any prohibition in the company's articles.
- The Act has nothing at all to say on some matters, which are therefore left to be addressed in the articles – a prime example is the division of powers, as regards the management of the company's business, between the shareholders and the directors, for the Act is silent on this most fundamental of questions.

4.3.3 This may seem an unduly confusing approach, but its rationale is to be found in the web of balancing acts in which the company law regime is engaged. On the one hand, it seeks to ensure that there is a degree of consistency in the way in which companies are run; on the other hand, it recognises that an overly prescriptive approach would reduce the attractiveness of the company as a vehicle for doing business.

4.3.4 This chapter will not attempt the Herculean task of listing every matter which should, or might, be dealt with in the articles. It is sufficient for present purposes to note that the articles of most private companies will be built around a number of core topics:

- the limited liability of the company's shareholders;
- the division of powers between the shareholders and the directors;
- the means by which directors take decisions;
- the conduct of general meetings; and
- the company's shares, including the procedure for declaring a dividend.

4.3.5 Key provisions of the model articles

4.3.5.1 Since most private companies will either adopt the model articles for private companies limited by shares in their entirety, or at least use them as a starting point for drafting a set of bespoke articles, anyone who works with private companies needs to be familiar with the main provisions of the model articles. This section contains brief commentary on selected provisions, dealing both with their effect as they stand and, in some cases, with options for supplementing them.

4.3.5.2 The full text of the model articles for private companies limited by shares and the model articles for public companies is set out in Appendix 3.

Article 2 – Liability of members
The liability of the members is limited to the amount, if any, unpaid on the shares held by them.

4.3.5.3 It is difficult to overstate the importance of this article. It ensures that the company is a 'company limited by shares' within the meaning of CA2006 s.3, which in turn ensures that the liability of its shareholders is limited in accordance with the Insolvency Act 1986 s. 74(2)(d). If article 2 is omitted, the shareholders face the prospect of being liable to contribute any amount necessary to pay off the company's debts in the event that it fails (see section 3.3 for a discussion of the legal basis of shareholders' limited liability).

Article 3 – Directors' general authority
Subject to the articles, the directors are responsible for the management of the company's business, for which purpose they may exercise all the powers of the company.

Article 4 – Shareholders' reserve power
(1) The shareholders may, by special resolution, direct the directors to take, or refrain from taking, specified action.
(2) No such special resolution invalidates anything which the directors have done before the passing of the resolution.

4.3.5.4 These two articles concern the fundamental division of powers between the shareholders and the directors, a question which is not addressed by CA2006.

4.3.5.5 Article 3 confers on the directors a wide-ranging power to run the company's business. This extends, for example, to responsibility for the company's day-to-day management, taking decisions as to whether to diversify the company's business, considering the merits of proposed acquisitions or disposals, managing staffing levels, instituting legal proceedings in the company's name and setting the company's long-term objectives.

4.3.5.6 Article 4 retains for the shareholders a so-called 'reserve power', which enables them, through the use of a special resolution, to take decisions which would normally be left to the board. It is designed to ensure that, if there is a serious disagreement between the shareholders and the board, the former will ultimately prevail.

4.3.5.7 Most private companies will retain both of these articles, although it is not uncommon to qualify article 3, so as to carve out certain matters from the delegation to the board. For example, the article may be supplemented by a proviso that substantial transactions may be entered into only with the prior approval of the shareholders, or that the company will not enter a new jurisdiction or a new line of business without such approval (Article 3 is discussed further in section 5.5. Article 4 is discussed further in paragraph 8.2.4).

> **Article 5 – Directors may delegate**
> (1) Subject to the articles, the directors may delegate any of the powers which are conferred on them under the articles –
>   (a) to such person or committee;
>   (b) by such means (including by power of attorney);
>   (c) to such an extent;
>   (d) in relation to such matters or territories; and
>   (e) on such terms and conditions;
>   as they think fit.
> (2) ...
> (3) ...

4.3.5.8 Article 5 recognises that it may not be practicable for the board to exercise all of its powers all the time, and so gives the directors a very wide power to delegate.

4.3.5.9 This power includes a power to delegate functions to executive directors, and in this connection article 5 should be read in conjunction with article 19(1), which provides for the appointment of executive directors. A point to note is that if the board does not expressly delegate powers to an executive director, the scope of his powers will be unclear. This is because no set list of the powers which will be taken to have been impliedly delegated to particular types of executive director by virtue of their appointment emerges from the case law. (In *Smith v Butler* [2012] EWCA Civ 314, a case concerning a managing director, Arden LJ held that 'in principle, the implied powers of a managing director are those that would ordinarily be exercisable by a managing director in his position', but that this was subject to the company's articles and any express agreement. The question as to whether an executive director would ordinarily possess a particular power will not always be easy to answer (the law on executive directors is considered further in section 5.6.5)). If the shareholders are concerned that the board may fail to take advantage of article 5 to delegate power expressly, the articles can be amended so as to specify, perhaps in non-exhaustive fashion, the powers which any executive directors will have.

Article 7 – Directors to take decisions collectively
(1) The general rule about decision-making by directors is that any decision of the directors must be either a majority decision at a meeting or a decision taken in accordance with article 8.
(2) If –
  (a) the company only has one director, and
  (b) no provision of the articles requires it to have more than one director,
  the general rule does not apply, and the director may take decisions without regard to any of the provisions of the articles relating to directors' decision-making.

Article 8 – Unanimous decisions
(1) A decision of the directors is taken in accordance with this article when all eligible directors indicate to each other by any means that they share a common view on a matter.
(2) Such a decision may take the form of a resolution in writing, copies of which have been signed by each eligible director or to which each eligible director has otherwise indicated agreement in writing.
(3) ...
(4) ...

4.3.5.10 These two articles form the basis of the model articles' provisions dealing with the means by which the board takes decisions (in practice, most decisions concerning the day-to-day conduct of a company's business are taken by individual directors. Major decisions are, however, taken by the board, and it is to such decisions that articles 7 and 8 apply). They provide two main options: a decision may be taken either by majority vote at a board meeting or unanimously by means of a directors' written resolution.

4.3.5.11 Article 8 is, in fact, wide enough to encompass unanimous decisions taken much less formally than by means of a directors' written resolution. For example, it would allow the board to take a unanimous decision by means of an exchange of text messages. Article 15 requires a written record to be kept of any decision taken by informal means, but in practice directors who are in the habit of acting informally are unlikely to comply with article 15, in which case there will be no paper trail to provide evidence of their decision. As a matter of good practice, therefore, boards should normally confine themselves either to acting at a board meeting or by means of a directors' written resolution.

Article 9 – Calling a directors' meeting
(1) Any director may call a directors' meeting by giving notice of the meeting to the directors or by authorising the company secretary (if any) to give such notice.
(2) Notice of any directors' meeting must indicate –
 (a) its proposed date and time;
 (b) where it is to take place; and
 (c) if it is anticipated that directors participating in the meeting will not be in the same place, how it is proposed that they should communicate with each other during the meeting.
(3) Notice of a directors' meeting must be given to each director, but need not be in writing.
(4) ...

4.3.5.12 This article is uncontroversial and largely self-explanatory. Some companies may wish to supplement it by requiring meetings to be held on a regular basis, for example once a month or on a quarterly basis.

4.3.5.13 A question may arise as to the timing of the notice, since the article does not specify a notice period. The position at common law is that the courts will be guided by the company's usual practice in this regard. In *Browne v La Trinidad* (1887) 37 Ch D 1 Lindley LJ was not convinced that notice given a matter of minutes before a board meeting was insufficient, given the board's practice of meeting on very short notice. In *Re Homer District Consolidated Gold Mines, ex parte Smith* (1888) 39 Ch D 546, by contrast, North J took a dim view of a notice period of three hours in light of the company's practice of giving notice the day before the meeting.

Article 10 – Participation in directors' meetings
(1) Subject to the articles, directors participate in a directors' meeting, or part of a directors' meeting, when –
 (a) the meeting has been called and takes place in accordance with the articles, and
 (b) they can each communicate to the others any information or opinions they have on any particular item of the business of the meeting.
(2) In determining whether directors are participating in a directors' meeting, it is irrelevant where any director is or how they communicate with each other.
(3) ...

4.3.5.14 This is an extremely important provision in practice, for it allows directors to attend meetings remotely, for example by telephone.

Article 11 – Quorum for directors' meetings
(1) At a directors' meeting, unless a quorum is participating, no proposal is to be voted on, except a proposal to call another meeting.
(2) The quorum for directors' meetings may be fixed from time to time by a decision of the directors, but it must never be less than two, and unless otherwise fixed it is two.
(3) If the total number of directors for the time being is less than the quorum required, the directors must not take any decision other than a decision –
  (a) to appoint further directors, or
  (b) to call a general meeting so as to enable the shareholders to appoint further directors.

4.3.5.15 The effect of paragraphs (1) and (2) is that no substantive business can be conducted at a board meeting unless at least two directors are present (or participating remotely). In practice, it is common to amend article 11(2), because a quorum of two directors will not meet every company's needs. For example, if a company has a large board, the shareholders may want to set the quorum at a higher level. In some cases, the quorum requirement is to the effect not only that a certain number of directors must be participating, but also that a particular named director (perhaps the founder of the company, who wishes to retain some measure of control over the board's activities) must be among their number.

4.3.5.16 Another issue concerning article 11 arises in relation to companies with a sole director. Under the Act, a private company is permitted to have a board consisting of a single director (s. 154(1)), but is free to specify a higher minimum number of directors in its articles. Although article 7(2) of the model articles (see paragraph 4.3.5.10) contemplates that the company can have just one director, article 11 as it stands can be interpreted as preventing the board from acting unless it has at least two directors. The correct analysis of the relationship between these two provisions is probably that article 7(2) prevails over article 11, so as to allow companies which adopt the model articles to operate with a sole director, but there are different views on this point (in fact, the relationship between articles 7(2) and 11 has proved to be the most controversial aspect of the model articles), and so a company which wants to have a sole director may choose to err on the side of caution and amend article 11 in order to make it clear that it can, indeed, operate in that way. Tailored articles may provide, for example, that, in the event that the company has just one director, the quorum for board meetings is set at one.

Article 13 – Casting vote
(1) If the numbers of votes for and against a proposal are equal, the chairman or other director chairing the meeting has a casting vote.
(2) ...

4.3.5.17 This is an easy provision to overlook, but potentially it can be very important. Companies need to be aware of its existence, so that they can decide whether in their particular circumstances they do, indeed, want the chairman to have a casting vote.

Article 14 – Conflicts of interest

(1) If a proposed decision of the directors is concerned with an actual or proposed transaction or arrangement with the company in which a director is interested, that director is not to be counted as participating in the decision-making process for quorum or voting purposes.

(2)–(7) ...

4.3.5.18 Article 14 is a long provision and looks formidable, but in essence it is simple. It relates to CA2006 ss. 177 and 182, which provide that a director who has a personal interest in a transaction with the company must declare that interest to the board (ss. 177 and 182 are discussed in section 7.3.24). Article 14 supplements that disclosure requirement by providing that the director in question will not normally be permitted to vote on the transaction.

4.3.5.19 Article 14 is the only provision in the model articles which directly concerns the statutory directors' duties, but tailored articles will sometimes deal with other aspects of the duties. In connection with a director's duty under s. 175 to avoid situations in which his interests may conflict with those of the company, for example, the articles may confirm that the board can authorise the entry by a director into such a situation (the board's power to authorise situations of conflict exists automatically by virtue of s. 175(5)(a), but it is good practice to confirm it expressly in the articles). They may also lay down rules governing the position of a director who has been duly authorised to enter into a situation of conflict; the rules may, for example, provide that he is not permitted to vote on any matters to which the conflict is relevant.

Article 17 – Methods of appointing directors

(1) Any person who is willing to act as a director, and is permitted by law to do so, may be appointed to be a director –
   (a) by ordinary resolution, or
   (b) by a decision of the directors.

(2) ...

(3) ...

4.3.5.20 The Act does not deal with the procedure for appointing directors. Article 17 fills this gap, and it does so in a fashion which will be appropriate to most companies' needs, allowing the appointment to be made either by the shareholders or by the existing directors. Some companies may choose to supplement it with a provision allowing the majority shareholders to make an appointment simply by sending a written notice to the company; this option relieves the shareholders of the need to go through the process of passing a formal resolution (the procedure for appointing directors is discussed in section 5.4).

Article 18 – Termination of director's appointment
A person ceases to be a director as soon as –
(a) that person ceases to be a director by virtue of any provision of CA2006 or is prohibited from being a director by law;
(b) a bankruptcy order is made against that person;
(c) a composition is made with that person's creditors generally in satisfaction of that person's debts;
(d) a registered medical practitioner who is treating that person gives a written opinion to the company stating that that person has become physically or mentally incapable of acting as a director and may remain so for more than three months;

... [Paragraph 18(e) was deleted from the model articles by the Mental Health (Discrimination) Act 2013 with effect from 28 April 2013. It read as follows: '(e) by reason of that person's mental health, a court makes an order which wholly or partly prevents that person from personally exercising any powers or rights which that person would otherwise have'.]

(f) notification is received by the company from the director that the director is resigning from office, and such resignation has taken effect in accordance with its terms.'

4.3.5.21 This article is narrower in scope than it might appear on a first reading. It specifies that a director ceases to hold office upon the occurrence of certain events, but it does *not* set out a procedure by which the shareholders can remove a director from office.

4.3.5.22 Technically, there is no need to include a removal procedure in the articles, for s. 168 contains a statutory procedure. However, the s. 168 procedure can be unsatisfactory from the shareholders' perspective, because although it gives them the power to remove a director by means of an ordinary resolution at any time, it requires the resolution to be passed at a general meeting (as opposed to by means of a written resolution), imposes an unusually long notice period in relation to the holding of the general meeting and gives the director in question the right to protest against his proposed removal (the procedure for removing directors is discussed in section 5.4). Some companies therefore choose to supplement s. 168 with a bespoke removal procedure in their articles. One option is to provide for removal by means of an ordinary resolution, just as s. 168 does, but not to include any requirement for a meeting to be held or for the director to be given the right to protest. Another option is to allow the majority shareholders to remove a director simply by sending a written notice to the company.

Article 22 – Powers to issue different classes of share

(1) Subject to the articles, but without prejudice to the rights attached to any existing share, the company may issue shares with such rights or restrictions as may be determined by ordinary resolution.

(2) ...

4.3.5.23 Article 22(1) is an important provision, because companies often find it useful to be able to attract potential investors by offering them special rights, for example in the form of weighted voting rights or preferential rights in respect of dividends. In practice, though, the rights attached to different classes of shares are often set out in the articles themselves rather than in an ordinary resolution.

Article 26 – Share transfers

(1)–(4) ...

(5) The directors may refuse to register the transfer of a share, and if they do so, the instrument of transfer must be returned to the transferee with the notice of refusal unless they suspect that the proposed transfer may be fraudulent.

4.3.5.24 One of the means by which shareholders can realise their investment in a company is by selling their shares to a third party. Individual shareholders will, therefore, want as much freedom as possible to transfer their shares. On the other hand, the body of shareholders as a whole may well want to ensure that there is some control over who is allowed to join the company (this is likely to be the case in smaller companies, in particular, for shareholders in such companies may work together quite closely). Article 26(5) strikes a balance between these needs by giving the board a wide discretion to refuse to register a transfer. Some companies will be content with this arrangement. Others may choose to modify it, for example by removing the board's discretion where the proposed transfer is to the shareholder's spouse or children, or by supplementing it with a pre-emption right in respect of transfers, which requires a shareholder who wishes to dispose of his shares to offer them to his fellow shareholders before seeking outside buyers.

Article 30 – Procedure for declaring dividends

(1) The company may by ordinary resolution declare dividends, and the directors may decide to pay interim dividends.

(2) A dividend must not be declared unless the directors have made a recommendation as to its amount. Such a dividend must not exceed the amount recommended by the directors.

(3)–(7) ...

4.3.5.25 The Act deals with various matters concerning dividends, including the profits out of which they may be paid, but does not lay down rules governing the procedure for declaring a dividend.

4.3.5.26 The rules concerning the declaration and payment of a dividend in articles 30 to 35 reflect standard practice. The basic structure, as set out in article 30(1) and (2), is that there are two ways for a company to declare a dividend: by means of an ordinary resolution of the shareholders following a board recommendation as to its amount, or by means of a board decision. A dividend which is declared by the board is known as an 'interim dividend'.

4.3.5.27 A dividend declared by the shareholders may be paid in cash or, by virtue of article 34, in non-cash assets. An interim dividend may only be paid in cash (the law governing dividends is discussed in section 9.3.4).

4.3.6 Part 4: Decision-making by shareholders (articles 37 to 47)

4.3.6.1 Part 4 of the model articles is entitled 'Decision-making by shareholders'. This is an accurate description of its contents, but also a misleading one. While Part 4 certainly deals with decision-making by shareholders, it deals with only one of the several means by which shareholders take decisions, namely by passing a resolution at a general meeting. In practice, shareholders' decisions in private companies are often taken by means of the statutory written resolution procedure (the statutory procedure is contained in CA2006 Chapter 2 of Part 13, which is discussed in section 8.3.5) and the model articles have nothing at all to say on written resolutions.

4.3.6.2 The reason why Part 4 deals with general meetings and not written resolutions is because whereas the Act's rules on written resolutions are almost entirely self-contained, leaving very little room for adjustments to be made in the articles, its rules on general meetings provide much more scope for tailoring. In fact, the statutory provisions on general meetings are exceedingly complex, comprising a mixture of mandatory rules and rules which establish a default position, and in some areas leave gaps which may be plugged by provisions in the articles.

4.3.6.3 Given that most private companies, at least those which are commercial companies, are unlikely ever to hold a general meeting (the situations in which private companies may want, or need, to hold a general meeting are discussed in paragraph 8.3.7.1), Part 4 of the model articles does not warrant close examination in this handbook. The principal provisions are, however, worth noting.

- *Article 37 – Attendance and speaking at general meetings.* This article provides for meetings to be attended remotely. It undoubtedly permits attendance through the use of technology which creates an audio-visual link between the shareholder who is not present in person and the meeting. It is less clear, despite the apparently broad scope of the article, whether a court would be persuaded that a shareholder who is not present in person, but who has a purely audio link with the meeting, could be said to be in attendance. In *Byng* v *London Life Association Ltd* [1990] 1 Ch 170, in which the Court of Appeal took the view that shareholders who are linked with a meeting by audio-visual means form part of the meeting, the question as to whether a purely audio link would suffice to establish attendance was not in issue. However, the judgments indicate that shareholders who are not present in person must be able to both hear and see the proceedings (see 183E (per Sir Nicolas Browne-Wilkinson VC) and 192C (per Mustill LJ)).

- **Article 38 – Quorum for general meetings.** The quorum for a general meeting is dealt with in CA2006 s. 318, which sets it at two (unless the company has just one shareholder, in which case it sets it at one). The effect of article 38 is that business can only be conducted at a general meeting which is quorate. Companies are free to specify a different quorum in their articles, and some companies will want to modify article 38 to that effect.
- **Article 42 – Voting: general/Article 44 – Poll votes.** There are two ways in which votes on a resolution may be taken at a general meeting: on a show of hands and on a poll. With the former, each shareholder normally has just one vote, regardless of how many shares he holds, and it can therefore be a crude way of assessing the extent of support for a resolution. The latter involves counting every vote held by every shareholder, and so provides an accurate measurement of the level of support.

  Article 42 states that votes are to be taken on a show of hands unless a poll is demanded, and article 44 lists the persons who are entitled to demand a poll. Tailored articles may modify the list in article 44, although s. 321 of the Act places restrictions on a company's ability to make it difficult for shareholders to demand a poll.
- **Article 47 – amendments to resolutions.** As part of the process of calling a general meeting, the shareholders have to be notified of the wording of any special resolution which is to be proposed (s. 283(6)), and in practice are also often notified of the wording of any ordinary resolution which is to be proposed. Article 47 sets out the very limited circumstances in which the wording of resolutions may be amended after they have been circulated to the shareholders. The fact that the article is drawn so narrowly should serve to encourage those who are involved in preparing documentation for general meetings to take every step to ensure that the text of resolutions as circulated is correct.

Article 52 – Indemnity

(1) Subject to paragraph (2), a relevant director of the company or an associated company may be indemnified out of the company's assets against –
    (a) any liability incurred by that director in connection with any negligence, default, breach of duty or breach of trust in relation to the company or an associated company,

(b) any liability incurred by that director in connection with the activities of the company or an associated company in its capacity as a trustee of an occupational pension scheme (as defined in CA2006 s. 235(6)),
(c) any other liability incurred by that director as an officer of the company or an associated company.
(2) This article does not authorise any indemnity which would be prohibited or rendered void by any provision of the Companies Acts or by any other provision of law.
(3) ...

4.3.6.4 Section 232(2) of the Act severely restricts a company's ability to indemnify its directors against liability in respect of a breach of duty or negligence. Article 52 allows the company to indemnify its directors to the extent permitted by s. 232(2).

4.3.6.5 The article is a merely permissive provision, and does not, in itself, constitute an indemnity. Although it can be amended so as to constitute an indemnity, directors are, in fact, unlikely to be able to enforce an indemnity contained within the articles (the difficulties surrounding the enforcement by directors of provisions in the articles are discussed in paragraph 4.5.2.1), and so will normally prefer to be given an indemnity in the form of a standalone contract.

4.3.6.6 The article may also be amended so as to extend its scope to parties other than directors. For example, the company may wish to have the power to indemnify members of its senior management team.

Article 53 – Insurance
(1) The directors may decide to purchase and maintain insurance, at the expense of the company, for the benefit of any relevant director in respect of any relevant loss.
(2) ...

4.3.6.7 The restrictions in s. 232(2) on a company's freedom to indemnify its directors against liability in respect of a breach of duty or negligence do not extend to a prohibition on buying insurance for them against such liability (ss. 232(2)(a) and 233). Article 53 gives the directors the power to purchase such insurance on the company's behalf.

4.3.6.8 Some companies may wish to modify the scope of the article so as to allow the directors to buy insurance for other parties, such as senior managers, too.

4.4 Amending the articles

4.4.1 The substantive law

4.4.1.1 The main rule governing amendments to a company's articles of association is that they may be made by means of a shareholders' special resolution (s. 21(1); although s. 21(1) perhaps does not make this as clear as it might have done, it specifies the only means by which the articles may be amended. In other words, there is no way to amend the articles other than by means of a special resolution).

4.4.1.2 This simple rule is, however, subject to a number of qualifications:

- **Any amendment must be made in what the shareholders believe to be the company's interests.** Normally, when shareholders exercise their voting rights, they are entitled to act entirely in their own interests, even if by so doing they damage their fellow shareholders or the company itself. However, the courts have long taken the view that since amendments to the articles bind all the shareholders, even those who did not support them, it would not be right to allow the shareholders who voted in favour of the change to act solely in their own interests. At common law, therefore, the power to alter the articles under s. 21 is qualified by the proviso that the amendment will be effective only if those who voted for it were acting 'bonâ fide for the benefit of the company as a whole' (*Allen v Gold Reefs of West Africa, Ltd* [1900] 1 Ch 656, at 671).

  The question arises as to whether the amendment has to be objectively for the company's benefit or whether it suffices that the shareholders themselves felt that it was for the company's benefit. The courts have taken the view that the latter analysis is correct (*Citco Banking Corporation NV v Pusser's Ltd* [2007] UKPC 13). Only if the amendment is 'such that no reasonable men could consider it for the benefit of the company' (*Shuttleworth v Cox Brothers and Company (Maidenhead), Ltd* [1927] 2 KB 9, at 18) will it be struck down.

  In practice, therefore, an amendment to the articles duly made in accordance with s. 21(1) is likely to be susceptible to challenge on the basis of this common law qualification only if there is evidence that the majority shareholders were acting oppressively or maliciously, motivated not by a desire to advance the company's interests, but by a desire to harm the minority shareholders. By way of example, consider the case of a company consisting of four equal shareholders, each of whom has a seat on the board, and one of whom is based in South America. In what circumstances might an amendment to the articles so as to prevent directors from attending board meetings remotely be at risk? If the amendment is made because the shareholders feel that face-to-face discussions at board meetings are likely to produce more measured decisions than meetings held over the telephone, it will be allowed to stand. If, on the other hand, three of the parties are motivated by a desire to squeeze the party who is based in South America out of the decision-making process because they have fallen out with him on a personal level, a challenge to the amendment might well succeed.

- **Some provisions of the articles may be 'entrenched'.** Companies are permitted to specify that certain provisions in their articles may be amended only if conditions in addition to the passing of a special resolution are satisfied. This power is contained in s. 22(1), which reads as follows:

    'A company's articles may contain provision ("provision for entrenchment") to the effect that specified provisions of the articles may be amended or repealed only if conditions are met, or procedures are complied with, that are more restrictive than those applicable in the case of a special resolution.'

    There are various ways of entrenching a provision. An obvious way is to specify that a provision may be amended only with the support of a higher percentage of the shareholders than the 75% required to pass a special resolution. For example, a provision may be expressed to be alterable only if, say, 90% of the shareholders agree to the change. Another way is to state that a provision is alterable only if a named shareholder agrees to the change; the provision could then be amended only if a special resolution were passed *and* the shareholder in question supported the amendment.

    Two points should be noted in connection with the power to entrench provisions. First, it is not an unbounded power, for it does not allow provisions to be made unalterable: the shareholders acting unanimously are always competent to amend the articles (s. 22(3)(a)). Second, a provision which specifies that other provisions of the articles are entrenched is ineffective unless it is entrenched itself, for otherwise the protection afforded to the latter could be removed by the simple expedient of removing the former by means of a special resolution in the usual way.

- **An amendment which imposes on a shareholder a financial obligation to the company will not be binding unless he agrees to be bound by it.** The law on this point is stated clearly in s. 25:

    '(1) A member of a company is not bound by an alteration to its articles after the date on which he became a member, if and so far as the alteration –
      (a) requires him to take or subscribe for more shares than the number held by him at the date on which the alteration is made, or
      (b) in any way increases his liability as at that date to contribute to the company's share capital or otherwise to pay money to the company.
    (2) Subsection (1) does not apply in a case where the member agrees in writing, either before or after the alteration is made, to be bound by the alteration.'

    The aim of this restriction is not to prevent a shareholder from agreeing to take more shares or otherwise increase his liability to pay money to the company, but rather – bearing in mind that an amendment to the articles does not

require unanimity on the part of the shareholders – to prevent him from being made subject to such obligations without his consent. It may be regarded as part of the much wider efforts of the company law regime to ensure that minority shareholders are not treated oppressively.
- **An amendment which varies the rights attached to a class of shares may require the consent of the holders of those shares.** It was noted in paragraph 4.3.5.23 that if a company has more than one class of shares, the rights attached to the different classes are often set out in the articles. An amendment to the articles which purports to vary the rights attached to a class of shares will be effective only if:
(a) a special resolution is passed in the normal way; and
(b) pursuant to s. 630 of the Act, (s. 630 is discussed in paragraph 9.2.5.9). either (i) any provision in the articles dealing with the variation of the rights is complied with, or (ii) if the articles do not contain any such provision, the holders of the shares in question consent to the variation. For these purposes, consent does not mean unanimous consent. What is required, instead, is either written consent from the holders of at least 75% in nominal value of the issued shares of the class in question or a special resolution passed at a general meeting of the holders of the shares of that class (s. 630(2) and (4)).

By way of illustration of the effect of s. 630, consider the case of a company with two classes of shares: 'A Shares', which carry one vote each, and 'B Shares', which carry preferential rights in respect of dividends but no right to vote. Assuming the company's articles do not specify a procedure for varying the rights attached to the shares, if the company wishes to amend its articles so as to vary the preferential dividend rights attached to the B Shares, not only will a special resolution of the company as a whole be required (in effect, since they are the only shareholders with a right to vote, this will be a special resolution of the holders of the A Shares), but 75% of the holders of the B Shares (who would otherwise have no say in the matter) will need to consent to the variation.

4.4.2 Filing requirements

4.4.2.1 The filing requirements associated with an amendment of the articles of association are potentially quite extensive. Not only must the special resolution effecting the amendment be filed (ss. 29(1)(a) and 30), but so must the revised articles themselves (s. 26), and in certain cases a notice concerning the amendment must also be filed. The notice requirements are contained in the following sections of the Act:

- Section 23 (which requires the registrar to be notified if the articles are amended so as to insert or remove a provision for entrenchment) (see Companies House Form CC01 ('Notice of restriction on the company's articles') and Companies

House Form CC02 ('Notice of removal of restriction on the company's articles')).
- Section 24 (which requires a statement of compliance to be sent to the registrar if articles which contain an entrenched provision are amended) (see Companies House Form CC03 ('Statement of compliance where amendment of articles restricted')).
- Section 31 (which requires the registrar to be notified if the articles are amended so as to insert, remove or alter an objects clause) (see Companies House Form CC04 ('Statement of company's objects')).
- Sections 636 and 637 (which require the registrar to be notified if a class of shares is renamed or if the rights attached to shares are varied) (see Companies House Form SH08 ('Notice of name or other designation of class of shares') and Companies House Form SH10 ('Notice of particulars of variation of rights attached to shares')).

4.5 Enforcing the articles

4.5.1 Direct enforcement

4.5.1.2 There is some scope for enforcing the articles of association directly, since they are treated by virtue of CA2006 as constituting a contract of sorts. The relevant provision is s. 33(1):

> 'The provisions of a company's constitution bind the company and its members to the same extent as if there were covenants on the part of the company and of each member to observe those provisions.'

The law governing the direct enforcement of the articles is, however, both unsatisfactory in its scope and uncertain in its detail.

4.5.2 Direct enforcement

Directors' rights

4.5.2.1 As is apparent from the wording of s. 33(1), the articles are not treated as constituting a contract to which the directors or other 'outsiders' are party. A provision which confers a right on an outsider – a director's right to a certain amount of remuneration, for instance – will, therefore, generally be unenforceable. Thus, in *Eley v The Positive Government Security Life Assurance Company, Ltd*, (1875–76) LR 1 Ex D 88 the Court of Appeal held that an individual who had been named in the company's articles as its solicitor could not enforce the provision.

Shareholders' rights

4.5.2.2 Despite the wording of s. 33(1) and its predecessors, the courts have taken the view that even a shareholder is not entitled to enforce all the provisions of the articles. What is more, there is considerable uncertainty as to what provisions, precisely, a shareholder does have the power to enforce.

4.5.2.3 The position, as distilled from a rather chaotic body of case law, may be summed up as follows: a shareholder can enforce a provision in the articles only if two conditions are met:

- the provision confers on him a right in his capacity as a shareholder; and
- the right is of a personal nature.

Each of these conditions warrants some elaboration.

4.5.2.4 In relation to the first condition, consider the common scenario in which a shareholder is also a director of the company. The effect of the condition is that whereas a shareholder-director would no doubt be able to enforce a provision giving him a right to a fixed dividend or multiple voting rights on certain types of shareholders' resolutions, he would not be able to enforce a provision giving him a right to an indemnity in connection with his activities as a director. In the leading case on this point, *Hickman v Kent or Romney Marsh Sheep-Breeders' Association*, the court summarised the law as follows: 'no right merely purporting to be given by an article to a person, whether a member or not, in a capacity other than that of a member, as, for instance, as solicitor, promoter, director, can be enforced against the company' ([1915] 1 Ch 881, at 900).

4.5.2.5 The position is, however, complicated by the fact that the courts have on occasion shown themselves to be willing to allow a shareholder who is also a director to enforce a right which is apparently conferred on him in his capacity as a director. In *Quin & Axtens, Ltd v Salmon* [1909] AC 442 (this was a decision of the House of Lords, approving the decision of the Court of Appeal in *Salmon v Quin & Axtens, Ltd* [1909] 1 Ch 311), for example, where a company's two principal shareholders were also managing directors, and each had a right under the articles to veto certain resolutions at board meetings, one of the shareholders was permitted to enforce that right (see also *Pulbrook v Richmond Consolidated Mining Company* (1878) 9 Ch D 610, at 612). How are such cases to be reconciled with the statement of the law in *Hickman v Kent or Romney Marsh Sheep-Breeders' Association*? The answer seems to lie in the fact that in some companies the shareholders' rights are closely intertwined with their rights as directors. If that is the case, it seems, the courts might take the view that a shareholder's rights as a director essentially form part of his rights as a shareholder, and that he is, therefore, permitted to enforce them.

4.5.2.6 As far as the second condition is concerned, the courts have drawn a distinction between provisions in the articles which confer rights on shareholders which are personal in nature and provisions which concern procedural matters.

Provisions of the former variety can be enforced by an individual shareholder, while provisions dealing with companies' internal affairs can be enforced only by the company.

4.5.2.7 This distinction is sound in principle – a failure to comply with procedural matters is a wrong done to the company rather than a wrong done to an individual shareholder, and since the company is a person in its own right, it alone should be able to complain about the failure – but it raises the question as to what rights are personal in nature and what rights are not. There is no list of personal rights to be found either in the case law or in CA2006. The decided cases do, however, provide some guidance. They indicate, for example, that a shareholder's right to have his vote counted is a right of a personal nature (*Pender v Lushington* (1877) 6 Ch D 70, at 81) while a right to demand that a vote be taken on a poll rather than on a show of hands is not (*MacDougall v Gardiner* (1875) 1 Ch D 13).

4.5.3 Indirect enforcement

4.5.3.1 The fact that certain rights conferred by the articles may not be enforceable presents a problem. A shareholder or director who is aware of the difficulties involved in basing a cause of action on s. 33 is in a position to take steps to protect his rights at the outset. A director who wants to be indemnified in respect of his activities on the company's behalf, for example, will try to ensure that the indemnity is given to him in the form of a standalone contract with the company, rather than in the articles. Similarly, shareholders who are concerned that aspects of their arrangements for the conduct of the company's internal affairs may not be directly enforceable if they are dealt with in the articles may opt to deal with them in a shareholders' agreement, which will be enforceable in the same way as any other contract.

4.5.3.2 A director or shareholder who did not fully appreciate the problems associated with s. 33, or did not have the bargaining power to ensure that his rights were set out in a separate agreement, will have to consider whether there are any other means by which he can indirectly enforce them, whether by compelling those concerned to abide by the articles or by obtaining a remedy in respect of any failure to do so.

4.5.3.3 A director is in a difficult position. As a matter of general law, it is possible that the relevant provision in the articles will form an implied contract between him and the company (*Re New British Iron Company, ex parte Beckwith* [1898] 1 Ch 324). Otherwise, he is likely to find that he is unable to enforce the right in question (although the Contracts (Rights of Third Parties) Act 1999 gives third parties the right to enforce provisions in contracts in certain circumstances, articles of association are specifically excluded from its scope (see s. 6(2))).

4.5.3.4 A shareholder is in a slightly more powerful position, in that a breach of the articles is one of the grounds upon which an unfair prejudice petition under s. 994 of the Act (the unfair prejudice remedy is discussed in section 8.4.7) may be based (*O'Neill v Phillips* [1999] 2 BCLC 1, at 7–8). The court has an extremely wide power to grant relief in respect of a successful petition (s. 996), and so in theory it could order the parties who are in default to comply with the articles. In practice, however, a petition under s. 994 is often used as a weapon of last resort on the part of a shareholder who is so dissatisfied with his relationship with the company that he wishes to have his stake in it bought out. A buy-out order will not protect his rights under the articles directly, but it will ensure that he will no longer have to remain associated with parties who are failing to abide by the company's internal rules.

4.5.3.5 The discussion in the paragraphs above of shareholder enforcement has focused on the position of an individual shareholder. It is worth noting, however, that if the shareholders act collectively (i.e. if at least a bare majority of them are acting together), they are in a very strong position indeed.

4.5.3.6 Consider a failure on the part of the directors to comply with the articles, for example by failing to hold regular board meetings or by failing to restrict the company's activities to specified lines of business. Direct enforcement under s. 33 will normally be impossible, on the basis that the directors are not contractually bound by the articles. The shareholders should not, however, encounter undue difficulty in forcing the board to comply with the provisions in question. A threat to remove from office any director who persists in ignoring his obligations under the articles (the shareholders' power to remove a director from office is discussed in section 5.4.2) or to procure that proceedings are brought against any such director for breach of duty (s. 171(a) contains a specific duty to comply with the articles), should, in most cases, suffice to force the directors who are in default to mend their ways.

5

Directors – the fundamentals

> **Summary**
> - A private company must have at least one director.
> - Although there is no requirement for a director to possess a formal qualification of any sort, there are a number of restrictions on the categories of person who may be a director.
> - CA2006 provides a mechanism for removing directors from office, but does not provide a mechanism for appointing directors.
> - In most companies, the role of the directors is to manage the company's business.

5.1 Introduction

5.1.1 The law governing directors is too wide-ranging a topic to be addressed comfortably in a single chapter. It has, therefore, been split into three parts for the purposes of this handbook. Chapters 6 and 7 deal, respectively, with the means by which directors make decisions and the statutory statement of directors' duties, while this chapter lays the foundations for those discussions by identifying the fundamental features of the legal framework. Specifically, this chapter answers the following questions:

- How many directors is a company required to have?
- Are there any restrictions on who may be a director?
- How are directors appointed and removed?
- What is the role of a director?
- What is the difference between a de jure director, a de facto director and a shadow director?
- What is the difference between an executive director and a non-executive director?

5.1.2 A feature of the law concerning directors is that it is derived largely from a company's articles and from case law. That is not to say that there is no statutory intervention; the statutory directors' duties are the most obvious example of the importance of CA2006 to this area of the law. On the whole, however, and particularly when it comes to the topics covered in this chapter and in Chapter 6, the Act plays a less prominent role than one might expect. As a policy matter, the view is taken that the activities and functions of directors are largely matters for companies to regulate internally.

5.2 Minimum number of directors

5.2.1 The law concerning the number of directors which a company is required to have illustrates the point made in the paragraph above. Although the Act is not entirely silent on this matter, its intervention is minimal, and for the most part it is up to companies to devise rules to suit their needs.

5.2.2 As far as the Act is concerned, then, the relevant provision is s. 154, which states that a private company must have at least one director (an enforcement mechanism in respect of this requirement is set out in s. 156). The section does not set an upper limit on the number of directors a company may have.

5.2.3 Not surprisingly, companies cannot reduce the number of directors they must have below the statutory minimum. Companies cannot opt, in other words, to function without a board. They are, however, free to provide in their articles for a higher minimum and/or a maximum.

5.2.4 Many companies will be content with the statutory default position, but the freedom to adjust it is useful where a company's shareholder base comprises a number of different factions, each with its own interests. In the case of a company with a shareholder base which is made up of members of three families, for example, the parties may choose to provide in the articles that the company must have three directors, each one nominated by a different family. Assuming the articles also specify that the quorum for board meetings is three (so that each family will always be represented when a decision is taken), this arrangement will give each family a degree of confidence that its interests will be protected.

5.3 Restrictions on who may be a director

5.3.1 The Act does not impose any qualification requirements on directors. There is no body to which a prospective director must belong, no training – whether in management practices, company law or accounting – which he must undertake and no particular experience which he must have accumulated. The logic behind this approach is that companies are designed to encourage entrepreneurship and business activity, and the imposition on directors of a requirement to gain a qualification would deter people from choosing to run their business through a corporate vehicle and constitute an unnecessary burden on companies. This issue was considered by the government in the wake of the financial crisis. See the discussion in paragraphs 186–188 and 194 of 'Transparency & trust: enhancing the transparency of UK company ownership and increasing trust in UK business – Government response' (BIS, April 2014).

5.3.2 There are, however, some restrictions on the categories of persons who may be a director. The principal restrictions are as follows:

- **The Act imposes restrictions on corporate directors.** The notion that a company might act as a director of another company is, on one analysis, unobjectionable. Since a company is a legal person, which can certainly own shares and property, for example, why should it not also be permitted to act as a director? On another analysis, it is fanciful to suggest that a company can, in any real sense, fulfil the administrative obligations attached to the office of a director, act loyally and competently in accordance with the statutory directors' duties and play a part in running the company's business. After all, a company is not a real person, with a mind, a conscience, skills and experience. Somewhere behind the company, perhaps shielded by multiple layers of other companies, are real human beings, and ultimately the company's actions as a director are the actions of those individuals.

    At present, the Act resolves the tension between these analyses largely in favour of the former, providing that a company may be a director of another company as long as that company has at least one 'natural person' (i.e. one human being) on its board (s. 155). Corporate directors are, in fact, a common feature of the business world, not only among the largest corporate groups, but also in the context of smaller groups.

    However, in the interests of increasing transparency in the corporate world, the law in this area is in the process of being reformed. The Small Business, Enterprise and Employment Act 2015 imposes a general prohibition on corporate directors, but gives the Secretary of State the power to provide in regulations for situations in which they will be permitted (subject to the proviso that a board must not be composed entirely of corporate directors). The government consulted on the scope of possible exceptions to the general prohibition in November 2014 and March 2015, but has yet to publish its conclusions. In any event, the reforms are expected to take effect in October 2015.
- **A person who is subject to a disqualification order is not permitted to be a director without the court's leave.** The Company Directors' Disqualification Act 1986 sets out various grounds on which the court may make a disqualification order. The grounds include general unfitness to be involved in the management of a company (Company Directors Disqualification Act 1986 s. 6), persistent failure to comply with the Act's filing requirements (Company

Directors' Disqualification Act 1986 s. 3) and involvement in wrongful trading, Company Directors' Disqualification Act 1986 s. 10). The effect of a disqualification order is that, for a specified period, the person is not permitted without the court's leave to be a director or to 'in any way, whether directly or indirectly, be concerned or take part in the promotion, formation or management of a company' Company Directors' Disqualification Act 1986 s.1 (1)). The Act also provides for voluntary disqualification undertakings, by which a person undertakes not to be a director or to be involved in the promotion, formation or management of a company for a specified period without the court's leave.

The sanctions attached to a breach of a disqualification order or undertaking are severe. A disqualified person who is appointed as a director commits a criminal offence and assumes personal responsibility for debts incurred by the company while he acts as a director (Company Directors' Disqualification Act 1986 ss. 13 and 15).

A register of disqualified persons is available as part of the WebCHeck service on the Companies House website.

- The disqualification regime is in the process of being strengthened, although it has not yet been announced when the reforms, which are set out in Part 9 of the Small Business, Enterprise and Employment Act 2015, will come into force.
- **An undischarged bankrupt is not permitted to be a director without the court's leave (Company Directors Disqualification Act 1986 s. 11).**
- **A person who is under the age of 16 is not permitted to be a director. (CA2006 s. 157).**

5.3.3 A company's articles may impose additional restrictions on the categories of persons who may be a director. They may, for example, specify that a person may not be appointed to be a director unless he holds a certain number of shares in the company. In practice, however, such provisions are rare.

5.4 Appointment and removal of directors

5.4.1 Appointment

5.4.1.1 The Act does not contain a mechanism for appointing directors, so this is a matter for companies to deal with in their articles.

5.4.1.2 Article 17 of the model articles for private companies provides for appointment by means of either an ordinary resolution or a board decision, and many companies will be content to adopt that approach.

5.4.1.3 Other companies will want to adapt article 17 or replace it altogether. For example:

- **It is not uncommon to give the majority shareholders the right to appoint a director simply by giving written notice to the company.** Since this option obviates the need for a formal shareholders' resolution to be passed, it reduces the administrative burden on the company. More importantly, it assists the shareholders in the event of a dispute with the existing directors as to the identity of the proposed director. Directors are normally responsible for initiating the means by which shareholders pass formal resolutions, and although shareholders have the power under the Act to force the board's hand (see CA2006 ss. 292 and 293 in relation to the shareholders' right to require the directors to circulate a proposed written resolution, and ss. 303 and 304 in relation to the shareholders' right to require the directors to call a general meeting), if the existing directors disapprove of the shareholders' proposed appointee, and if the articles give the shareholders the power to appoint a director only by means of a formal resolution, the directors can at least delay the appointment by refusing to initiate the shareholder decision-making process until they are forced to do so. If, however, the articles give the shareholders the power to appoint a director by written notice, they are not reliant on the co-operation of the existing directors.
- **Where the shareholder base consists of different factions, each faction may want the power to appoint a director.** The articles may provide, for example, that a named shareholder from each faction has the power to appoint one director by giving written notice to the company, or that the majority of shareholders within each faction have such a power.

5.4.2 Removal

5.4.2.1 Whereas companies are left entirely to their own devices as far as the procedure for appointing directors is concerned, the Act provides a mechanism for removing directors. This statutory procedure can be supplemented in the articles by an alternative removal procedure, but it cannot be excluded. The statutory removal procedure is contained in ss. 168 and 169. The sections are set out in full in Figure 5.1.

Figure 5.1 Text of CA2006 ss. 168 and 169

Section 168 – Resolution to remove director

'(1) A company may by ordinary resolution at a meeting remove a director before the expiration of his period of office, notwithstanding anything in any agreement between it and him.

(2) Special notice is required of a resolution to remove a director under this section or to appoint somebody instead of a director so removed at the meeting at which he is removed.

(3) A vacancy created by the removal of a director under this section, if not filled at the meeting at which he is removed, may be filled as a casual vacancy.

(4) A person appointed director in place of a person removed under this section is treated, for the purpose of determining the time at which he or any other director is to retire, as if he had become director on the day on which the person in whose place he is appointed was last appointed a director.

(5) This section is not to be taken –
  (a) as depriving a person removed under it of compensation or damages payable to him in respect of the termination of his appointment as director or of any appointment terminating with that as director, or
  (b) as derogating from any power to remove a director that may exist apart from this section.'

Section 169 – Director's right to protest against removal

'(1) On receipt of notice of an intended resolution to remove a director under section 168, the company must forthwith send a copy of the notice to the director concerned.

(2) The director (whether or not a member of the company) is entitled to be heard on the resolution at the meeting.

(3) Where notice is given of an intended resolution to remove a director under that section, and the director concerned makes with respect to it representations in writing to the company (not exceeding a reasonable length) and requests their notification to members of the company, the company shall, unless the representations are received by it too late for it to do so –
  (a) in any notice of the resolution given to members of the company state the fact of the representations having been made; and
  (b) send a copy of the representations to every member of the company to whom notice of the meeting is sent (whether before or after receipt of the representations by the company).

(4) If a copy of the representations is not sent as required by subsection (3) because received too late or because of the company's default, the director may (without prejudice to his right to be heard orally) require that the representations shall be read out at the meeting.

(5) Copies of the representations need not be sent out and the representations need not be read out at the meeting if, on the application either of the company or of any other person who claims to be aggrieved, the court is satisfied that the rights conferred by this section are being abused.

(6) The court may order the company's costs (in Scotland, expenses) on an application under subsection (5) to be paid in whole or in part by the director, notwithstanding that he is not a party to the application.'

5.4.2.2 The statutory procedure has three key features:

- **The resolution to remove the director must be passed at a general meeting (s. 168(1)).** The Act states expressly that a resolution under s. 168 cannot be passed in the form of a written resolution (s. 288(2)(a)), and case law indicates that a decision by a sole shareholder pursuant to s. 357 will not be effective to pass such a resolution, either (see the discussion of the High Court's decision in *Bonham-Carter v Situ Ventures Ltd* [2012] EWHC 230 (Ch) in paragraph 8.3.6.4).
- **'Special notice' of the resolution must be given to the company (s. 168(2)).** A general meeting can only be called if notice of the meeting is given to the shareholders in advance in accordance with the Act. The notice period for private companies is 14 days, although companies are free to specify a longer notice period in their articles (s. 307(1) and (3)).

  'Special notice', as the expression is used in s. 168, is quite distinct from notice of the meeting. It is notice of the intention to propose the removal resolution, and must be given *to the company* at least 28 days before the meeting is held (s. 312). The company, in turn, must then give notice of the proposed resolution to the director in question (s. 169(1)) and to the shareholders (s. 312(2) and (3)).
- **The director has the right to protest against his proposed removal (s. 169).** The Act gives the director whose position is under threat the opportunity to make the case against his removal. He is entitled not only to make written representations to the shareholders, but also to speak at the general meeting (s. 169(2) to (4)).

5.4.2.3 Companies cannot use their articles to deprive their shareholders of the option of removing a director using the statutory procedure. A provision in the articles stating that a director may be removed only by means of a special resolution, for example, will not prevent the shareholders from removing a director by means of an ordinary resolution pursuant to s. 168. Similarly, the fact that a director has a service contract with the company will not prevent the shareholders from removing him using the statutory procedure (although any contractual liability incurred by the company as a result of the removal is preserved by virtue of s. 168(5)(a)).

5.4.2.4 Companies can, however, use their articles to adjust the balance of power between shareholders and directors which is established by the statutory procedure.

- **On the one hand, the articles can be used to make it easier to remove a director.** Since s. 168(5)(b) states that the statutory procedure does not derogate from any other power to remove a director, companies are free to insert an alternative removal mechanism into their articles.

  The statutory procedure is problematic from the shareholders' perspective, not only because it is time-consuming (because of the requirement for special notice) and administratively burdensome (because it involves a general meeting), but also because the director in question has the right to argue against his proposed removal. Many companies choose, therefore, to include in their articles a power to remove a director by means of an ordinary resolution, and some will supplement this with a power to remove a director by means of written notice from the majority shareholders. The difference between an ordinary resolution under an alternative removal procedure in the articles and an ordinary resolution under s. 168 is that the former may be passed as a written resolution, is not subject to the special notice requirement and is not accompanied by a right on the part of the director to protest.

- **On the other hand, the articles can also be used to make it more difficult to remove a director, at least if he is also a shareholder.** A director who holds enough shares to block an ordinary resolution is, of course, safe from the threat of removal under the statutory procedure.

Even a director with a minority stake can, however, be protected by the use of weighted voting rights. Since the Act does not exclude the use of weighted voting rights on a s. 168 resolution, companies are free to provide in their articles that a director's shares carry extra votes on any s. 168 resolution to remove him from office.

The use of weighted voting rights in this way was considered by the House of Lords in *Bushell v Faith* [1970] AC 1099. The case concerned a private company with three shareholders (A, B and C), two of whom (A and B) were the company's only directors. Each of A, B and C held 100 of the company's 300 shares. Under the company' articles, each share carried one vote, except on a resolution to remove a director, in relation to which each share held by that director carried three votes. B and C sought to remove A from his office as a director by means of an ordinary resolution under a predecessor to s. 168. The question for the court was whether the provision in the articles conferring extra voting rights on a removal resolution was valid, in which case A had defeated the resolution by a margin of 300 votes to 200. The House of Lords concluded that the statutory procedure did not prevent the use of weighted voting rights in this way and that, therefore, the provision in the articles was valid and the resolution to remove A had failed.

Given that s. 168 is designed to give shareholders the power to remove directors with whom they are dissatisfied, it may seem strange that companies can so easily strengthen the position of directors. In fact, in *Bushell v Faith* itself, Lord Morris delivered a dissenting judgment in which he argued that the use of weighted voting rights in this way made a mockery of the statutory procedure. The majority view, however, was that the statutory procedure did not seek to set in stone the balance of power between shareholders and directors; it was, rather, a starting point from which companies could establish a balance which met their needs.

5.5 The role of a director

5.5.1 The Act goes some way towards describing what directors actually do, in that it allocates various responsibilities and powers to them. For example:

- section 30 imposes upon them responsibility for ensuring that the company complies with its obligation to file special resolutions with the registrar;
- section 288 confers upon them a power to initiate the process by which shareholders pass written resolutions;
- section 394 imposes upon them responsibility for preparing the company's accounts; and
- section 550 confers upon them a limited power to allot shares without shareholder authorisation.

5.5.2 It does not, however, deal with the fundamental question as to the extent to which the directors are responsible for running the company's business. This general division of powers between shareholders and directors is, therefore, left to companies to address in their articles.

5.5.3 Article 3 of the model articles for private companies gives the directors an extremely wide power to run the company's business.

> **Article 3 – Directors' general authority**
> 'Subject to the articles, the directors are responsible for the management of the company's business, for which purpose they may exercise all the powers of the company.'

5.5.4 Under this provision, the directors are responsible not only for day-to-day management decisions, but also, among other things, for setting the company's longer-term strategy, for taking decisions as to whether to invest more heavily in some strands of the company's business than in others, for considering the merits of potential acquisitions and disposals and for initiating legal proceedings in the company's name. For all intents and purposes, it is they and not the shareholders who run the company's business.

5.5.5 If a company is small, and its shareholders and directors are the same people, the shareholders may well be content to adopt article 3 wholesale. After all, in delegating management power to the board they are merely delegating power to themselves in another capacity, and so remain in full control of the business.

5.5.6 If a company has a large shareholder base, most of the shareholders will not also have a seat on the board. If, therefore, they adopt article 3 wholesale, they will be handing over control of the company to others, and this transfer of power carries risks. The directors may, for example, act not in the company's interests, but in their own. Thus, the directors of a company which runs a grocery shop might place a contract for the purchase of fruit with a farm in which they have a stake, rather than with a rival farm which offers the company better terms. Equally, the directors may simply be incompetent, or may wish to take the company in a direction of which the shareholders disapprove.

5.5.7 In order to reduce their exposure to these risks, shareholders may choose to adapt article 3 so as to restrict the board's role. A family company which has recently put outside directors on its board, for example, may not wish to give the directors an unfettered power to set the company's long-term strategy, and so may want to specify that no decision to venture into new lines of business or new jurisdictions may be taken without the shareholders' prior approval in the form of an ordinary resolution. Restrictions on the board's freedom to exercise the company's borrowing powers, too, are not uncommon. For example, article 3 may be made subject to a proviso that no decision to borrow more than £100,000 may be taken without the sanction of an ordinary resolution.

5.6 Terminology

5.6.1 Overview

5.6.1.1 The terminology surrounding the office of director can be confusing, not least because many of the expressions which one encounters regularly in this connection are neither defined, nor even referred to, in CA2006. Of the five expressions which will be examined in this section – namely 'de jure director,' 'de facto director', 'shadow director', 'executive director' and 'non-executive director' – the only one which is expressly referred to (and, in fact, defined) in the Act is 'shadow director'.

5.6.1.2 The five expressions may be divided into two categories. The question as to whether someone is a de jure director, a de facto director or a shadow director goes to his status as a director, in that a person who is not a director in any of those senses is not a director at all. The question as to whether someone is an executive director or a non-executive director, on the other hand, goes to the nature of the role within the company played by someone who is a director. Thus, the second question does not arise unless it has been determined that the person is, indeed, a de jure, de facto or shadow director.

5.6.2 De jure director

5.6.2.1 A 'de jure director' is someone who has been properly appointed as a director. Where, for example, a company has adopted article 17 of the model articles for private companies, which provides that a director may be appointed by an ordinary resolution or a decision of the directors, a director who was appointed by an ordinary resolution was properly appointed and is therefore known as a de jure director.

5.6.3 De facto director

5.6.3.1 The courts have declined to provide a single, universal definition of 'de facto director', and in fact they have taken the view that it is impossible to devise such a definition, since the expression may have different meanings in different contexts (*Holland v Commissioners for Her Majesty's Revenue and Customs* [2010] UKSC 51, at [39] (per Lord Hope) and [93] (per Lord Collins); *Smithton Ltd v Naggar* [2014] EWCA Civ 939 at [33] (per Arden LJ)). It is, however, clear that the essential question is whether the person has taken on the role of a director. In the words of Arden LJ in *Smithton Ltd v Naggar*: 'The question is whether he was part of the corporate governance system of the company and whether he assumed the status and function of a director so as to make himself responsible as if he were a director' ([2014] EWCA Civ 939 at [33]).

5.6.3.2 It will not always be easy to determine whether, in a particular case, a person is assuming the function of a director or, to put it another way, undertaking acts of a directorial nature, and ultimately this is a question of fact, and will therefore depend upon all the circumstances. The difficulty inherent in this exercise is illustrated by the most important decision on de facto directors, that of the Supreme Court in *Holland v Commissioners for Her Majesty's Revenue and Customs* [2010] UKSC 51. The issue before the court was whether a director of a corporate director of various companies was himself a de facto director of those companies, and although the judges broadly agreed as to the relevant legal principles, they were divided as to how to apply those principles to the facts. Three of the judges felt that the director was not a de facto director; the remaining two judges felt that he was.

5.6.3.3 Some guidance as to how to decide whether a person is assuming the function of a director can be gleaned from the case law. Two points, in particular, are worth noting. First, a job title will not decide the matter one way or the other (*Smithton Ltd v Naggar* [2014] EWCA Civ 939 at [38]); thus, where a relatively junior member of staff within a large multinational is given the job title 'Branch customer services director', he will not thereby fall to be classified as a de facto director. Second, a person may be classified as a de facto director even if he has not been involved in all aspects of the company's activities (*Smithton Ltd v Naggar* [2014] EWCA Civ 939 at [32]).

5.6.3.4 The position in relation to de facto directors may, then, be summed up as follows: a de facto director is someone who has not been properly appointed as a director, but who nevertheless acts as a director.

5.6.3.5 The expression encompasses both:

- a person who has purportedly been appointed a director, but whose appointment was defective in some way; and
- a person in relation to whom no effort has been made to appoint him a director in the normal way, but who nevertheless has taken on the role of a director.

5.6.3.6 The consequences of being found to be a de facto director are potentially serious. According to s. 250 of the Act, '"director" includes any person occupying the position of director, by whatever name called', so most (though perhaps not all) provisions of the Act which impose responsibilities or sanctions on directors must be read as imposing responsibilities or sanctions on de facto directors as well as de jure directors (while s. 250 is expressed in very wide terms, seeming to provide that every reference in the Act to a 'director' must be regarded as a reference not only to a de jure director but also to a de facto director, the courts have indicated that it may not be appropriate to read every reference to a 'director' in this way. In *Re Lo-Line Electric Motors Ltd* [1988] Ch 477, the High Court, when considering the position under CA1985, indicated (at 489B) that the statutory requirement to have a minimum number of directors, for example, must be read as a requirement to have a minimum number of de jure directors). Perhaps the most important implication of this is that de facto directors will be subject to the same statutory duties to the company as de jure directors.

5.6.3.7 The potential liabilities to which a de facto director is subject are not confined to CA2006. The wrongful trading provision in the Insolvency Act 1986 s. 214, for example, applies to de facto directors (*Re Hydrodam (Corby) Ltd* [1994] 2 BCLC 180 at 182), just as it does to de jure directors (and, indeed, shadow directors).

5.6.4 Shadow director

5.6.4.1 The expression 'shadow director' is defined in CA2006 s. 251, as amended by the Small Business, Enterprise and Employment Act 2015 with effect from 26 May 2015:

'(1) In the Companies Acts "shadow director", in relation to a company, means a person in accordance with whose directions or instructions the directors of the company are accustomed to act.

(2) A person is not to be regarded as a shadow director by reason only that the directors act –
 (a) on advice given by that person in a professional capacity;
 (b) in accordance with instructions, a direction, guidance or advice given by that person in the exercise of a function conferred by or under an enactment;

(c) in accordance with guidance or advice given by that person in that person's capacity as a Minister of the Crown (within the meaning of the Ministers of the Crown Act 1975).

(3) A body corporate is not to be regarded as a shadow director of any of its subsidiary companies for the purposes of –
Chapter 2 (general duties of directors)
Chapter 4 (transactions requiring members' approval), or
Chapter 6 (contract with sole member who is also a director),
by reason only that the directors of the subsidiary are accustomed to act in accordance with its directions or instructions.'

5.6.4.2 A similar definition is to be found in the Insolvency Act 1986 s. 251 and the Company Directors Disqualification Act 1986 s. 22 (in both cases as amended by the Small Business, Enterprise and Employment Act 2015 with effect from 26 May 2015), although neither of those sections contains a provision corresponding to CA2006 s. 251(3).5.6.4.3 The courts have taken the view that the statutory definition is to be given its natural meaning. What is required in order to show that a person is a shadow director is, therefore, nothing more nor less than that the company's de jure directors are accustomed to act on his directions or instructions.

5.6.4.4 The leading decision on shadow directors is that of the Court of Appeal in *Secretary of State for Trade and Industry v Deverell* [2001] Ch 340. In the course of concluding that two individuals were shadow directors for the purposes of the Company Directors' Disqualification Act 1986, Morritt LJ, who delivered the only substantive judgment, provided useful guidance as to the circumstances in which a person might be said to be a shadow director. In particular, he noted that:

- a shadow director is someone who has 'real influence in the corporate affairs of the company', although that influence need not cover the full range of the company's activities;
- it is not necessary to show that the de jure directors are subservient or surrender their discretion – all that is required is that, as a matter of fact, they act on the person's directions or instructions;
- it is not necessary that the directions or instructions are labelled as such; and
- a shadow director need not be someone who lurks in the shadows, but may instead give his directions or instructions quite openly.

5.6.4.5 The consequences of being found to be a shadow director are potentially serious, for numerous provisions of CA2006 and the Insolvency Act 1986 expressly extend liability beyond de jure and de facto directors to shadow directors. For example, if a company fails to comply with an order to change its name under CA2006 s.76 (under CA2006 s. 76, if a company's name gives a misleading indication of its activities, the Secretary of State may order the company to change it. See, further, paragraph 2.2.7.17), a criminal sanction is imposed on 'every officer' who is in default, and the Act specifies that a shadow director is an officer for these purposes CA2006 s. 76(6). Similarly, the wrongful trading provision in the Insolvency Act 1986 s. 214 is expressly extended so as to cover not just de jure directors and de facto directors, but also shadow directors (Insolvency Act 1986 s. 214(7)).

5.6.4.6 In its original form, CA2006 s. 170(5) provided for the statutory directors' duties to apply to shadow directors 'where, and to the extent that, the corresponding common law rules or equitable principles so apply', but unfortunately it was not entirely clear from the case law to what extent shadow directors were, in fact, subject to directors' duties. With effect from 26 May 2015, however, the Small Business, Enterprise and Employment Act 2015 amended CA2006 s. 170(5) to the effect that the statutory duties will generally apply to shadow directors just as they apply to de jure and de facto directors (see, further, paragraph 7.3.3).

5.6.5 Executive director

5.6.5.1 An 'executive director' is a director to whom particular responsibilities concerning the management of the company have been delegated. There is no list, either in the Act or in case law, of the different types of executive director a company may choose to appoint, but examples include the managing director (sometimes, especially in large companies, known as the chief executive officer (CEO) or simply the chief executive), finance director and commercial director.

5.6.5.2 Companies are under no obligation to have any executive directors. If, though, a company has more than a handful of directors, it may be impracticable for the board as a whole to take decisions concerning the day-to-day management of the company's affairs; it may be more efficient, instead, to allocate particular areas of responsibility to individual directors.

5.6.5.3 Since the Act does not deal with executive directors, it is left to companies to address such matters as their appointment and powers in their articles. One option is for the articles to specify that the company will have, say, a managing director, and to set out details of the powers which he will have and the remuneration which he will receive for his services. It is more common, however, for the articles to adopt a less prescriptive approach, giving the board a general power to appoint executive directors on such terms as they see fit, and this is the approach adopted in the model articles for private companies. The relevant provisions (though they do not mention executive directors in so many words) are articles 5(1) and 19(1) and (2). The latter gives the board the power to appoint any of its members to undertake services for the company and to remunerate them for their services, and the former gives the board a wide-ranging power to delegate its powers.

5.6.5.4 The scope of an executive director's role is for his company to decide, because his role will depend upon the extent of the powers which are delegated to him.

5.6.5.5 Ideally, there will be an express delegation of powers in writing, whether in the articles, the board resolution appointing him or his service contract. For example, if a company has adopted the model articles, the board may pass a resolution which not only appoints a managing director, but also states that he will be responsible for managing the company's business save that he must refer specified matters – for example, decisions to commit the company to expenditure over a certain level – to the board.

5.6.5.6 Many smaller companies are, however, run on far less formal lines, and there may well not be any express delegation of powers (indeed, it is not uncommon in the context of small private companies for a director to act as an executive director (normally a managing director) despite never having been formally appointed as such). In such cases, the precise boundaries of the executive director's role will be unclear, because case law does not provide a comprehensive statement of the powers which will be taken to have been impliedly delegated to the various types of executive director. According to Arden LJ in *Smith v Butler* [2012] EWCA Civ 314, a managing director to whom powers have not been expressly delegated will be taken to have, as implied powers, those powers 'that would ordinarily be exercisable by a managing director in his position'. Although this is a clear enough statement of the law, the test which it establishes is not always easy to apply in practice, for it raises the question as to what powers are ordinarily exercisable by executive directors. No doubt a managing director will normally have the powers which he needs in order to manage the company's day-to-day affairs, and a finance director will normally have the powers which he needs in order to manage the company's finances, but what powers, exactly, are those? Some guidance as to the usual powers of executive directors can be gleaned from the case law (in *Smith v Butler* [2012] EWCA Civ 314 itself, the Court of Appeal held that a managing director did not, on the facts, have the power to dismiss the chairman, and Arden LJ suggested further that it will not normally be for a managing director to set the company's strategy) but unfortunately the courts have not had many opportunities to consider this matter.

5.6.6 Non-executive director

5.6.6.1 A 'non-executive director' is a director who does not have any executive functions. The Act does not distinguish expressly between executive and non-executive directors, so a non-executive director is just as much a director as an executive director, in the sense that he is subject to the numerous obligations and responsibilities under the Act which are imposed on 'directors'. In particular, a non-executive director must comply with the statutory directors' duties, which are stated to be 'owed by a director of a company' (s. 170(1)).

5.6.6.2 The expression 'non-executive director' was traditionally used primarily in the context of listed companies, and non-executive directors of such companies will normally be in receipt of sufficient legal advice to be in no doubt as to the importance of their role in the corporate governance framework. Non-executive directors of those listed companies which are subject to the UK Corporate Governance Code, in particular, will be well aware of the nature of their responsibilities, for the Code deals with their role in some detail. For example, one of the Code's Main Principles reads as follows: 'As part of their role as members of a unitary board, non-executive directors should constructively challenge and help develop proposals on strategy' (section. A.4, UK Corporate Governance Code (September 2014)).

5.6.6.3 There is a growing tendency among directors of smaller, private companies who do not have an executive function to refer to themselves as non-executive directors. This is unobjectionable in principle, but such directors must not fall into the trap of believing that they are, in effect, sleeping directors, with no real role in the life of the company. In fact, although they may not be engaged in day-to-day decisions concerning the company's business, they play an important role in overseeing the activities of the executive directors, and a failure to familiarise themselves with the company's business and to challenge the executive directors where appropriate may well constitute a breach of their duty under s. 174 to act with care and diligence. In *Lexi Holdings plc (in administration) v Luqman* [2009] EWCA Civ 117, a failure on the part of two directors to exercise an appropriate degree of oversight over the company's managing director constituted a breach of the common law predecessor to the duty of care under s. 174 (s. 174 is discussed in paragraphs 7.3.12).

6
Decision-making by directors

> **Summary**
> - The rules governing the means by which directors make decisions are set out primarily in companies' articles.
> - The rules set out in the model articles establish a sensible framework, which many companies will either adopt in its entirety or use as a starting point for producing bespoke rules.
> - Directors generally take decisions either by majority vote at a board meeting or unanimously in the form of a directors' written resolution.
> - The statutory directors' duties play an important role in the decision-making process.

6.1 Introduction

6.1.1 Most decisions concerning a company's business are taken by individual directors in the course of their day-to-day management of its affairs. A managing director, for example, might renew a contract with an existing supplier, and a finance director might agree modifications to the terms of the company's relationship with its bank. CA2006 contains no rules on the means by which such decisions are taken and does not require them to be recorded, and most companies' articles, too, will be silent on these points. A director is, of course, free to record any decisions which he feels are of a relatively significant nature – and, indeed, he would be well-advised to do so – but the form which any such record takes will be a matter for his discretion.

6.1.2 Some decisions, however, are taken by the full board. It will not always be clear, in the context of the division of powers within a particular company, whether a particular decision should be taken by the full board or, for instance, by the managing director (see paragraph s 5.6.5.4 to 5.6.5.6), but in general the more significant a decision is, the more likely it is that it will need to be taken by the board as a whole.

6.1.3 The Act contains two important provisions concerning the recording of decisions taken at board meetings (see ss. 248 and 249, concerning, respectively, the obligation to keep minutes of meetings and the evidential value of minutes), but otherwise board decisions are governed primarily by companies' articles. The model articles for private companies, for example, deal both with the procedure governing the taking of such decisions and, albeit to a lesser extent, the means by which they are to be recorded.

6.1.4 This chapter examines various aspects of the law and rules concerning board decisions. Specifically, it discusses the following matters:

- the framework governing decision-making by directors;
- the procedure for taking decisions at board meetings;
- the procedure for taking decisions by means of a directors' written resolution; and
- the impact of the statutory directors' duties on the decision-making process.

6.2 Terminology

6.2.1 Decisions taken by directors are described formally as 'resolutions'. Whereas shareholders' resolutions are divided into ordinary resolutions and special resolutions – the former being a resolution passed by a bare majority and the latter being a resolution passed by a 75% majority – no such corresponding terminology is employed in relation to directors' resolutions. Thus, there is no such thing as an 'ordinary resolution of the board' or a 'special resolution of the board'.

6.3 The framework

6.3.1 The approach adopted in the model articles for private companies as regards the procedure for taking decisions is typical, and many companies adopt the wording of the relevant provision, namely article 7(1), wholesale.

6.3.2 Article 7(1) is in the following terms: *'The general rule about decision-making by directors is that any decision of the directors must be either a majority decision at a meeting or a decision taken in accordance with article 8.'*

6.3.3 The effect of this provision, when read with article 8, is that the directors may take decisions either at a board meeting (in which case a resolution is passed if a majority of those present vote in favour of it) or, if they are acting unanimously, in any other way. In practice, unanimous decisions are normally passed in the form of a directors' written resolution.

6.3.4 If a company's articles are along the lines of the model articles, there is no difference, in terms of the effectiveness of the decision, between a board resolution passed at a board meeting and a board resolution passed in the form of a directors' written resolution. Both are perfectly valid decisions of the board.

6.3.5 As a general rule, however, it is advisable to take the most important decisions at a board meeting rather than by means of a written resolution.

- This is partly because board meetings are likely to produce more measured decisions than those which are taken in writing. After all, a meeting affords the participants an opportunity to engage in a collaborative process, in which the proposals under consideration are debated thoroughly and various points of view are aired and tested. When directors pass written resolutions, by contrast, they may make their minds up in isolation, without the benefit of their colleagues' opinions.
- Another important advantage of board meetings concerns the directors' obligation to comply with statutory duties of loyalty and care. A director whose decision on a particular matter is subsequently challenged may find that it is easier to show that he complied with the duties if he was part of a meeting at which the resolution in question was subject to a detailed examination than if the resolution was passed in writing.

    Take the case of a board decision to acquire a rival business. If the business fails a few months after the acquisition, pushing the company into insolvency, its directors will be in a strong position to defend themselves against a claim by the liquidator that they acted negligently if they can point to minutes of a board meeting at which the managing director, an independent expert on business acquisitions and the company's solicitors reported on the proposed transaction and were subjected to probing questions as to the soundness of the target business, the expected benefits of the acquisition and the key provisions of the legal documentation. The directors would be on less comfortable ground if they could point instead only to a written resolution which was accompanied by written reports, for the court would be well aware that they could have signed the written resolution without so much as glancing at the reports, let alone giving them careful consideration.

6.3.6 Many companies, especially those at the smaller end of the scale, will be content to leave it to their board to decide on an ad hoc basis whether a particular decision warrants a board meeting. Some, though, may wish to exercise greater control over the decision-making process, for example by providing in the articles or in internal policy documents that certain types of decisions must be passed at a board meeting.

6.4 Board meetings

6.4.1 Procedure

6.4.1.1 Although the procedure for taking decisions at board meetings is determined by individual companies' articles rather than by the Act, most companies will either adopt the relevant provisions of the model articles in their entirety, or at least use them as a base upon which to build a set of bespoke rules. The following points outline the procedure which is prescribed in the model articles.

- A meeting may be called by any of the directors (article 9(1)).
- Notice of the meeting must normally (see article 9(4) in relation to a director's right to waive his entitlement to receive notice) be given to each director (article 9(3)). It must specify when and where the meeting will be held, and how any directors who are not expected to be present in person will be participating (article 9(2)). There is no requirement to give the notice a set number of days before the meeting; in the event of a dispute as to whether sufficient notice of a particular meeting was given, the courts will be guided by the company's usual practice in this regard (see paragraph 4.3.5.13). The notice need not be in writing (article 9(3)), and may be given by any means to which the director has agreed (article 48(2)).
- The meeting must be chaired, either by a director who has been appointed to be the chairman on an ongoing basis or, if no such appointment has been made or if the chairman is absent, by one of the directors who is participating in the meeting (article 12).
- The directors do not have to be present at the meeting in person. In fact, the model articles adopt a very permissive approach to attendance, providing simply that each director must be able to communicate with the others (article 10). Thus, a director is permitted to attend a board meeting by telephone, say, or by means of a videoconferencing facility.
- In order for the meeting to proceed, it must be quorate, which is to say that at least two directors must be present in person or participating remotely (article 11). Anyone who is charged with the task of attending to the procedural aspects of a board meeting will need to check the quorum requirement very carefully. Not only do the model articles provide for the directors to raise (though not lower) the threshold at their discretion, but in practice article 11 is one of the provisions of the articles which is most likely to be modified by the company to meet its particular needs (see the discussion of article 11 in paragraph 4.3.5.15).
- Resolutions proposed at a board meeting are passed if a majority of the directors who are entitled to vote support them (article 7(1)).

    There are two points to note in connection with voting. First, certain directors may be subject to restrictions on their entitlement to vote on particular resolutions. The model articles, for example, provide that if a resolution concerns a transaction with the company in which a director has a personal interest (for example, if he is a shareholder in a supplier with whom the company is considering doing business), that director is not entitled to vote on it (article 14) (Restrictions on directors' entitlement to vote are discussed in paragraphs 4.3.5.19 and 6.6.5). Second, the articles may confer a casting vote on one of the directors in the event that there are an equal number of votes for and against a resolution. The model articles, for example, confer a casting vote on the director who is chairing the meeting (article 13).

6.4.2 Minutes

6.4.2.1 In a rare intervention in the sphere of directors' decision-making, the Act imposes upon companies an obligation to keep a record of proceedings at board meetings in the form of minutes (s. 248(1)).

6.4.2.2 The Act goes on to provide that the minutes must be retained for at least ten years (s. 248(2)), and in fact it is good practice to keep them indefinitely, for minutes serve as an important historical resource for both the company and its directors. On a general note, clearly it can be helpful for purely internal purposes to have an accurate record of the directors' deliberations on important matters. If, for example, a newly installed board is contemplating an expansion into a new line of business, a record of a failed attempt at diversification by the previous board could be of great assistance in identifying potential pitfalls. A somewhat narrower, but equally important, reason for keeping minutes is that they can play an important role in protecting directors in the event of an allegation that, in reaching a particular decision, they breached their duties to the company. Assuming they did, indeed, comply with their duties, a well-drafted set of minutes, which identifies the relevant aspects of their compliance in clear, unambiguous terms, would afford them a powerful defence against any such attack. Note, in this connection, that minutes which are signed by the director who chaired the meeting are evidence of the proceedings at the meeting (s. 249 and, in relation to the term 'authenticated' as it is used in that section, s. 1146).

6.4.2.3 The task of drafting board minutes can seem daunting, because it is not always clear which aspects of the proceedings should be recorded in detail. There is no simple solution to this problem, since it is a matter of judgement as to what matters deserve particular attention in the minutes, and good judgement comes from experience. It may, however, be helpful to bear in mind the main purposes served by minutes, as outlined in the paragraph above. It should also be borne in mind that, like any other document, minutes should be written clearly and concisely, and should adopt a logical structure. It perhaps goes without saying that they must include an accurate statement of any resolutions passed by the board.

6.4.2.4 The Act does not prescribe a format for board minutes, and it is extremely unlikely that a company's articles will fill this gap. In practice, however, most companies' minutes conform to a fairly standard template, along the lines of the sample minutes set out in Figure 6.1.

Figure 6.1 Sample board minutes

[name of company]
Registered number: [ ]

Minutes of a board meeting held at [address] at [time] on [date]

Directors in attendance: [ ]

1. Formalities
   - appointment of chairman
   - confirmation by chairman that the meeting had been properly called in accordance with the articles of association
   - confirmation by chairman that a quorum was present (including a reference to any directors who were attending by telephone, etc., and to any directors who were in attendance but who did not count towards the quorum)
2. Purpose of the meeting
   Chairman's summary of:
   - the events leading up to the meeting, including a reference to previous board meetings concerning the proposed transaction
   - the specific purpose for which the meeting had been called (for example, to consider internal and external reports concerning the proposed transaction, and to consider a resolution to proceed with it)
3. Declarations of interest
   - details of any declarations by directors that they had an interest in the proposed transaction [In the case of a board meeting to consider a proposal to enter into a transaction, any declarations will be made pursuant to the directors' duty under s. 177 of the Act to declare any interest in a proposed transaction with the company. In relation to other types of decisions, declarations may relate to the duty under s. 182 to declare any interest in an existing transaction to which the company is a party, and to the duty under s. 175 to avoid situations of conflict. For a discussion of the impact of these duties on the decision-making process, see paragraph 6.6.5].
   - chairman's confirmation as to whether, in the light of the declarations, the directors in question counted towards the quorum and were able to vote at the meeting

4. Documents
   - list of any documents which were discussed at the meeting
5. Reports
   - summary of the key points made in any reports presented by directors or external advisers (for example, a report by the managing director on the benefits and risks of the proposed transaction, a report by an environmental consultant on the environmental impact of the proposed transaction and a report by the company's solicitors on the draft transaction documents)
   - summary of the board's discussion of the reports, including details of any significant questions raised
6. Directors' duties
   - reference to the directors' compliance with any of their statutory duties that are particularly relevant (for example, a reference in connection with s. 171(b) to the purpose for which a power is being exercised and a reference to the directors' consideration of any of the mandatory factors listed in s. 172 in relation to which the proposed transaction raises particular issues)
7. Resolutions
   - clear, concise statement of the resolutions passed – for example: 'having carefully assessed the proposed transaction, the directors resolved:
   - pursuant to s. 172 of CA2006, that the transaction would promote the success of the company for the benefit of its members as a whole
   - that, accordingly, the managing director was authorised to sign the transaction documents in the form attached to these minutes on the company's behalf'
8. Minutes
   - instruction to the company secretary to prepare minutes of the meeting
9. Conclusion of meeting
   - chairman's declaration that the meeting was closed

_____   _____
Chairman   Date

6.4.2.5 In many private companies, minutes will be prepared in the traditional manner. That is to say, the company secretary or other designated person will attend the meeting, take detailed notes of the proceedings, prepare draft minutes and submit them to the chairman for approval by the board.

6.4.2.6 In some larger companies, however, and especially in relation to meetings concerning matters of particular importance, a slightly different approach might be adopted, such that draft minutes will be prepared by the company's solicitors or in-house legal team in advance of the meeting and will then be used as an agenda for the meeting. The company secretary or other designated person will still attend the meeting and take detailed notes of the proceedings, but instead of having to write up a complete set of minutes at that stage will simply have to amend the draft minutes to ensure that they reflect accurately what transpired at the meeting before submitting them to the chairman. The principal advantage of this approach is that it provides the directors with useful guidance as to the matters which they must consider in reaching their decisions, thus increasing the likelihood that they will comply with any relevant provisions of the Act (including those which set out their duties) and with the company's articles.

6.5 Directors' written resolutions

6.5.1 Most companies want their directors to have the option of taking decisions otherwise than at a board meeting, and it is customary for private companies to include in their articles a provision along the lines of article 8 of the model articles, which allows directors to take decisions outside board meetings if they are acting unanimously.

6.5.2 Article 8 reads as follows:

'(1) A decision of the directors is taken in accordance with this article when all eligible directors indicate to each other by any means that they share a common view on a matter.
(2) Such a decision may take the form of a resolution in writing, copies of which have been signed by each eligible director or to which each eligible director has otherwise indicated agreement in writing.
(3) References in this article to eligible directors are to directors who would have been entitled to vote on the matter had it been proposed as a resolution at a directors' meeting.
(4) A decision may not be taken in accordance with this article if the eligible directors would not have formed a quorum at such a meeting.'

6.5.3 Article 8 goes well beyond merely giving the directors the option of using a written resolution. All that is required for a valid decision under the article is that 'all eligible directors *indicate to each other by any means* that they share a common view on a matter' (emphasis added). This generous approach reflects the position at common law, which is that the courts are willing to allow directors who act unanimously to act informally (*Runciman v Walter Runciman plc* [1992]

BCLC 1084 at 1092). A unanimous decision taken by the directors during a brief chat at the office coffee machine, for example, would constitute a valid decision of the board under article 8, as would a unanimous decision reached by means of an exchange of text messages.

6.5.4 If directors take a decision by informal means, they are required by article 15 to record it in writing, thus creating a paper trail for future reference. However, it is open to question whether directors who are in the habit of taking decisions in a relatively casual fashion will then take the trouble to ensure that a written record is prepared. It is, therefore, best practice for directors to resist the temptation to take advantage of the full flexibility of article 8 and, if they wish to take a decision otherwise than at a board meeting, to do so by means of a formal written resolution.

6.5.5 The procedure for passing a directors' written resolution is set out in article 8(2). It is, in essence, extremely straightforward: all the directors must sign the written resolution or otherwise indicate in writing that they agree with it.

6.5.6 There are, however, two points to note in relation to written resolutions.

- First, article 8(2) (and, in fact, article 8 in general) requires only unanimity as among 'eligible directors'. In this context, an 'eligible director' is a director who would have been entitled to vote on the resolution had it been considered at a board meeting (article 8(3)). Thus, a director who, pursuant to article 14 (article 14 is discussed in paragraph 4.3.5.18), has been stripped of his entitlement to vote on a resolution which concerns a transaction with the company in which he has a personal interest is not an 'eligible director' for these purposes, and the resolution may be passed as a written resolution even if he opposes it.
- Second, the written resolution procedure cannot be used to bypass the quorum requirement which applies in relation to board meetings. The effect of article 8(4) is that if the eligible directors would not have formed a quorum at a board meeting to consider a resolution, they are not competent to pass that resolution in the form of a written resolution. Take the case of a company with six directors and articles which set the quorum for board meetings at four. If, in relation to a particular resolution, four of the directors are prevented from counting in the quorum or voting by virtue of article 14, the other two directors would not be able to pass the resolution at a board meeting, because the meeting would be inquorate. Article 8(4) prevents those two directors from seeking instead to pass the resolution as a written resolution on the basis that unanimity among the eligible directors (i.e. among the two of them) has been achieved. (There are various ways to resolve a situation in which the directors are unable to act. For example, the shareholders can lower the quorum requirement or appoint additional directors.)

6.5.7 Most companies' articles will not supplement article 8(2) with rules as to the content or format of a directors' written resolution. As far as content is concerned, the key point to bear in mind when drafting a written resolution is that it will serve the same purpose as board minutes, in that it will be a historical resource to be drawn upon both generally in the course of the company's future activities and specifically by the directors in the event that their decision is subsequently challenged. As far as format is concerned, most written resolutions will be drafted along the lines of the sample written resolutions set out in Figure 6.2.

Figure 6.2 Sample directors' written resolutions

[name of company]
Registered number: [ ]

Directors' written resolutions

These are resolutions in writing of the directors of [name of company], passed in accordance with article [ ] of the company's articles of association.

1. Background
   - summary of the events leading up to the written resolutions, including a reference to the board's previous decisions concerning the proposed transaction
2. Declarations of interest
   - details of any declarations by directors that they have an interest in the proposed transaction [in the case of written resolutions concerning a proposed transaction, any declarations will be made pursuant to the directors' duty under s. 177 of the Act to declare any interest in a proposed transaction with the company. In relation to other types of decisions, declarations may relate to the duty under s. 182 to declare any interest in an existing transaction to which the company is a party, and to the duty under s. 175 to avoid situations of conflict. For a discussion of the impact of these duties on the decision-making process, see paragraph 6.6.5].
   - explanations of the consequences of the declarations (for example, that the directors in question are not 'eligible directors' for the purposes of the written resolutions)
3. Documents
   - list of documents accompanying the written resolutions
   - summary of the key points made in the documents

4. Directors' duties
   - discussion of any of the statutory directors' duties that are particularly relevant (for example, a reference in connection with s. 171(b) to the purpose for which a power is being exercised and a reference to any of the mandatory factors listed in s. 172 in relation to which the proposed transaction raises particular issues)
5. Resolutions
   - text of the resolutions – for example:
     'having carefully assessed the proposed transaction, the directors resolve:
   - pursuant to section 172 of CA2006, that the transaction would promote the success of the company for the benefit of its members as a whole
   - that, accordingly, the managing director is authorised to sign the transaction documents in the form attached to these written resolutions on the company's behalf'

_____   _____
[name of director]   Date

_____   _____
[name of director]   Date

_____   _____
[name of director]   Date

6.6 Impact of directors' duties on decision-making

6.6.1 The duties which are imposed on directors by CA2006 (the duties are examined in detail in Chapter 7 (Directors' duties)) play a significant role in the decision-making process. Not only must the directors comply with the duties when they participate in the process, but they will also want to ensure that the fact of their compliance has been properly recorded, so that they are in a position to defend themselves against any future allegations that their conduct fell below the required standard.

6.6.2 A director is subject to his statutory duties whenever he is acting in his capacity as a director (in fact, the duties can also affect a director's conduct when he is acting in an entirely private capacity. See the discussion of the duty under s. 175 to avoid situations of conflict in paragraph 7.3.2.2). When he is participating in the process by which the board takes decisions, therefore, he will need to bear in mind the nature and scope of the duties and take all necessary steps to ensure that he is complying with them. The duty under s. 174 to act with care and skill, for example, will require him to ensure that he has at his fingertips all the information which a reasonable man would wish to examine before he reaches a decision, while compliance with the duty under s. 172 to promote the company's success will require him to be acting, when he votes on a resolution, in what he genuinely believes are the company's best interests. In some instances, compliance will involve a declaration to the rest of the board; under s. 177, for example, a director must declare any interest he has in a proposed transaction with the company.

6.6.3 Although different companies and directors (and law firms, for that matter) may have slightly different views as to how, precisely, to record compliance with the duties, the underlying objective is to have a written record – whether in board minutes or in a directors' written resolution – documenting clearly the fact of the directors' compliance.

6.6.4 There is normally no need expressly to record compliance with every duty. Thus, if the board minutes or director's written resolution disclose the fact that the directors have considered various reports on a proposed transaction, a separate statement that they have thereby complied with their duty under s. 174 to act with care and skill would be superfluous. Similarly, if a decision is taken pursuant to a provision in the articles, a reference to that fact will normally obviate the need to record separately the fact that the directors were complying with their duty under s. 171(a) to act in accordance with the company's articles of association.

6.6.5 The duties which those charged with preparing board minutes or directors' written resolutions should normally consider referring to explicitly are as follows:

- **The duty to exercise powers only for the purposes for which they are conferred (s. 171(b)).** In fact, this duty is *not* customarily referred to in board minutes or directors' written resolutions, and certainly there is no need to record in relation to every power exercised by the directors the fact that it was exercised for a proper purpose. Where, however, the directors are aware that their exercise of a particular power (the power to issue shares, for example) may be challenged, it is sensible to record in writing the fact that they had sought to identify the purpose for which the power could legitimately be exercised and had duly exercised the power for that purpose. An illustration of the potential benefits of dealing expressly with the duty in s. 171(b) in appropriate cases is to be found in *Eclairs Group Ltd v JKX Oil & Gas plc* [2013] EWHC 2631 (Ch). Although the case subsequently went to appeal (see paragraph s 7.3.9.3 to 7.3.9.4 for a discussion of the Court of Appeal's decision), the High Court's decision is notable for the lengths to which the judge had to go in order to ascertain the purpose for which directors had exercised a particular power. Since the relevant board minutes were apparently silent on the point, and since it was not addressed to any great extent in the witness statements, Mann J was left to try to identify the purpose primarily by means of a close examination of the evidence given at the trial.

- **The duty to promote the success of the company (s. 172).** This is the core duty of directors, and as such is the one duty to which all board minutes or directors' written resolutions concerning significant decisions will refer. Thus, the resolution in paragraph 7 of the sample board minutes in Figure 6.1 states that the directors considered, pursuant to s. 172, that the proposed transaction would promote the company's success. It is not necessary actually to cite s. 172 in the resolution. Some companies prefer simply to state that the directors considered that the act in question would promote the company's success.

    Section 172 specifies that, in acting in such a way as to promote the company's success, a director must have regard to a non-exhaustive list of factors, including the interests of the company's employees, the company's relationship with its suppliers and the impact of the company's activities on the environment. Assuming directors have duly considered each of these factors, the question arises as to how compliance with this aspect of the duty should be recorded. There are two views on this point. On one view, it is sensible to record the fact that each of the factors has been taken into account, and perhaps even to list them all. The contrary view is that such an approach might give the impression that the directors are engaging in a box-ticking exercise, simply listing the factors automatically and not giving them proper consideration. On this view, the better approach is to refer only to those factors (if any) which are of particular relevance to the decision in question. Thus, if the directors were voting on a proposal to reorganise the company's business, the record might well refer to the fact that they took into account the interests of employees, but would probably not need to report that they had considered the impact of the decision on the environment. This latter approach is widely, though not universally, favoured in practice, and is reflected in paragraph 6 of the sample board minutes in Figure 6.1.

- **The duty to avoid situations of conflict (s. 175).** Although s. 175 does not normally affect the decision-making process, on the rare occasions on which it is relevant it will need to be addressed in the board minutes or directors' written resolution.

    Under s. 175, a director is not permitted to enter into a situation in which his interests conflict with those of the company. The shareholders (and, in some instances, the board) can, however, authorise a director to enter into such a situation, and an authorisation of a s. 175 conflict may go on to specify that the director in question is not permitted to vote or count in the quorum in relation to any matter to which the conflict of interest relates. Take the case of a director who is invited to buy a small stake in a rival company. The shareholders may choose to allow him to acquire the stake, but may specify that he will not be permitted to vote or count in the quorum in relation to any decision to which his interest in the rival company may be relevant. If the board subsequently considers a proposal to launch a marketing campaign designed to attack the rival company, for example, the director will not be permitted to vote on it.

If a director's ability to vote is compromised in this way, the board minutes or directors' written resolution will need to record that fact. In the example above, they would note that the director had reminded the rest of the board of his interest in the rival company, that his interest had been authorised subject to a restriction on his right to vote and that, as a result, he was disenfranchised in relation to the marketing campaign resolution.

- **The duty to declare an interest in a proposed or existing transaction with the company (ss. 177 and 182).** Naturally, if a director has an interest which he is required to declare in accordance with this duty (if, for example, the board is voting on a resolution to acquire a company in which his wife owns a stake), that declaration should be reflected in the board minutes or the directors' written resolution. If, as is often the case, the statutory obligation to make a declaration is supplemented by a provision in the articles preventing a director who has an interest from voting or counting in the quorum in relation to the transaction in question, the documentation will also need to note the fact of the director's disenfranchisement. Declarations under ss. 177 and 182 are usually dealt with in a dedicated paragraph in the documentation (see, for example, paragraph 3 of the sample board minutes in Figure 6.1), and the fact that the director does not count in the quorum may also be dealt with at the outset of the meeting (see paragraph 1 of the sample minutes).

7
Directors' duties

> **Summary**
> - Directors owe various duties to their company.
> - The duties, which are set out in CA2006, are designed to ensure a director's loyalty and competence. The core duty of loyalty is a duty to promote the success of the company. The question of a director's competence is addressed by a duty to exercise reasonable care, skill and diligence.
> - A breach of duty is essentially an internal matter. A company can bring proceedings against a director for a breach of duty, but equally it can choose to ignore a breach or formally to excuse it by authorising it in advance or ratifying it after the fact.

7.1 Introduction

7.1.1 CA2006 imposes a number of duties on directors.

7.1.2 The law in this area is regarded as one of the most difficult aspects of the company law regime, primarily because the duties are expressed not in the form of detailed rules with which a director must comply, but in the form of broad principles, compliance with which requires both good judgement and an understanding of their underlying rationale. In essence, however, the duties are very simple, and seek only to ensure that a director is loyal to his company and meets a minimum standard of competence.

7.1.3 This chapter is divided into three sections:

- Background – this section outlines the background to the statutory duties.
- The duties – this section examines each of the duties in turn, with a particular emphasis on the duty only to exercise powers for the purposes for which they are conferred (s. 171(b)), the duty to promote the success of the company (s. 172), the duty to exercise reasonable care, skill and diligence (s. 174) and the duty to avoid conflicts of interest (s. 175).

- Consequences of breach – it is impossible to gauge accurately the impact of the duties in practice without understanding the consequences which may flow from their breach, and this section explores both the means by which a breach may be excused by the company through authorisation or ratification, and the means by which a director who commits a breach may be held to account.

7.2 Background

7.2.1 The duties owed by directors to their company were originally devised by the courts. Thus, CA1985 (the predecessor to CA2006) had very little to say on the subject: it required directors to have regard not only to the interests of shareholders, but also to the interests of employees (CA1985 s. 309), and to disclose any interests they had in transactions with the company (CA1985 s. 317), but it did not set out the core duties, such as the duty to act in the company's best interests and the duty to avoid conflicts of interest.

7.2.2 The decision to codify the common law duties in CA2006 was controversial, because it constituted a departure from the approach which the company law regime had adopted for more than a century, but the motivation behind the exercise, which was principally to make the duties more accessible, was sensible. Whereas previously a director with no background in company law would have found it next to impossible to identify the duties to which he was subject without legal advice, such a director now has access to a concise statutory statement of the nature and scope of his duties.

7.2.3 A director who believes that the law on directors' duties is now contained exclusively in the relevant provisions of the Act is, however, operating under a misapprehension. Although it is true that the statutory provisions contain a definitive statement of the duties, the wording of the individual duties is subject to the interpretation of the courts on an ongoing basis. Take, for example, s. 171(b), which requires a director to exercise powers only for the purposes for which they are conferred. It is not for the courts, plainly, to modify the scope of the duty; it is, however, for them to determine the purposes for which particular powers are given to directors. What is more, it is not only the courts' pronouncements on the wording of the statutory provisions which a director must bear in mind. Section 170 notes that the statutory duties are based on, and replace, the duties which the courts had devised (s. 170(3)) and, more importantly, adds that 'regard shall be had to the corresponding common law rules and equitable principles in interpreting and applying the general duties [i.e. broadly speaking, the statutory duties]' (s. 170(4)). In other words, a director who wishes to understand fully the nature of the duties needs to take into account judicial consideration both of the statutory duties and of their common law predecessors.

7.2.4 The discussion of the individual duties in this chapter contains references both to cases which deal with the statutory duties and to cases which were decided on the basis of their common law predecessors.

7.3 The duties

7.3.1 Overview

7.3.1.1 The duties are set out in ss. 172 to 177 and 182 in outline comprise the following:

- a duty to act in accordance with the company's constitution (s. 171(a));
- a duty only to exercise powers for the purposes for which they are conferred (s. 171(b));
- a duty to promote the success of the company (s. 172);
- a duty to exercise independent judgment (s. 173);
- a duty to exercise reasonable care, skill and diligence (s. 174);
- a duty to avoid situations in which personal interests conflict with those of the company (s. 175);
- a duty not to accept benefits from third parties (s. 176); and
- a duty to declare to the board any personal interest in a proposed or existing transaction with the company (ss. 177 and 182).

7.3.1.2 The duties are owed by 'a director of a company' (s. 170(1)). In this context, the term 'director' encompasses both properly appointed directors (so-called de jure directors) and any persons who have taken on the role of a director (so-called de facto directors). (See the partial definition of the term 'director' in s. 250. De jure and de facto directors are discussed in sections 5.6.2 and 5.6.3, respectively.) As far as shadow directors are concerned, s. 170(5) originally left the question of the extent of the application of the duties to shadow directors to the courts, but unfortunately the common law did not contain a clear answer to it. With effect from 26 May 2015, however, s. 170(5) was amended so as to read as follows: 'The general duties apply to a shadow director of a company where and to the extent that they are capable of so applying.' The Small Business, Enterprise and Employment Act 2015, which introduced the amendment, also gave the Secretary of State the power to make regulations concerning the application of the duties to shadow directors, but since no such regulations have yet been forthcoming the current position is that the duties apply to shadow directors in much the same way as they apply to de jure or de facto directors.

7.3.1.3 Save in the case of s. 182, breach of the duties does not constitute a criminal offence, and so it is for the party to whom the duties are owed to hold the directors to account in the event of any transgression. Under the Act, the duties are owed to the company (s. 170(1)), and so enforcement is in the hands of the company, rather than individual shareholders, creditors, employees or other stakeholders.

7.3.1.4 This is an exceedingly important feature of the regime, because its effect is that the duties are, for the most part, an entirely internal matter. In other words, just as a company can choose to hold a director who has breached his duties to account by bringing legal proceedings against him, so too it can choose to approve a breach, whether by authorising it in advance (authorisation in advance of conduct which would otherwise constitute a breach of duty can normally be given only by the shareholders (s. 180(4)(a)) or by ratifying it after the fact (a breach of duty can be ratified after the fact only by the shareholders (s. 239)). Consider the case of a director who wishes to take a 'sabbatical', such that he will withdraw from any involvement in the company's affairs for a year. Such conduct would normally constitute a breach of the duty under s. 174 to exercise reasonable care, skill and diligence, but it is open to the company to take the view that he deserves a break from his responsibilities and accordingly to authorise or ratify the breach. In fact, many breaches are, in practice, neither authorised nor ratified, but simply ignored. A director whose breaches have not been sanctioned does, however, run the risk of being pursued at a later date if the company changes hands or falls into insolvency, for the new board or the liquidator may take a less charitable view of his conduct.

7.3.1.5 The following paragraphs examine each of the duties in turn, but the duties should not be regarded as separate and unconnected obligations. For one thing, the Act specifically provides that more than one duty may apply in a particular case (s. 179), which means that a particular act or series of acts may constitute a breach of more than one of the duties. More generally, though, it is difficult to appreciate fully the scope of the regime without understanding how the duties interrelate. In this connection, the following analysis may be helpful:

- a director's core duty, as set out in s. 172, is to do what he thinks will benefit the company; but
- his freedom to do so is constrained by the other duties, which place restrictions on his conduct.

7.3.1.6 Thus, a director who genuinely believes that the company would benefit from the experience he would gain if he accepted an offer to join the board of a larger rival would be acting in accordance with his duty under s. 172, but would be prevented from taking the new role by virtue of his obligation under s. 175 to avoid situations in which he has a personal interest (in this case, his interest in ensuring the success of the rival) which conflicts with the company's interests.

7.3.2 The duty to act in accordance with the company's constitution (s. 171(a))

>Section 171 – Duty to act within powers
>A director of a company must –
>(a) act in accordance with the company's constitution, and
>(b) ...

7.3.2.1 As far as the duty to act in accordance with the company's constitution is concerned, the question arises as to what 'constitution' means for these purposes. As a matter of common sense, it would seem obvious that it includes, at least, the company's articles of association, but the matter is, in fact, dealt with in the Act, which provides a two-part non-exhaustive definition of the term.

7.3.2.2 Section 17 provides a general definition, which is supplemented for the purposes of the part of the Act which contains the statutory duties by s. 257. The sections are set out in full in Figure 7.1.

Figure 7.1 Text of CA2006 ss. 17 and 257

Section 17 – A company's constitution
Unless the context otherwise requires, references in the Companies Acts to a company's constitution include –
(a) the company's articles, and
(b) any resolutions and agreements to which Chapter 3 applies (see section 29).

Section 257 – References to company's constitution
(1) References in this Part to a company's constitution include –
 (a) any resolution or other decision come to in accordance with the constitution, and
 (b) any decision by the members of the company, or a class of members, that is treated by virtue of any enactment or rule of law as equivalent to a decision by the company.
(2) This is in addition to the matters mentioned in section 17 (general provision as to matters contained in company's constitution).

7.3.2.3 The principal effect of the sections is that a company's articles do, indeed, form part of its constitution, and as such the duty in s. 171(a) serves to ensure that directors comply with the articles.

7.3.2.4 However, a director who is seeking to ensure that he complies with the duty needs to be aware that the definition of 'constitution' goes well beyond the company's articles. The reference in s. 17(b) to s. 29 is to a list of certain types of shareholders' decisions which must be notified to the registrar, and the effect of the reference is that every decision on the list – which includes special resolutions – is part of the company's constitution. Section 257 broadens the definition still further, and although the scope of the provision is somewhat unclear, it would certainly seem to encompass decisions of the board. The duty to act in accordance with the constitution therefore incorporates, among other things, a requirement that a director must comply with special resolutions and board resolutions.

7.3.3 The duty to exercise powers only for the purposes for which they are conferred (s 171(b))

> Section 171 – Duty to act within powers
> A director of a company must –
> (a) ...
> (b) only exercise powers for the purposes for which they are conferred.

7.3.3.1 The duty only to exercise powers for the purposes for which they are conferred (the common law predecessor to the duty in s. 171(b) was generally described as a duty not to exercise powers for improper purposes) illustrates perfectly the limits of the codification process, for the wording of s. 171(b) gives no clue as to either the powers to which the duty applies or the purposes for which any particular power are conferred. These matters, then, are left to be decided by the courts.

7.3.3.2 As to the powers to which s. 171(b) applies, the traditional view is that it applies in respect of most, perhaps all, powers which a director may exercise, whether under the articles or CA2006. Certainly, the courts have, over the years, held that the duty applies to the exercise of a wide variety of powers, including the power to issue shares (*Howard Smith Ltd v Ampol Petroleum Ltd* [1974] AC 821) the power to refuse to register a transfer of shares (*Re Smith and Fawcett, Ltd* [1942] 1 Ch 304) and the power to deal with the assets of the company (*Extrasure Travel Insurances Ltd v Scattergood* [2003] 1 BCLC 598).

7.3.3.3 A recent decision has, however, cast some doubt on the traditional wide view of the duty's scope. In *Eclairs Group Ltd v JKX Oil & Gas plc* [2014] EWCA Civ 640 the Court of Appeal held by a majority that the duty did not apply, at least on the facts before it, to a power under a company's articles to restrict a shareholder's voting rights in certain circumstances.

7.3.3.4 There are two reasons why a director should, notwithstanding the decision in *Eclairs Group Ltd v JKX Oil & Gas plc*, operate on the assumption that most, if not all, of his powers fall within the duty's compass. First, while the brief judgment of the majority in that case contains some indications as to the circumstances in which a power might be held to fall outside the duty, it does not by any means provide a clear test which directors can use to determine which powers it catches and which it does not. Second, the dissenting judgment, delivered by Briggs LJ, sets out a powerful argument for regarding the duty as being of general application, and it is quite possible that his analysis will prevail in the long run, such that judges will in future confine the majority's decision to the specific facts of the case, and continue to take the view that most powers fall within the purview of s. 171(b).

7.3.3.5 From a compliance perspective, the main problem with the duty in s. 171(b) is that it will not always be obvious for what purposes a particular power was conferred on the directors. For example, there will normally be no explicit statement as to the purposes for which the powers to issue shares, to bring legal proceedings or to enter into agreements are conferred. Directors are, therefore, faced with the potentially difficult task of trying to discern from the context of the company's articles and CA2006, and from any relevant case law, why they were given particular powers.

7.3.3.6 In relation to some powers, case law provides specific guidance. It is clear, for example, that the power to issue shares is conferred on directors primarily – though not exclusively – in order to enable them to raise money for the company (*Punt v Symons & Co, Ltd [1903] 2 Ch 506, at 515–516*).

7.3.3.7 Where the power in question has not been the subject of extensive consideration by the courts, the starting point should be to consider the following general principles derived from the case law on the duty generally.

- If the power concerns the board's role in managing the company's business, the courts may be inclined to take the view that it was conferred for no special purpose beyond that of seeking to ensure the company's success. As Briggs LJ put it in his dissenting judgment in *Eclairs Group Ltd v JKX Oil & Gas plc*: 'In relation to purely managerial powers, concerned with the planning and conduct of the company's business, the court will be slow to identify bespoke restrictions, and will afford the greatest respect to the directors' skill and judgment ...' ([2014] EWCA Civ 640, at [100]). A director who exercises a managerial power in what he believes are the company's interests is, then, likely to be acting in compliance with s. 171(b).
- Powers are generally not conferred on directors for the purpose of allowing them to adjust the balance of power between the board and the shareholders. This principle underpinned the decision of the Privy Council in *Howard Smith Ltd v Ampol Petroleum Ltd* [1974] AC 821, where directors issued shares to a third party in order to dilute the majority shareholders' stake. Lord Wilberforce, delivering the court's conclusion that they had thereby used their power to issue shares for an improper purpose, noted that 'it must be unconstitutional for directors to use their fiduciary powers over the shares

in the company purely for the purpose of destroying an existing majority, or creating a new majority which did not previously exist. To do so is to interfere with that element of the company's constitution which is separate from and set against their powers.'

- Powers are not conferred on directors in order to enable them to pursue their own interests (*Howard Smith Ltd v Ampol Petroleum Ltd* [1974] AC 821, at 834H). A director who acts in his own interests rather than those of the company will, therefore, fall foul of s. 171(b).

7.3.3.8 Ultimately, the question as to the purposes for which a power was conferred on directors is one for the courts to decide. A director who diligently undertakes the task of trying to identify the purposes for which a particular power was conferred on him and duly exercises the power for those purposes will, therefore, find that he has breached s. 171(b) if a court disagrees with his conclusion.

7.3.3.9 Compliance with some of the statutory duties is a relatively straightforward matter, and a director who has given them due consideration should need to seek legal advice on their application only in exceptional circumstances. Given the difficulties involved in defining its scope, however, the duty in s. 171(b) is one of those duties in relation to which a director may need to be prepared to seek expert assistance more often.

7.3.4 The duty to promote the success of the company (s. 172)

Section 172 – Duty to promote the success of the company

(1) A director of a company must act in the way he considers, in good faith, would be most likely to promote the success of the company for the benefit of its members as a whole, and in doing so have regard (amongst other matters) to –
   (a) the likely consequences of any decision in the long term,
   (b) the interests of the company's employees,
   (c) the need to foster the company's business relationships with suppliers, customers and others,
   (d) the impact of the company's operations on the community and the environment,
   (e) the desirability of the company maintaining a reputation for high standards of business conduct, and
   (f) the need to act fairly as between members of the company.

(2) Where or to the extent that the purposes of the company consist of or include purposes other than the benefit of its members, subsection (1) has effect as if the reference to promoting the success of the company for the benefit of its members were to achieving those purposes.

(3) The duty imposed by this section has effect subject to any enactment or rule of law requiring directors, in certain circumstances, to consider or act in the interests of creditors of the company.

7.3.4.1 The duty to promote the success of the company – generally known, prior to the introduction of the Act, as the duty to act in the company's best interests – is the most important of the statutory duties, for it expresses in the purest form the fundamental principle that a director should be loyal to his company. It is also arguably the easiest duty with which to comply, for in essence it requires nothing more from a director than that he does what he thinks is best for the company.

7.3.4.2 The two defining characteristics of the duty are that it is subjective in nature and that it requires directors to place shareholders' interests above those of any other stakeholders (such as employees). The following paragraphs examine each of these characteristics in turn.

7.3.4.3 The reference immediately above to the duty's subjective nature is to the fact that it requires a director to do what *he* believes is in the company's best interests. This is apparent from the wording of s. 172(1), which requires a director to 'act in the way *he* considers, in good faith, would be most likely to promote the success of the company' (emphasis added).

7.3.4.4 If it were needed, confirmation of the duty's subjective nature has been provided by the courts. In *McKillen v Misland (Cyprus) Investments Ltd, Re Coroin Ltd*, the judge cited the following well-known description of the nature of the common law duty to act in the company's best interests in *Regentcrest plc (in liquidation) v Cohen*, and held that it applied equally to the statutory duty:

> 'The question is not whether, viewed objectively by the court, the particular act or omission which is challenged was in fact in the interests of the company; still less is the question whether the court, had it been in the position of the director at the relevant time, might have acted differently. Rather, the question is whether the director honestly believed that his act or omission was in the interests of the company. The issue is as to the director's state of mind. No doubt, where it is clear that the act or omission under challenge resulted in substantial detriment to the company, the director will have a harder task persuading the court that he honestly believed it to be in the company's interest; but that does not detract from the subjective nature of the test.' (*Regentcrest plc (in liquidation) v Cohen* [2001] 2 BCLC 80, at [120], cited in *McKillen v Misland (Cyprus) Investments Ltd, Re Coroin Ltd* [2012] EWHC 2343 (Ch), at [567]) (The latter case went to appeal, but the judges in the Court of Appeal did not comment on this point.)

7.3.4.5 The robustness of the principle is illustrated by the decision in *Regentcrest plc (in liquidation) v Cohen* [2001] 2 BCLC 80 itself. The case concerned a resolution by the board of a company which was in financial difficulties to waive a claim, potentially worth £1.5 million, against three individuals. When the company was wound up shortly thereafter, its joint liquidators alleged that, in voting in favour of the waiver, a director had been acting not in the company's interests, but in those of the three individuals, two of whom were fellow directors and one of whom was a former director. The court took the view that the director had been motivated by a desire to preserve the board's unity at a time when the company was experiencing financial problems, and that he genuinely felt that the waiver was in the company's best interests, and it held that he had therefore not breached the duty.

7.3.4.6 Although it is, thus, relatively easy to comply with the duty, it might be assumed that a director who does not even consider his company's interests must be in breach of it. After all, a director who does not ask himself whether a particular course of action will help the company surely cannot be said to be acting loyally.

7.3.4.7 In fact, the courts have shown themselves to be willing to relax the duty in these circumstances, such that the director will not be found to have breached the duty as long as the decision in question was one which an intelligent man could reasonably have believed to be in the company's interests. In *Re HLC Environmental Projects Ltd (in liquidation)*, for instance, the deputy judge commented as follows: 'the subjective test only applies where there is evidence of actual consideration of the best interests of the company. Where there is no such evidence, the proper test is objective, namely whether an intelligent and honest man in the position of a director of the company concerned could, in the circumstances, have reasonably believed that the transaction was for the benefit of the company' ([2013] EWHC 2876 (Ch), at [92]). The courts' willingness to relax the duty in this way stems from Pennycuick J's decision in *Charterbridge Corporation Ltd v Lloyds Bank Ltd* [1970] Ch 62 (although it has to be said that it is far from clear that the case – which did not concern directors' duties – provides a sound basis for their approach).

7.3.4.8 Consider the case of a director of a subsidiary who resolves to lend money to its parent company. Even if, in so doing, he does not consider the subsidiary's interests, he will not be in breach of s. 172 as long as the loan could, on an objective analysis, be thought to benefit it. If, for example, a reasonable man could take the view that the subsidiary was securing its own future by supporting the parent company, the director will not be in breach of the duty.

7.3.4.9 As helpful as this lenient approach to the duty is from a compliance perspective, a director should not allow it to obscure the fact that, fundamentally, he must be loyal to his company. For one thing, the relaxation is narrowly confined; a director who considers his company's interests and chooses to sacrifice them to his own interests or to those of some other party will certainly find himself in breach of s. 172. Quite apart from that, a director who falls into the habit of failing to consider whether his actions would promote the company's success is unlikely to retain the support of the shareholders, in which case he may simply be removed from office.

7.3.4.10 The second defining characteristic of the duty, namely that it requires directors to place shareholders' interests above those of anyone else, may not be immediately apparent from the wording of s. 172. A casual reader might assume that the effect of the list in s. 172(1) of matters to which a director must have regard (sometimes known as the 'mandatory factors') is that the director must act not only in the interests of the shareholders, but also in the interests of, among others, employees, suppliers and customers. On closer examination, however, the section makes it clear that shareholders' interests are paramount. The duty is to act in the way which the director feels will promote the company's success for the benefit of its shareholders and only 'in doing so' to have regard to the factors on the list. In other words, the duty requires a director to take into account the mandatory factors (and, since the list is non-exhaustive, any other relevant matters) in the course of deciding whether a particular act would serve the shareholders' interests.

7.3.4.11 As is the case with the subjective nature of the duty, the notion of shareholder primacy, too, has been confirmed by the courts. *R (on the Application of People and Planet) v HM Treasury* [2009] EWHC 3020 (Admin) was an unusual case from a company law perspective, because it was an application for permission to bring judicial review proceedings. At issue was the extent to which the government, as the majority shareholder in the Royal Bank of Scotland, should try to force the company to adopt more rigorous corporate social responsibility ('CSR') policies. In the course of refusing the application, Sales J considered the extent to which the directors of the bank should take into account environmental and social considerations in connection with their duty under s. 172. His view was that they should adopt more rigorous CSR policies only if the bank's existing policies compared unfavourably with those of its competitors and thereby damaged its value. He felt, in other words, that the directors' obligation was to take into account environmental and social matters only to the extent that was necessary in order to protect the company's value.

7.3.4.12 This aspect of s. 172 does not merely prevent a director from acting purely in the interests of parties other than shareholders. It also entitles – indeed, obliges – him to harm the interests of such parties if he feels that to do so would benefit the shareholders. Take the case of a company which owns several factories, one of which is making heavy losses. Not only must the company's directors refrain from keeping the factory open purely because they are reluctant to make the workers there redundant, but they are actually obliged to close it down if they believe the closure to be in the shareholders' interests.

7.3.4.13 Quite simply, a director's one and only concern under s. 172 must be to serve the interests of the shareholders.

7.3.4.14 If the interests referred to in the mandatory factors are, in effect, trumped by the interests of shareholders, what purpose, if any, does the list in s. 172(1) serve?

7.3.4.15 The answer to this question is that the list is intended to encourage directors to appreciate that shareholders' interests – generally, the long-term financial success of the company – are normally bound up in the interests of the company's other stakeholders. Thus, a director who is considering whether to proceed with a round of redundancies, for example, should pause to consider whether the job cuts are really in the interests of the shareholders. True, they might reduce the company's outgoings in the short term, but might they also damage the reputation of the company to such an extent that it would find it more difficult to attract good workers in the future? This more reflective, rounded approach to the company's success – as opposed to an approach which is based on ensuring that the company is as profitable as possible in the short term – is sometimes said to be based on the concept of 'enlightened shareholder value'.

7.3.4.16 From a compliance perspective, the list of mandatory factors may be said to work at once for and against directors.

7.3.4.17 On the one hand, it is certainly a burden of sorts, for a director must take the factors – or, at least, those of them that are relevant (in *Parry v Bartlett* [2011] EWHC 3146 (Ch), at [76], the High Court indicated that a director does not need to consider factors which are self-evidently irrelevant in the circumstances) – into account whenever he takes any decision, whether large or small. In relation to decisions which are sufficiently important to be taken by the whole board, this will involve considering each of the factors in turn, either at the board meeting or in the course of reading and reflecting on the directors' written resolution. In relation to minor, everyday decisions, it will not normally be practicable to adopt such a measured approach, but at the very least a director will need to have the list at the back of his mind and be prepared to consider it more carefully if any of the mandatory factors appear to be relevant to a particular decision.

7.3.4.18 On the other hand, the list may be of assistance to a director who is taking a decision which he believes will benefit the company in the long run, but which will not necessarily enhance its value in the short term. If he is called upon to defend the decision, he will be able to point to the fact that, in the course of seeking to promote the company's success, he is subject to a statutory obligation to consider the big picture by taking into account matters such as the long-term implications of the decision, the company's reputation and the interests of employees.

7.3.4.19 This discussion of the duty in s. 172 has so far addressed only s. 172(1). The effect of s. 172(2) and (3) is to derogate from the usual rule that the company is to be run for the benefit of its shareholders.

7.3.4.20 Section 172(2) recognises the fact that some companies exist otherwise than for the benefit of their shareholders. A not-for-profit company set up in order to provide free advice to local unemployed people, for example, will have as its objective the successful provision of that service. By virtue of s. 172(2), a director of such a company must focus his efforts on furthering that objective, rather than on generating profits for the shareholders.

7.3.4.21 More importantly, at least as far as commercial companies are concerned, s. 172(3) recognises that, in certain circumstances, a director should be acting in the interests of the company's creditors, and not its shareholders. The reference in the subsection to any 'enactment' is to the wrongful trading provision in the Insolvency Act 1986 s. 214, under which a director will normally be expected to ensure that the company stops trading as soon it becomes clear that it is going to fail (the wrongful trading provision is discussed in section 3.5.2). The reference to any 'rule of law' is to the common law principle that creditors' interests displace those of shareholders when the company is approaching insolvency (*Colin Gwyer & Associates Ltd v London Wharf (Limehouse) Ltd* [2002] EWHC 2748 (Ch), at [74]). When a company is wound up, its creditors must be paid before any surplus assets are distributed to the shareholders; this means that once a company's financial condition has deteriorated to such an extent that it is unlikely to have any surplus assets left over for its shareholders when it is wound up, the shareholders cease to have any meaningful interest in it, and the wrongful trading provision and the common law principle ensure that, in such circumstances, a director is no longer running the company for their benefit. In practice, the main effect of s. 172(3) is that the directors of a failing company may need to cause it to stop trading at an earlier date than they would have done had they been acting in the shareholders' interests. This is because a director acting in the shareholders' interests will be tempted to gamble every last penny of the company's funds on an attempt to turn its fortunes around – after all, the shareholders no longer have anything to lose – while a director acting with creditors in mind might decide to cut the company's losses at some point in order to ensure that the creditors recover at least a portion of the sums owed to them.

7.3.5 The duty to exercise independent judgment (s. 173)

Section 173 – Duty to exercise independent judgment
(1) A director of a company must exercise independent judgment.
(2) This duty is not infringed by his acting –
  (a) in accordance with an agreement duly entered into by the company that restricts the future exercise of discretion by its directors, or
  (b) in a way authorised by the company's constitution.

7.3.5.1 This duty is self-explanatory inasmuch as it simply requires a director to use his own judgment when taking decisions or otherwise acting in relation to the company's affairs.

7.3.5.2 It does not prevent a director from following the advice of external experts, such as lawyers and financial advisers, provided that he first gives careful consideration to the advice itself and to the extent to which it may be prudent to rely on the opinion of the expert in question. Indeed, a director who fails to take professional advice on matters beyond his own area of expertise might well be in breach of his duty under s. 174 to act with care and skill.

7.3.5.3 Some companies have internal arrangements pursuant to which particular shareholders have the right to appoint one or more directors. Although the rationale for such arrangements is that the so-called 'nominee director' will be in a position to protect the interests of the appointing shareholder, nominee directors run the risk of breaching certain of the statutory duties, in particular the duty to exercise independent judgement, the duty to promote the company's success (s. 172), the duty to act with care and skill (s. 174) and possibly also the duty to avoid situations in which their interests conflict with those of the company (s. 175). (One of the points made by BIS in its 2013/2014 review of the transparency of companies was that nominee directors are subject to the same statutory duties as any other director. The review's discussion of nominee directors can be found at pp. 46 to 49, 'Transparency & Trust: Enhancing the Transparency of UK Company Ownership and Increasing Trust in UK Business – Discussion Paper' (BIS, July 2013), and pp. 47 to 51, 'Transparency & Trust: Enhancing the Transparency of UK Company Ownership and Increasing Trust in UK Business – Government Response' (BIS, April 2014)). There is no doubt that the courts take a dim view of nominee directors who act in their nominator's interests at the expense of those of the company (see, for example, the courts' comments on the responsibilities of nominee directors in *Scottish Co-operative Wholesale Society Ltd v Meyer* [1959] AC 324, at 367 (per Lord Denning) and *Hawkes v Cuddy* [2009] EWCA Civ 291, at [32] and [33], per Stanley Burnton LJ), and certainly a director who acts merely as a mouthpiece for a shareholder cannot be said to be exercising his own judgement. In practice, however, a nominee director who places the interests of his nominator above those of the company may be more likely to be in breach of ss. 172 or 174 than s. 173, because s. 173(2) provides a safe harbour for directors who are acting in accordance with an agreement entered into by the company or in accordance with the company's constitution. As long as a nominee director is permitted to act on his nominator's instructions by virtue of an agreement or a provision in the company's articles, therefore, he will not be in breach of his duty to exercise independent judgement.

7.3.6 The duty to exercise reasonable care, skill and diligence (s. 174)

> Section 174 – Duty to exercise reasonable care, skill and diligence
> (1) A director of a company must exercise reasonable care, skill and diligence.
> (2) This means the care, skill and diligence that would be exercised by a reasonably diligent person with –
>   (a) the general knowledge, skill and experience that may reasonably be expected of a person carrying out the functions carried out by the director in relation to the company, and
>   (b) the general knowledge, skill and experience that the director has.

7.3.6.1 Most of the statutory duties are fiduciary in nature, which is to say that they stem from and reflect the relationship of trust which exists between a director and his company. They are designed to ensure that the director remains loyal to the company. Thus, he must do what he thinks will promote the company's success (s. 172), for example, and refrain from allowing his own interests to jeopardise his ability to act in the company's interests (s. 175).

7.3.6.2 The duty to exercise care and skill is the only duty which is not fiduciary in nature. It is designed to ensure not a director's loyalty, but his competence.

7.3.6.3 Section 174 measures a director's conduct against that of a 'reasonably diligent person' who has a particular degree of knowledge, skill and experience, namely:

- the knowledge, skill and experience which a person carrying out his role in a similar company would be expected to possess (s. 174(2)(a)); and
- any additional knowledge, skill and experience which the director himself happens to possess (s. 174(2)(b)).

7.3.6.4 The effect of the first limb of s. 174(2) is to set a minimum threshold of competence below which a director must not fall. The effect of the second limb is to raise that threshold if the director in question has particular knowledge, skill or experience, for example by reason of his long career in the industry in which the company operates.

7.3.6.5 The chief difficulty with s. 174 from a director's perspective is that it does not specify at what level the minimum threshold of competence is set. In other words, it does not set out the standard of competence which every director must meet. There has, however, been a good deal of judicial analysis of the duty and its common law predecessor (which it reflects faithfully), and the courts have also provided useful commentary on the standards which they expect directors to live up to in the context of wrongful trading proceedings under the Insolvency Act 1986 s. 214 and disqualification proceedings under the Company Directors' Disqualification Act 1986. The following principles can be discerned from the case law.

- There is, in fact, no single minimum threshold, because the standard expected of a director will vary depending upon the nature of his role within the company and the nature of the company itself (*Re Produce Marketing Consortium Ltd* (1989) 5 BCC 569, at 594H; *Brumder v Motornet Service and Repairs Ltd* [2013] EWCA Civ 195, at [55]). Thus, the managing director of a large multinational company will be subject to a higher minimum standard of competence than a director of a small, family company who has no executive role.
- A director is expected to understand the company's business (*Re Barings plc (No 5)* [2000] 1 BCLC 523, at [36]; *Weavering Capital (UK) Ltd (in liquidation) v Dabhia* [2012] EWHC 1480 (Ch), at [174]).
- A director is expected to seek to ensure that both he and the company comply with their statutory obligations. Thus, the point was made by Knox J in *Re Produce Marketing Consortium Ltd* (1989) 5 BCC 569, at 595A–B that directors must ensure that they and the company comply with their accounting obligations, while in *Brumder v Motornet Service and Repairs Ltd* [2013] EWCA Civ 195, at [45]–[47] the Court of Appeal held that a director who had paid no attention to the company's obligations in relation to health and safety matters had breached s. 174.
- A director is expected to be aware of the company's financial circumstances (*Re Produce Marketing Consortium Ltd* (1989) 5 BCC 569; *Re Kudos Business Solutions Ltd (in liquidation)* [2011] EWHC 1436 Ch).
- A director who delegates responsibilities is subject to an ongoing obligation to supervise the discharge of those responsibilities (*Re Barings plc (No 5)* [2000] 1 BCLC 523, at [36]. See also Jonathan Parker J's discussion of this point in his first instance decision in that case: *Re Barings plc (No 5)* [1999] 1 BCLC 433, at 486–489). In other words, it is not open to a director, having passed responsibilities to a manager, to wash his hands of them. On the contrary, he is likely to be required to ensure not only that the manager is subject to appropriate controls, but also that the manager does, indeed, discharge the responsibilities in question.
- A director must be prepared to challenge his fellow directors, especially if there are any grounds for concern about their honesty or trustworthiness. In *Re*

Westmid Packing Services Ltd [1998] 2 All ER 124, the Court of Appeal noted as follows: 'It is of the greatest importance that any individual who undertakes the statutory and fiduciary obligations of being a company director should realise that these are inescapable personal responsibilities. The appellants [two directors of a private company] may have been dazzled, manipulated and deceived by Mr Griffiths [their fellow director] but they were in breach of their own duties in allowing this to happen.' In another decision of the Court of Appeal, *Lexi Holdings plc (in administration) v Luqman* [2009] EWCA Civ 117, a managing director who had past criminal convictions misappropriated nearly £60 million of his company's money. Two of his fellow directors, both of whom knew of his convictions, were held to have breached their duty of care and skill by virtue of having failed properly to challenge his conduct of the company's affairs.

7.3.6.6 The minimum threshold of competence required of a director by virtue of s. 174(2)(a) is objective in nature, since it is based on the knowledge, skill and experience which a person carrying out the director's functions in a similar company would be expected to possess. By contrast, the threshold of competence required by virtue of s. 174(2)(b) is subjective in nature, since it is based on the level of knowledge, skill and experience of the director in question.

7.3.6.7 The effect of s. 174(2)(b) is that even if two directors of a company have identical roles, they will be judged by different standards if one of them has more knowledge, skill or experience than the other. Take the case of two directors of a software company, one of whom is a computer scientist and the other of whom is a corporate lawyer specialising in mergers and acquisitions. If they commit the company to an agreement to buy a rival's business, but it subsequently transpires that the agreement does not adequately protect the company's interests, such that it loses a significant amount of money on the deal, proceedings may be brought against them under s. 174. The computer scientist, who has no special skills in legal matters, will be judged by the minimum standard of competence in s. 174(2)(a), and the court may feel that he was entitled to rely on the assurances of the company's legal advisers that the agreement was properly drafted. In accordance with s. 174(2)(b), however, the corporate lawyer will be judged by a higher standard, and the court may conclude that, in the light of his expertise in corporate matters, he should have examined the document more carefully, and should have realised that it was flawed.

7.3.6.8 The duty under s. 174 should give prospective directors pause for thought. Some people simply do not possess the basic attributes which are needed in order to run a company properly. An individual who has such a poor grasp of financial matters that he would not be able to assess his company's financial health on an ongoing basis, even with the benefit of advice from accountants, will fall into this category. So, too, will an individual who is incapable of organising his time properly, such that he will not be able to remember to attend board meetings or to read any documents relating to the company's affairs. There is nothing to prevent such people from investing in companies as shareholders, but they run a serious risk of being in breach of the duty to exercise care and skill if they accept a role as a director, whether in an executive or a non-executive capacity.

7.3.6.9 Assuming a director has the required level of knowledge, skill and experience, the key to ensuring compliance with s. 174 is to be diligent. He should take steps to ensure that he understands the company's business and is aware of its financial condition. He should apprise himself of the legal and regulatory framework in which the company operates, and should be alert to the possibility that he will need to take expert advice on some matters. He should supervise his subordinates, and be prepared to question his fellow directors if he has any concerns about their conduct. He should attend board meetings, peruse any documentation concerning the company's affairs with due care and read documents before he signs them. He should, in short, apply himself conscientiously to the company's affairs.

7.3.6.10 Thus, although the duty does not prevent a person from being a non-executive director, whose role is to oversee the activities of the executive directors, a 'sleeping director', who declines to play any part at all in the company's affairs, will be in breach of s. 174.

7.3.7 The duty to avoid conflicts of interest (s. 175)

Section 175 – Duty to avoid conflicts of interest

(1) A director of a company must avoid a situation in which he has, or can have, a direct or indirect interest that conflicts, or possibly may conflict, with the interests of the company.

(2) This applies in particular to the exploitation of any property, information or opportunity (and it is immaterial whether the company could take advantage of the property, information or opportunity).

(3) This duty does not apply to a conflict of interest arising in relation to a transaction or arrangement with the company. [This subsection is considered in paragraphs 9.3 to 7.3.9.3, as part of the discussion of the duty under ss. 177 and 182 to declare personal interests in transactions with the company]

(4) This duty is not infringed –
  (a) if the situation cannot reasonably be regarded as likely to give rise to a conflict of interest; or
  (b) if the matter has been authorised by the directors.

(5) Authorisation may be given by the directors –
   (a) where the company is a private company and nothing in the company's constitution invalidates such authorisation, by the matter being proposed to and authorised by the directors; or
   (b) where the company is a public company and its constitution includes provision enabling the directors to authorise the matter, by the matter being proposed to and authorised by them in accordance with the constitution.
(6) The authorisation is effective only if –
   (a) any requirement as to the quorum at the meeting at which the matter is considered is met without counting the director in question or any other interested director, and
   (b) the matter was agreed to without their voting or would have been agreed to if their votes had not been counted.
(7) Any reference in this section to a conflict of interest includes a conflict of interest and duty and a conflict of duties.

7.3.7.1 This duty requires a director to avoid entering into a situation in which his own interests conflict, or may conflict, with those of the company. It stems from the overriding principle that a director must be loyal to his company, in that it is based on the assumption that a director who allows a situation to arise in which a desire to further his own interests may compromise his ability to focus wholeheartedly on the company's interests cannot be said to be acting loyally.

7.3.7.2 Section 175 could scarcely have been given a wider scope. Not only does it encompass both direct and indirect interests on the part of the director, but it also prevents him from entering into situations in which there is a mere possibility of conflict. The duty's wide-ranging nature means that it acts as a significant restriction on the freedom of a director to take advantage of opportunities outside the company. On the other hand, it also means that a director will normally not need legal advice to assist him in deciding whether, in any given scenario, he is at risk of breaching it. The only question he has to consider is whether his own interests are fully aligned with those of the company.

7.3.7.3 Before turning to a detailed examination of the scope of the duty, it is worth pausing to note that some of the case law decided on the common law predecessor to s. 175 should be treated with caution.

7.3.7.4 There was no doubt, prior to the introduction of CA2006, that directors were subject to a duty to avoid situations of conflict. More than a century and a half ago, in *Aberdeen Rail Co v Blaikie Brothers*, Lord Cranworth LC famously described the common law duty in the following terms: 'it is a rule of universal application that no one having such duties [i.e. fiduciary duties] to discharge shall be allowed to enter into engagements in which he has or can have a personal interest conflicting or which possibly may conflict with the interests of those whom he is bound to protect' ([1843 – 60] All ER Rep 249, at 252).

7.3.7.5 Much of the case law on the common law duty referred, however, not only to a 'no conflict rule', but also to a 'no profit rule', which stated that a director must not make any outside profit by virtue of his office. The relationship between the two rules was not entirely clear: although the 'no profit rule' was probably best regarded as forming part of the wider 'no conflict rule' (*Boardman v Phipps* [1967] 2 AC 46, at 123D (per Lord Upjohn)), some of the case law seemed to suggest that they were separate, albeit related, rules. If, indeed, they were separate rules, it could be argued that the effect of the 'no profit rule' was that a director could not profit from his office *under any circumstances*, regardless of whether by so doing he was placing himself in a situation of conflict.

7.3.7.6 A detailed consideration of the position at common law, and the extent to which it has been preserved in s. 175, is beyond the scope of this handbook. It suffices to say that, whatever the precise boundaries of the common law duty might have been, the statutory duty is a 'no conflict rule' which incorporates a 'no profit rule', and that s. 175 will prevent a director from profiting from his office only if by so doing he is placing himself in a situation of conflict. To the extent, therefore, that older cases appear to suggest that there is a standalone 'no profit rule', they must be treated as out of date.

7.3.7.7 The scope of the duty is set out primarily in s. 175(1), which states that a director 'must avoid a situation in which he has, or can have, a direct or indirect interest that conflicts, or possibly may conflict, with the interests of the company'. Section 175(2) specifies that the prohibition encompasses the exploitation of any property, information or opportunity of the company.

7.3.7.8 It is impossible to list every situation which might give rise to a breach of the duty. However, the following scenarios, all of which will attract the application of the duty, serve to illustrate its scope.

- **The director becomes involved with a rival company.** Take the case of a director of a company which runs an independent bookshop in London. If he buys shares in a property development company which specialises in the Scottish market, he has nothing to fear from s. 175, because his financial interest in the property development company will not threaten his loyalty to the bookshop. If, however, he buys shares in a company which operates a national chain of bookshops which has many outlets in London, his interest in the success of the national chain will certainly compromise his ability to do his best for the independent bookshop, and therefore his purchase of the shares will have placed him in a situation in which his own interests conflict with those of his company.

Much the same analysis would apply if, instead of buying shares in the national chain, he joins its board. It is quite possible that he would feel that, in taking on the new position, he is gaining valuable experience in the industry which he can then put to use in promoting the success of the independent bookshop, but his belief that he is acting in the best interests of the independent bookshop does not alter the fact that a situation of conflict has been created, and he will therefore be in breach of s. 175. The case law in this area is somewhat unhelpful, in that in two well-known cases (*London and Mashonaland Exploration Co Ltd v New Mashonaland Exploration Co Ltd* [1891] WN 165 and *In Plus Group Ltd v Pyke* [2002] EWCA Civ 370) the courts sanctioned a director's involvement with a rival company. In both of those cases, however, the person in question was a director in name only, and so on the facts there was no real conflict of interest. The decisions do not, therefore, detract from the proposition that a director who involves himself in a rival business will normally be in breach of s. 175.

In fact, such is the breadth of the duty that a director would probably find himself in breach if it was not he, but, say, his wife who was involved in the rival business. After all, if his wife has a financial interest in the success of the rival, that fact will surely compromise his ability to be single-mindedly loyal to his company.

- **The director uses the company's property for his own benefit.** This point requires little elaboration. Plainly, a director who uses an asset belonging to the company for his own ends is allowing his own interests to conflict with those of the company. Thus, a director of a company which runs a gardening business will be in breach of his duty under s. 175 if he uses its tools and equipment in maintaining his own garden.

- **The director diverts opportunities belonging to the company to himself.** As a matter of principle, this point, too, requires little elaboration, for it is obvious that a director who takes for himself an opportunity which belongs to the company is allowing his own interests to conflict with those of the company.

The question arises, though, as to the circumstances in which an opportunity will be classified as one which belongs to the company.

In some cases, it will be obvious that a director has exploited a corporate opportunity. *Cook v Deeks* [1916] AC 554 concerned four individuals who ran a railway construction company as directors and (broadly) equal shareholders. When they fell out, three of the directors undertook negotiations for a new contract with a regular customer of the company in the normal way, but then entered into the contract in their own names. The Privy Council had no doubt that they had breached their duty to the company, commenting that 'men who assume the complete control of a company's business must remember that they are not at liberty to sacrifice the interests which they are bound to protect, and, while ostensibly acting for the company, divert in their own favour business which should properly belong to the company they represent'.

In other cases, the position may appear to be less clear. However, the courts have adopted a very strict approach to the law in this area, taking the view that any opportunity which might be of interest to the company will be treated as a corporate opportunity. In *Bhullar v Bhullar* [2003] EWCA Civ 424, the two groups of shareholders behind a company which owned various properties had decided that they no longer wished to work together, and the directors had agreed that the company would not buy any more properties. Two of the directors subsequently bought a property adjacent to one of the company's existing properties. Despite the fact that the board had agreed not to engage in further property acquisitions, the court took the view that since the opportunity to purchase the property would, given its location, have been attractive to the company, the directors had breached their duty by buying it for themselves.

7.3.7.9 Wide though the scope of the duty undoubtedly is, it is not without its limits. Pursuant to s. 175(4), it will not be breached 'if the situation cannot reasonably be regarded as likely to give rise to a conflict of interest'. What is required, therefore, is 'a real sensible possibility of conflict'(*Boardman v Phipps* [1967] 2 AC 46, at 124 (per Lord Upjohn)); the duty will not be breached simply because it is possible to imagine a scenario, no matter how far-fetched, in which the director's personal interests might conflict with those of the company.

7.3.7.10 Under s. 175(2), the duty applies to the exploitation of corporate opportunities, etc. regardless of whether the company itself could have exploited them. It will be apparent that there is a tension between this rule and s. 175(4)(a), since one might imagine that, if the company cannot exploit an opportunity, there can be no real conflict of interest. This tension is not new, for both provisions reflect the previous position at common law, but the fact remains that a director who is seeking to comply with the duty is faced with the difficulty of resolving it one way or the other. On one view, s. 175(4)(a) should be regarded as the overriding provision, purely as a matter of statutory interpretation. However, the courts have been at pains over the years to stress the importance of the rule against exploiting corporate opportunities (the courts' approach was expressed in memorable terms by Sir W M James LJ in *Parker v McKenna* (1874) 10 Ch App 96, at 124: 'I do not think it is necessary, but it appears to me very important, that we should concur in laying down again and again the general principle that in this Court no agent in the course of his agency, in the matter of his agency, can be allowed to make any profit without the knowledge and consent of his principal; that that rule is an inflexible rule, and must be applied inexorably by this Court, *which is not entitled, in my judgment, to receive evidence, or suggestion, or argument as to whether the principal did or did not suffer any injury in fact by reason of the dealing of the agent; for the safety of mankind requires that no agent shall be able to put his principal to the* *danger of such an inquiry as that'* (emphasis added)), and so the sensible approach is to assume that, if the opportunity is one in which the company might, in theory, be interested, a director cannot take advantage of it in his personal capacity.

7.3.7.11 A director who wishes to take advantage of a corporate opportunity, but who is conscious of his obligations under s. 175, might feel that the solution is to resign from the board before he exploits the opportunity. However, s. 170(2)(a) expressly extends the reach of s. 175(2) to former directors.

7.3.7.12 Section 170(2) provides as follows:

'A person who ceases to be a director continues to be subject –
(a) to the duty in section 175 (duty to avoid conflicts of interest) as regards the exploitation of any property, information or opportunity of which he became aware at a time when he was a director, and
(b) to the duty in section 176 (duty not to accept benefits from third parties) as regards things done or omitted by him before he ceased to be a director.
To that extent those duties apply to a former director as to a director, subject to any necessary adaptations.'

7.3.7.13 The decision in *Killen v Horseworld Ltd* [2012] EWHC 363 (QB) illustrates the effect of s. 170(4)(a). In that case, a director of a company which had broadcast the 2008 Badminton Horse Trials over the internet subsequently left the company and secured the rights to broadcast the 2009 event over the internet and on television. The judge found that she had become aware of the broadcasting opportunity in relation to the Badminton Horse Trials while she was a director, had useful information about the business model used by the company in connection with its broadcast of the 2008 event and knew that the company was hoping to secure the internet broadcasting rights for the 2009 event. In the circumstances, the judge was in no doubt that by taking the rights for the 2009 event for herself, the former director had breached her duty under s. 175.

7.3.8 The duty not to accept benefits from third parties (s. 176)

Section 176 – Duty not to accept benefits from third parties
(1) A director of a company must not accept a benefit from a third party conferred by reason of
    (a) his being a director, or
    (b) his doing (or not doing) anything as director.
(2) A 'third party' means a person other than the company, an associated body corporate or a person acting on behalf of the company or an associated body corporate.

(3) Benefits received by a director from a person by whom his services (as a director or otherwise) are provided to the company are not regarded as conferred by a third party.

(4) This duty is not infringed if the acceptance of the benefit cannot reasonably be regarded as likely to give rise to a conflict of interest.

(5) Any reference in this section to a conflict of interest includes a conflict of interest and duty and a conflict of duties.

7.3.8.1 This duty prevents a director from accepting a benefit from a third party (that is, broadly, anyone other than the company or another company in the same group) which is given to him either because he is a director or because he does, or fails to do, something in his capacity as such. The expression 'third party' is defined in s. 176(2). (The expression 'associated body corporate', as it is used in s. 176(2), is, in turn, defined in s. 256.)

7.3.8.2 The following points may be noted in relation to the scope of the duty:

- the prohibition applies to the acceptance of both financial and non-financial benefits;
- a director may be in breach of the duty even if his behaviour was not influenced by the benefit in any way;
- a director may be in breach of the duty despite the fact that neither he nor the third party acted in bad faith; and
- a director will not be in breach of the duty 'if the acceptance of the benefit cannot reasonably be regarded as likely to give rise to a conflict of interest' (s. 176(4)).

7.3.8.3 The most obvious application of the duty is to bribes. Thus, a director who accepts £10,000 from a rival company in return for voting against a proposal to launch an aggressive campaign to take business away from the rival company will clearly be in breach of s. 176.

7.3.8.4 However, the duty also potentially applies to rather less blameworthy conduct, and in particular the question arises as to whether it prevents a director from accepting corporate hospitality. The key provision in this context is s. 176(4), for a director will be permitted to accept hospitality as long as he is not thereby placing himself in a situation in which his interests conflict with those of the company. Unfortunately, there is no fixed rule as to what types of hospitality, if any, fall below this threshold, because the question as to whether the acceptance of the hospitality will put the director's loyalty to his company at risk will always depend on the particular circumstances. While it is probably safe to say that a director who accepts modest hospitality – for example, a celebratory meal at the conclusion of a transaction or tickets to a local sporting event as a gesture of gratitude from a satisfied client – will not normally be in breach of the duty, ultimately, if his conduct is challenged, it will be for a court to take a view as to whether, on the facts, he compromised his ability to serve his company loyally. A director who is considering whether a particular instance of hospitality falls within the scope of s. 176(4) should, therefore, err on the side of caution and, if there is any doubt, assume that it does not.

7.3.8.5 A director who is in breach of s. 176 will also necessarily be in breach of s. 175, since, as noted immediately above, he will be in breach of the former only if by accepting the benefit he is placing himself in a situation of conflict (he may well also be in breach of certain other of his duties, including his duty under s. 172 to promote the company's success). It does not follow, however, that s. 176 is therefore redundant. The crucial difference between the two duties is that whereas the statute provides a mechanism by which the board of directors can authorise conduct which would otherwise be a breach of s. 175 (ss. 175(4)(b), (5) and (6)), it confers no such power on the board in relation to the duty under s. 176. It is, however, open to the shareholders to authorise what would otherwise be a breach of s. 176. The law governing the authorisation and ratification of breaches of the statutory duties generally is discussed in section 7.4.3.

7.3.9 The duty to declare personal interests in transactions with the company (ss. 177 and 182)

Section 177 – Duty to declare interest in proposed transaction or arrangement
(1) If a director of a company is in any way, directly or indirectly, interested in a proposed transaction or arrangement with the company, he must declare the nature and extent of that interest to the other directors.
(2) The declaration may (but need not) be made –
(a) at a meeting of the directors, or
(b) by notice to the directors in accordance with –
(i) section 184 (notice in writing), or
(ii) section 185 (general notice).
(3) If a declaration of interest under this section proves to be, or becomes, inaccurate or incomplete, a further declaration must be made.
(4) Any declaration required by this section must be made before the company enters into the transaction or arrangement.
(5) This section does not require a declaration of an interest of which the director is not aware or where the director is not aware of the transaction or arrangement in question.
For this purpose a director is treated as being aware of matters of which he ought reasonably to be aware.

(6) A director need not declare an interest –
  (a) if it cannot reasonably be regarded as likely to give rise to a conflict of interest;
  (b) if, or to the extent that, the other directors are already aware of it (and for this purpose the other directors are treated as aware of anything of which they ought reasonably to be aware); or
  (c) if, or to the extent that, it concerns terms of his service contract that have been or are to be considered –
    (i) by a meeting of the directors, or
    (ii) by a committee of the directors appointed for the purpose under the company's constitution.

Section 182 – Declaration of interest in existing transaction or arrangement

(1) Where a director of a company is in any way, directly or indirectly, interested in a transaction or arrangement that has been entered into by the company, he must declare the nature and extent of the interest to the other directors in accordance with this section.

This section does not apply if or to the extent that the interest has been declared under section 177 (duty to declare interest in proposed transaction or arrangement).

(2) The declaration must be made –
  (a) at a meeting of the directors, or
  (b) by notice in writing (see section 184), or
  (c) by general notice (see section 185).

(3) If a declaration of interest under this section proves to be, or becomes, inaccurate or incomplete, a further declaration must be made.

(4) Any declaration required by this section must be made as soon as is reasonably practicable. Failure to comply with this requirement does not affect the underlying duty to make the declaration.

(5) This section does not require a declaration of an interest of which the director is not aware or where the director is not aware of the transaction or arrangement in question.

For this purpose a director is treated as being aware of matters of which he ought reasonably to be aware.

(6) A director need not declare an interest under this section –
  (a) if it cannot reasonably be regarded as likely to give rise to a conflict of interest;
  (b) if, or to the extent that, the other directors are already aware of it (and for this purpose the other directors are treated as aware of anything of which they ought reasonably to be aware); or
  (c) if, or to the extent that, it concerns terms of his service contract that have been or are to be considered –

(i) by a meeting of the directors, or
(ii) by a committee of the directors appointed for the purpose under the company's constitution.

7.3.9.1 This duty, expressed as two complementary obligations, requires a director to declare to the rest of the board any personal interest he has in any proposed or existing transaction to which the company is a party. Although neither section provides for any consequences to flow from the declaration, some companies supplement them with a provision in their articles preventing a director who has an interest in a transaction from voting on any resolution concerning it.

7.3.9.2 The main features of the duty are as follows:

- **It encompasses direct and indirect interests of any description.** The duty thus has a very broad scope. Although it is narrowed somewhat by the proviso that the obligation to make a declaration does not arise if the interest 'cannot reasonably be regarded as likely to give rise to a conflict of interest' (ss. 177(6)(a) and 182(6)(a)) it will be a matter of fact in each case as to whether a particular interest is likely to give rise to a conflict, and there will be situations in which the answer to the question is not entirely clear-cut. Unless it is obvious that an interest will not affect the director's loyalty to his company, the prudent course is to err on the side of caution and make a declaration.
- **The declaration must be made to the other directors.**
- **The 'nature and extent' of the interest must be declared (ss. 177(1) and 182(1)).** It will not suffice for a director to report simply that he has an interest. Take the case of a company in the food retail sector which is considering entering into a contract with a vegetable supplier. If a director owns a 25% stake in the supplier, he will not comply with his duty by reporting the bare fact that he has 'an interest' in the proposed transaction. His declaration should, instead, be along the following lines: 'I declare that I am interested in the proposed transaction by virtue of the fact that I own 25% of the shares in [the vegetable supplier].'
- **If the declaration is, or becomes, inaccurate or incomplete, the director must make a further declaration (ss. 177(3) and 182(3)).**
- **Whereas a breach of the duty under s. 177 is primarily an internal matter for the company to deal with as it sees fit, a breach of the duty under s. 182 constitutes a criminal offence (s. 183).**

7.3.9.3 The relationship between the duty under ss. 177 and 182 and the duty under s. 175 to avoid conflicts of interest is addressed in s. 175(3), which states that the latter 'does not apply to a conflict of interest arising in relation to a transaction or arrangement with the company'.

7.3.9.4 Take the case of a director of a company which owns a bookshop. If the company is considering appointing as its auditor a firm of accountants in which his son is a partner, the effect of s. 175(3) is that s. 175 does not apply, and he will simply have to declare his interest in the proposed contract with the accountancy firm pursuant to s. 177.

7.3.9.5 Section 175(3) does not, however, prevent both duties from applying in some cases. Staying with the example of the bookshop, assume now that it has long had a local rival in which the director's daughter owns a 50% stake, and that the rivals are currently contemplating a joint venture to open a bookshop in Paris. The effect of s. 175(3) is that only the duty under s. 177 will apply in respect of the proposed joint venture agreement. However, the underlying situation of conflict which stems from the daughter's involvement with the rival company is not affected by s. 175(3), and the director will have been in breach of s. 175 all along unless his fellow directors or the company's shareholders had authorised the conflict.

7.3.9.6 The duty under ss. 177 and 182 does not exist in isolation. It forms part of a wider regime governing directors' interests in transactions with the company.

7.3.9.7 For one thing, companies often supplement the duty with a provision in their articles preventing a director who has an interest in a transaction from voting on it. Article 14(1) of the model articles for private companies, for example, provides as follows: 'If a proposed decision of the directors is concerned with an actual or proposed transaction or arrangement with the company in which a director is interested, that director is not to be counted as participating in the decision-making process for quorum or voting purposes.' (The article goes on to provide in paragraphs (2) to (4) that the rule is subject to a number of exceptions.)

7.3.9.8 There are also a number of provisions in the Act which require a company to obtain shareholder approval, in the form of an ordinary resolution, before it enters into certain types of transactions or arrangements with any of its directors. The provisions are complicated, and a detailed examination of them is beyond the scope of this handbook. In outline, though, the transactions or arrangements in question are as follows:

- a 'long-term service contract' for a director – that is, a service contract under which the director's term of employment is more than two years (s. 188);
- a 'substantial property transaction' with a director – that is, a contract under which the director buys from, or sells to, the company an asset which is (a) worth more than £5,000, provided that its value exceeds 10% of the value of the company's net assets; or (b) worth more than £100,000 (ss. 190 and 191);
- a loan to a director of more than £10,000 (ss. 197 and 207); and

- an extra-contractual payment to a director of more than £200 as compensation for the loss of his office as a director (ss. 215, 217, 220 and 221).

7.4 Consequences of breaching the duties

7.4.1 Overview

7.4.1.1 Given the effort that went into codifying the common law duties, and given the importance which lawyers habitually attach to compliance with the statutory provisions, it might be assumed that serious consequences must inevitably flow from any breach of duty. It might even be assumed that a breach exposes the director to the risk of criminal proceedings.

7.4.1.2 In fact, the only duty in respect of which a breach constitutes a criminal offence is the duty under s. 182 to declare any personal interest in an existing transaction to which the company is a party (s. 183), and in practice a director who breaches s. 182 is very unlikely to face criminal proceedings.

7.4.1.3 For the most part, therefore, a breach of duty is an internal matter. The duties are owed to the company (s. 170(1)), and so it is for the company to decide whether or not to pursue a director who fails to comply with them. Certainly, some breaches will be pursued with vigour. On the other hand, many breaches will either be formally excused or simply ignored.

7.4.2 Pursuing a director

7.4.2.1 The decision as to whether to bring civil proceedings against a director for a breach of duty will normally lie with the board of directors, in its role as the organ of the company responsible for managing the company's business (see, for example, article 3 of the model articles for private companies, which is discussed in paragraph 4.3.5.5).

7.4.2.2 When deciding whether to pursue a director, the rest of the board will, of course, be bound by the duties themselves, and so will be obliged to act purely in the company's interests and to set aside any desire they might have to protect their colleague. That is not to say, though, that they are required to bring proceedings in respect of every breach. For example, it may well be appropriate to deal with a relatively minor breach by reminding the director concerned of the scope of the statutory duties, and warning him that any future breaches will not be tolerated. Even serious breaches may not, on the facts, be felt to warrant legal proceedings. Consider the case of a director of a small manufacturing firm who, having previously been the managing director of a much larger rival firm, has excellent contacts among local suppliers and customers. If he were to divert a potentially lucrative opportunity from the company to himself in breach of his duty under s. 175, his fellow board members' instinct would no doubt be to take him to court in an effort to force him to disgorge any profits he made from the opportunity. On reflection, however, it might occur to them that if they were to sue him, he would certainly resign from the board and the company would lose the benefit of his expertise and contacts. If, in the light of such thoughts, they conclude that the company's interests would be best served by turning a blind eye to the misconduct on this occasion, they are perfectly entitled – indeed, obliged – to refrain from pursuing him in respect of the breach. In *Kleanthous v Paphitis* [2011] EWHC 2287 (Ch), at [71]–[75], the High Court was sympathetic to the notion that a board might legitimately choose not to pursue a high-profile director in respect of an alleged breach if it felt that legal proceedings would harm the company by reason of the fact that it would be impossible to replace him and that the company's reputation would suffer in turn if his reputation were tarnished.

7.4.2.3 The fact that the decision as to whether to bring proceedings against a director is generally one for the board does not mean that shareholders are entirely without a say in the matter. Shareholders who disagree with the board's decision not to institute proceedings in respect of a breach have various options.

- If they have sufficient support to pass a special resolution, they can either alter the articles so as to take the power to initiate proceedings away from the directors altogether, or, if the articles contain a reserve power, exercise that power to instruct the board to take action (see the discussion of the reserve power in article 4 of the model articles for private companies in paragraph 4.3.5.6, and the discussion of reserve powers generally in paragraph 8.2.4).
- If they only have sufficient support to pass an ordinary resolution, they cannot overrule the board directly, but they can adjust its composition, in the hope that the reconstituted board will decide that it is, after all, appropriate to take action. Thus, they can appoint new directors who may be more open to the idea of bringing legal proceedings and/or remove those directors who decided against action (the law governing the appointment and removal of directors is discussed in section 5.4). In practice, a threat to reconstitute the board may well be enough to persuade the existing directors to reconsider their decision.
- Even a solitary shareholder with a shareholding of just one share is not entirely powerless. In theory, he can seek to enforce the duty by bringing a so-called 'derivative claim', a statutory procedure under which he, in effect, usurps the power of the board by bringing proceedings against the director concerned on the company's behalf (the derivative claim is discussed in section 8.4.8). In order to bring a derivative claim, however, he will need the permission of the court, and in practice it is quite difficult to obtain permission. If, for example, he is acting against the will of the majority (as will often be the case – if the majority agreed with his view that the director should be pursued, they would

no doubt have sought to force the board to take action by the means discussed immediately above, namely by altering the company's articles, exercising a reserve power or threatening to reconstitute the board) the court will generally refuse to allow the claim to proceed.

A more practical solution may be for the shareholder to seek to enforce the duty indirectly, by applying to the court for an unfair prejudice order (the unfair prejudice remedy is discussed in section 8.4.7). If the breach has caused him prejudice, for example by reducing the value of his shares, the court has the power to order the other shareholders (who presumably support the director and, indeed, may include him among their number) to buy his shares from him at a price which reflects their value prior to the breach. In such a scenario, the director will not have been sanctioned directly for his breach of duty, in the sense that he will not have been ordered to pay any sum to the company itself, but he and his supporters will, in effect, have been forced to compensate the shareholder for the harm which he suffered as a result of the breach.

7.4.3 Excusing the breach

7.4.3.1 If the board and the shareholders agree that a director should not be pursued in respect of a particular breach, but take no steps formally to approve his misconduct, the director is exposed to the risk that he might be sued in the future. If, for example, the company is taken over, the new board may decide that it would, after all, be appropriate to bring proceedings against him. From a director's perspective, therefore, it is vital that any breach of any significance which the company is content not to pursue is either authorised or ratified.

7.4.3.2 If conduct which would otherwise constitute a breach of duty is approved in advance, it is said to have been 'authorised'.

7.4.3.3 Authorisation is normally a matter for the shareholders. Although the Act does not expressly confer on them the power to authorise breaches s. 180(4)(a) preserves their common law power to do so by means of an ordinary resolution. That provision reads as follows:

'(4) The general duties –
  (a) have effect subject to any rule of law enabling the company to give authority, specifically or generally, for anything to be done (or omitted) by the directors, or any of them, that would otherwise be a breach of duty ...'

7.4.3.4 Directors have a very limited statutory power to authorise a breach. Under s. 175(5)(a), the board of a private company may authorise a breach of the duty under s. 175 to avoid conflicts of interest unless its articles say otherwise. (The Act adopts a slightly different approach to public companies, providing in

s. 175(5)(b) that the board of a public company may authorise a breach of s. 175 only if its articles so provide.)

7.4.3.5 If conduct which constitutes a breach of duty is approved after the fact, it is said to have been 'ratified'. Ratification is, in all cases, a matter for the shareholders. The shareholders' power to ratify breaches is contained in ss. 239(1) and (2), which read as follows:

> '(1) This section applies to the ratification by a company of conduct by a director amounting to negligence, default, breach of duty or breach of trust in relation to the company.
>
> (2) The decision of the company to ratify such conduct must be made by resolution of the members of the company.'

7.4.3.6 Several features of the authorisation and ratification regime are worthy of note.

- **Authorisation by directors.** On a vote on a board resolution to authorise a breach of the duty under s. 175, the director in question and any other 'interested' directors are disenfranchised (s. 175(6)(b)). The Act does not contain any definition of a director who is 'interested' for these purposes. However, in the light of the importance which the courts have long attached to the duty to avoid conflicts of interest, they may well be inclined to give the term a wide interpretation, so as to ensure that only directors who are truly free from bias are permitted to vote on the resolution). The remaining directors will themselves be subject to the statutory duties, including the duty of loyalty under s. 172 and the duty of care under s. 174, and so they should not pass an authorisation resolution lightly.
- **Authorisation or ratification by shareholders – persons entitled to vote.** While the director in question (assuming he is a shareholder) is entitled to vote on a shareholders' authorisation resolution, both he and any shareholders who are 'connected' with him are disenfranchised on a shareholders' ratification resolution (ss. 239(3) and (4)). Section 252 identifies the categories of shareholders who are treated for these purposes as being 'connected' with a director).

    This inconsistency can assist a director who is contemplating undertaking acts which might amount to a breach of duty. If there is any doubt in his mind as to whether the independent shareholders will be prepared to ratify his conduct after the fact, he can seek authorisation of it in advance, knowing that he and his allies are entitled to vote on an authorisation resolution.
- **Authorisation or ratification by shareholders – 'unratifiable breaches'.** The shareholders' power to authorise or ratify a breach is wide ranging, but it is not without limits, for certain breaches either can never be approved or can be approved only in certain circumstances. The law on such breaches (which are

commonly referred to as 'unratifiable breaches') is both complex and uncertain, but it suffices for the purposes of this handbook to note the two most important categories of unratifiable breach.

First, the shareholders are not competent to authorise or ratify a breach by a director of his obligation under s. 172(3) to act in the interests of the company's creditors when the company is approaching insolvency (*Liquidator of West Mercia Safetywear Ltd v Dodd* [1988] BCLC 250. Section 172(3) is considered in paragraph 7.3.4.21). The rationale for this rule is that it would be wrong for shareholders to be permitted to excuse a breach which does not concern them.

Second, they are competent to authorise or ratify a breach which involves the appropriation by the director of company property only if they are acting unanimously and in what they perceive to be the company's interests. (The term 'property' is to be given a wide meaning in this context, in that it is not confined to physical assets, but extends, for example, to opportunities. Precisely what sort of opportunities it encompasses is, unfortunately, less than clear. By way of a general guideline, it may be said that it encompasses opportunities which the company would want to take for itself, but not opportunities which, although of interest to it, the company may not ultimately want to take for itself. A breach of duty involving the taking of the latter type of opportunity may, it seems, be susceptible to authorisation or ratification in the usual way (*Regal (Hastings) Ltd v Gulliver* [1967] 2 AC 134)). Thus, a bare majority of the shareholders is not competent to approve such a breach (on the basis that the breach is of so serious a character that it would be wrong to allow it to be approved against the minority's will) (*Cook v Deeks* [1916] AC 554, at 564), and nor, if they are not motivated by the interests of the company, are the shareholders acting unanimously (on the basis that even the shareholders acting unanimously must not be permitted so blatantly to harm the company) (*Madoff Securities International Ltd v Raven* [2011] EWHC 3102 (Comm), at [94]–[125]). In relation to the latter point, Lord Sumption noted as follows in *Prest v Petrodel Resources Ltd*: 'The sole shareholder or the whole body of shareholders may approve a foolish or negligent decision in the ordinary course of business, at least where the company is solvent ... But not even they can validly consent to their own appropriation of the company's assets for purposes which are not the company's ...' ([2013] UKSC 34, at 41). Realistically, therefore, a director is unlikely to be able to arrange matters in such a way that he can take the company's property for himself without breaching his duties.

7.4.3.7 The fact that most breaches can be authorised or ratified will give a director who is concerned about his possible liability under the directors' duties regime some comfort. Ideally, however, he will want to obtain a blanket protection against any such liability.

7.4.3.8 The Act takes a very strict approach to this matter. Under s. 232, the general rule is that any provision in the company's articles, in a contract or elsewhere which exempts a director from liability for a breach of duty or provides him with an indemnity against liability for a breach of duty is void (ss. 232(1) and (2)). This rule is, however, subject to several exceptions, the most important of which is that the company is permitted to take out insurance for the director against liability (s. 233). In terms of obtaining blanket protection, therefore, a director's best course of action will normally be to try to persuade the company to purchase insurance on his behalf.

8

Shareholders

> **Summary**
>
> - The role of shareholders in a company is supervisory in nature. They do not normally manage the company's business, but they have various means of controlling directors at their disposal.
> - Shareholders take decisions in the form of an ordinary resolution or a special resolution.
> - There are three formal means by which shareholders of a private company can pass a resolution: in the form of a shareholders' written resolution, pursuant to the procedure in s. 357 or at a general meeting.
> - One of the themes running through company law is the desire to protect minority shareholders from oppression by majority shareholders. Among the measures which are designed to protect minority shareholders are the unfair prejudice remedy and the derivative claim.

8.1 Introduction

8.1.1 The law governing shareholders is not as extensive as the law governing directors, not least because shareholders do not owe any duties corresponding to the statutory directors' duties, and so it can be addressed comfortably in a single chapter. In fact, its key features can be encompassed in the answers to three questions.

- **What is the role of shareholders?** This part of the chapter considers the division of powers between shareholders and directors, and the means by which shareholders retain ultimate control of the company's affairs.
- **How do shareholders take decisions?** The aspect of the law governing shareholders which those dealing with companies are most likely to encounter on a regular basis is its rules on decision-making. This part of the chapter deals with decisions made by means of a shareholders' written resolution, the written record procedure for single member companies (s. 357), general meetings and the unanimous consent rule (also known as the 'Duomatic principle').

- **How are minority shareholders protected?** One of the themes running through company law is the need to afford minority shareholders a degree of protection against the risk of oppression by majority shareholders. This part of the chapter examines the two most important mechanisms which are available to a minority shareholder who is seeking to defend his interests: the unfair prejudice remedy and the derivative claim.

8.2 The role of shareholders

8.2.1 CA2006 places the administration of the company in the hands of the directors. Thus, directors are responsible, for example, for ensuring that special resolutions are filed with the registrar (s. 30), for initiating the process by which shareholders take decisions using the shareholders' written resolution procedure (s. 288) and for preparing the company's accounts (s. 394).

8.2.2 Most companies also place the management of the company's business in the hands of the directors by adopting a provision in their articles along the lines of article 3 of the model articles for private companies. Article 3 reads as follows: 'Subject to the articles, the directors are responsible for the management of the company's business, for which purpose they may exercise all the powers of the company.' As is noted elsewhere in this handbook (see paragraphs 4.3.5.5 and 5.5.3), article 3 gives the directors an extremely wide-ranging power to run the company's business. Not only are they responsible for its day-to-day operation, but they also set its long-term strategy, take investment decisions and determine matters such as staffing levels, whether legal proceedings should be brought in a particular instance and even the location of the company's headquarters.

8.2.3 Given that the directors will normally be in charge of the administration of the company and the running of its business, it might be thought that the only role left to shareholders is that of passive owners of the company, who from time to time extract profits from it in the form of dividends. In fact, shareholders play a crucial role in the life of the company, in that they have the power to ensure that, in broad terms at least, it is being run in a manner of which they approve. Their role may, therefore, best be described as supervisory in nature.

8.2.4 The shareholders' supervisory function stems in large part from their power to determine the content of the company's articles and alter the composition of the board. Shareholders can use their power to amend the articles to control the board in a variety of ways (under s. 21, the shareholders have the power to amend the articles by means of a special resolution. This power is discussed in section 4.4.1). For example, they can:

- Carve out exceptions to the broad delegation of power to the board (this option is considered further in paragraph 4.3.5.7 (in the context of a discussion of articles 3 and 4 of the model articles for private companies) and paragraphs 5.5.6 to 5.5.7 (in the context of a discussion of the role of a director)). If, for example, the shareholders of a company feel that the directors are committing the company to too many risky transactions, they can specify that their prior approval is required before the board enters into any transactions worth more than, say, £50,000.
- Restrict the company's objects (the law governing objects clauses is discussed in section 3.6). If, for example, the shareholders of a company are concerned about the directors' propensity to expand the company's activities into fields which prove to be unprofitable, they can specify that the company's objects are restricted to the carrying on of particular types of business.
- Retain a 'reserve power' for themselves. If the shareholders of a company feel that they might on occasion need to overrule the directors on specific issues, they can add a proviso to the broad delegation of power to the effect that they can direct the board's actions in particular instances by means of a special resolution (see, for example, article 4 of the model articles for private companies, which is discussed in paragraph 4.3.5.6). In theory, there is no reason why they cannot reserve for themselves the right to overrule the board by means of an ordinary resolution, but such provisions are rarely, if ever, seen. This is no doubt because shareholders normally have sufficient confidence in their directors that they do not foresee the need to interfere with their discretion on a regular basis.

An express reserve power may be thought to be redundant, on the ground that a majority of the shareholders must surely have an inherent right to overrule the board. In fact, the principle that shareholders have no such right was established more than a century ago, in *Automatic Self-Cleansing Filter Syndicate Company, Ltd v Cuninghame* [1906] 2 Ch 34. The case concerned a company with articles which conferred general management power on the directors, subject to the shareholders' right to direct the board's actions by means of an 'extraordinary resolution' (i.e. a resolution passed by a 75% majority). A shareholders' resolution passed by a 55% majority directed the board to sell the company's business, but the board, taking the view that the sale would not be in the company's interests, refused to do so. The Court of Appeal felt that it would not be appropriate to allow a bare majority of the shareholders to, in effect, adjust the division of powers which was set out in the articles, and held that the board was not bound by the resolution.

8.2.5 The shareholders' power to alter the composition of the board consists of a statutory right to remove a director at any time and, usually, a right under the articles to appoint a director. (The statutory right to remove a director by means of an ordinary resolution is contained in s. 168. The articles usually give the shareholders the right to appoint a director by means of an ordinary resolution, and they sometimes also contain an alternative to the statutory removal procedure. The law governing the appointment and removal of directors is discussed in section 5.4.) The importance of this power in the context of the shareholders' supervisory function is obvious. In some cases, shareholders may need to go to the lengths of actually replacing board members in order to ensure that the board complies with their wishes. For the most part, though, the mere threat that they might be removed will be enough to persuade directors who are at odds with the shareholders to back down from a confrontation.

8.2.6 As important as the power to amend the articles and the power to alter the board's composition are, they are not the only means by which the company law regime ensures that ultimately it is the shareholders, and not the directors, who are in control of the company. For example, the Act provides that in many cases the directors cannot allot shares without the prior authorisation of the shareholders (s. 551; this provision is discussed in section 9.2.4) and the directors are generally obliged, as a result of their statutory duties, to act in the interests of the shareholders.

8.3 Decision-making by shareholders

8.3.1 The legal framework governing decision-making by shareholders is fundamentally different from that governing decision-making by directors, in that the former is set out primarily in CA2006, while the latter is set out primarily in companies' articles.

8.3.2 There are three ways in which shareholders of a private company can take decisions:

- by using the statutory written resolution procedure in Chapter 2 of Part 13 of the Act;
- by using the procedure in s. 357, pursuant to which a sole shareholder who takes a decision must simply notify the company of the decision after the fact; and
- by holding a general meeting in accordance with Chapter 3 of Part 13 of the Act (the position in relation to public companies is slightly different, in that their shareholders can take decisions only by using the s. 357 procedure or at a general meeting. The main statutory provisions concerning general meetings of public companies are in Chapters 3 to 5 of Part 13 of the Act).

8.3.3 None of these procedures is any more 'effective' than any of the others. That is to say, a decision which is taken by means, for example, of the s. 357 procedure is just as effective as a decision taken by means of a written resolution or at a general meeting.

8.3.4 Resolutions

8.3.4.1 Shareholders take decisions by passing resolutions. The Act provides for two types of shareholders' resolution: an 'ordinary resolution' and a 'special resolution'.

An ordinary resolution is a resolution which is passed by a simple majority (that is to say, by a majority of more than 50%) (s. 282(1)), while a special resolution is a resolution which is passed by a majority of 75% or more (s. 283(1)).

8.3.4.2 The question arises as to how it is determined whether the simple majority or three-quarters majority threshold has been reached. A curious feature of the law in this area is that the method used to calculate whether the necessary support for a resolution has been achieved differs depending upon whether the resolution was proposed as a written resolution or at a general meeting. If a resolution is proposed as a written resolution, it will be passed if the necessary proportion of *all the available votes* are cast in favour of it (see s. 282(2) in relation to ordinary resolutions and s. 283(2) in relation to special resolutions). If, on the other hand, it is proposed at a general meeting, it will be passed if the necessary proportion of *all the votes which are actually cast* are cast in favour of it (see s. 282(3) and (4) in relation to ordinary resolutions and s. 283(4) and (5) in relation to special resolutions).

8.3.4.3 CA1985 provided for a third type of shareholders' resolution, namely an 'extraordinary resolution'. Although such resolutions – which, like special resolutions, required the support of at least 75% of the shareholders CA1985 s. 378(1) – do not form part of the regime under CA2006, references to them may be encountered from time to time in companies' articles or in contracts, and such references continue to have effect (Paragraph 23, Schedule 3, Companies Act 2006 (Commencement No 3, Consequential Amendments, Transitional Provisions and Savings) Order 2007 (SI 2007/2194)).

8.3.5 Shareholders' written resolutions

8.3.5.1 The written resolution procedure is, in essence, very straightforward: a proposed resolution is circulated to the shareholders, and it is duly passed if a sufficient proportion of them inform the company that they support it.

8.3.5.2 Although the relevant statutory provisions are fairly prescriptive, the procedure is less administratively burdensome than the general meeting procedure, and shareholders in private companies should, therefore, regard it as the default means by which to take decisions.

8.3.5.3 The procedure may be used to pass any type of resolution save for:

- a resolution to remove a director under s. 168 (s. 288(2)(a). A resolution to remove a director not under s. 168, but under an alternative removal procedure set out in the company's articles, may, however, be passed as a written resolution. The law governing the removal of directors is discussed in section 5.4.2); and
- a resolution to remove an auditor under s. 510 (s. 288(2)(b)).

8.3.5.4 The statutory provisions leave very little scope for companies to use their articles to adapt the procedure to suit their own needs.

8.3.5.5 What is more, whereas companies were free to supplement the statutory written resolution procedure under CA1985 with an alternative written resolution procedure in their articles, CA2006 does not afford companies this option. Accordingly, while the articles of some older companies may still contain a non-statutory procedure, a resolution which purports to have been passed using such a procedure is invalid.

8.3.5.6 The core of the statutory regime is contained in Chapter 2 of Part 13. Its main features are as follows:

- **A written resolution may be proposed either by the directors or by the shareholders (s. 288(3)).** In the normal course of events, where the directors and the shareholders are in agreement about the need for a shareholders' resolution, it will be the directors who propose the written resolution. However, in the event of a dispute – consider, for example, a situation in which the shareholders are unhappy with the board's performance, and wish to amend the articles so as to restrict its powers – the shareholders have the power to force the directors to initiate the decision-making process (ss. 292 and 293).

    From an administrative perspective, it is important to note that, in any event, the board will need to pass a resolution approving the form of the proposed shareholders' written resolution. Thus, the shareholders' written resolution procedure involves at least two documents: (a) either board minutes or a directors' written resolution approving the form of the proposed shareholders' written resolution; and (b) the shareholders' written resolution itself.
- **Although there is no prescribed format for a written resolution, the Act imposes certain requirements as to its contents and as to accompanying documentation.** The Act specifies that a written resolution must be accompanied by a statement explaining to the shareholder how he can indicate his support for it and noting the last date on which the resolution may be passed (s. 291(4)). Although the Act uses the word 'accompanied', it would seem that the statement does not have to be contained in a separate document; certainly, it is common practice for it to be incorporated into the notes to the written

resolution. (See, for examples, Notes 1 and 3 to the sample shareholders' written resolution set out in Figure 8.1.) The means by which a shareholder may indicate his support for a resolution are discussed below. As regards the requirement to note the last date on which the resolution may be passed, s. 297 provides that a proposed written resolution will lapse if it is not passed within any period specified for that purpose in the company's articles or, if no such period is specified, within the period of 28 days beginning with the date on which it was sent to the shareholders (described in the Act as the 'circulation date') (s. 290).

If the proposed written resolution is a special resolution, it must state that it is being proposed as such (s. 283(3)).

In the case of certain types of resolution, the Act specifies that the proposed written resolution must be accompanied by additional documentation. For example, if the resolution is an ordinary resolution to approve a loan to a director pursuant to s. 197, s. 197(3)(a) specifies that it must be accompanied by a memorandum detailing various matters, including the amount of the loan and the purpose for which it is required.

A sample format for a written resolution is set out in Figure 8.1.

- **A proposed written resolution must be sent to every shareholder who is entitled to vote on it (s. 291(2)) (described in the Act as an 'eligible member') (s. 289) and to the company's auditor (s. 502(1)).** The Act provides for a proposed written resolution to be sent to the shareholders in hard copy, in electronic form or via a website (s. 291(3)). Whichever method the company adopts, it will need to comply with the Act's general provisions on communications, which are set out in ss. 1143 to 1148 and Schedules 4 and 5.
- **A written resolution is passed when the necessary majority of shareholders (i.e. a bare majority in the case of an ordinary resolution and a majority of 75% or more in the case of a special resolution) have agreed to it (s. 296(4)).** A shareholder agrees to a resolution 'when the company receives from him (or from someone acting on his behalf) an authenticated document – (a) identifying the resolution to which it relates, and (b) indicating his agreement to the resolution' (s. 296(1)). (The meaning of 'authenticated' for these purposes is set out in s. 1146). As noted in above, the written resolution must be accompanied by a statement explaining how the shareholder can indicate his support for it. It may specify, for example, that he can indicate his support by signing it and then either posting it to the company or emailing the company a scanned copy of it.

Once a shareholder has agreed to a proposed resolution, he cannot revoke his agreement (s. 296(3)).

Importantly, it is not necessary for a written resolution to be passed that all the shareholders have responded to it. It is passed as soon as the bare majority or three-quarters majority threshold has been reached.

Figure 8.1 Sample shareholders' written resolution

Companies Act 2006

[name of company]
Registered number: [ ]

Written resolutions
Circulation date: [ ]

The directors of [name of company] (the 'Company') propose, pursuant to Chapter 2 of Part 13 of CA2006, that the first resolution below is passed as a special resolution of the members of the Company and that the second resolution below is passed as an ordinary resolution of the members of the Company.

Special resolution

'That, in accordance with section 21 of CA2006, the articles of association attached to this written resolution and marked 'A' for identification purposes are adopted as the Company's articles of association in place of its current articles of association with immediate effect.'

Agree   ☐
Do not agree   ☐

Ordinary resolution

'That, in accordance with section 551 of CA2006, the directors of the Company are authorised to exercise any power of the Company to allot shares, provided that the maximum amount of shares that may be allotted under this authorisation is [amount], and provided also that this authorisation will expire on [date].'

Agree   ☐
Do not agree   ☐

I, the undersigned, being a member who is entitled to vote on the resolutions on the circulation date, [date], agree to the resolution or resolutions beneath which I have entered an 'X' in the 'Agree' box.

_____   _____
[Shareholder's name]   Date

Notes
1. If you agree to a proposed resolution, please enter an 'X' in the 'Agree' box beneath that resolution. If you do not agree to a proposed resolution,

please enter an 'X' in the 'Do not agree' box beneath that resolution. When you have completed that portion of the document, please sign and date the document and return it to the Company either by posting it to [name and address], or by emailing a scanned copy of it to [email address].
2. Once the Company has received the signed document, you may not revoke your agreement to a resolution to which you agreed.
3. If a proposed resolution is not passed by [date], it will lapse.

8.3.6 Decisions by sole shareholders

8.3.6.1 A sole shareholder of a private company has all three decision-making options open to him. He is perfectly entitled to take decisions by means of a written resolution or even at a general meeting, but the most efficient option is the procedure in s. 357.

8.3.6.2 Section 357 provides, in effect, that a sole shareholder can make his mind up about a particular matter and then simply inform the company of his decision. The text of the section is set out in full in Figure 8.2.

Figure 8.2 Text of CA2006 s. 357

Section 357 – Records of decisions by sole member
'(1) This section applies to a company limited by shares or by guarantee that has only one member.
(2) Where the member takes any decision that –
   (a) may be taken by the company in general meeting, and
   (b) has effect as if agreed by the company in general meeting,
   he must (unless that decision is taken by way of a written resolution) provide the company with details of that decision.
(3) If a person fails to comply with this section he commits an offence.
(4) A person guilty of an offence under this section is liable on summary conviction to a fine not exceeding level 2 on the standard scale.
(5) Failure to comply with this section does not affect the validity of any decision referred to in subsection (2).'

8.3.6.3 The s. 357 procedure may be used to pass both ordinary resolutions and special resolutions.

8.3.6.4 Although the Act does not expressly exclude any types of resolution from the scope of the procedure, it probably cannot be used to pass a resolution to remove a director under s. 168 or to remove an auditor under s. 510. In *Bonham-Carter v Situ Ventures Ltd* [2012] EWHC 230 (Ch) (the case subsequently went to appeal, but the Court of Appeal's decision did not deal with the matters under discussion in this paragraph) the High Court considered the scope of the unanimous consent rule, under which shareholders may take decisions informally (i.e. without complying with a formal decision-making procedure) as long as they are acting unanimously. The deputy judge took the view that a s. 168 resolution cannot be passed in accordance with the unanimous consent rule, on the basis that shareholders are not competent to, in effect, waive compliance with the accompanying measures in s. 169, which offer protection to the director in question (s. 169 is discussed in paragraph 5.4.2.2). Since the use of the s. 357 procedure to pass a s. 168 resolution would also involve a waiver of s. 169, it would seem to follow that the procedure cannot be used for that purpose. (There is no doubt, however, that a resolution to remove a director not under s. 168, but under an alternative removal procedure set out in the company's articles, can be passed using the s. 357 procedure. The law governing the removal of directors is discussed in section 5.4.2.) A similar analysis applies in relation to a resolution under s. 510, since that provision is supplemented by measures in s. 511 which appear to be designed to protect the auditor.

8.3.6.5 Section 357 does not prescribe the means by which the sole shareholder must inform the company of his decision. His obligation is merely to 'provide the company with details of that decision'. Athough in theory he could, therefore, convey his decision by means of, say, a text message or even a telephone call, best practice is to produce a formal written record of the decision, so as to ensure that there is no confusion about what was decided and when the decision was taken.

8.3.6.6 A sample format for a written record of a decision by a sole shareholder is set out in Figure 8.3.

Figure 8.3 Sample written record of a decision by a sole shareholder
Companies Act 2006

[name of company]
Registered number: [ ]

Record of a decision by the sole member

Pursuant to s. 357(2) of CA2006, this is a record of a decision taken by the sole member of [name of company] (the 'Company') on [date], being a decision that may be taken by the company in general meeting and that has effect as if agreed by the company in general meeting as an ordinary resolution.

> **Ordinary resolution**
>
> 'That, in accordance with article [ ] of the Company's articles of association, [name] is appointed to be a director of the Company with immediate effect.'
>
> _____   _____
> [Sole shareholder's name]   Date

8.3.7 General meetings

8.3.7.1 Shareholders in private companies should normally pass resolutions by means either of the written resolution procedure or, in the case of a sole shareholder, the s. 357 procedure. The general meeting procedure is not, however, obsolete.

- A general meeting will be required if the shareholders want to pass a resolution to remove a director under s. 168 or an auditor under s. 510, or if the company's articles specify that the company must hold an annual general meeting (such provisions are uncommon, but may be found in the articles of some older companies).
- In some cases, it may be felt that a general meeting provides an opportunity for shareholders with different views on a matter to debate the issues and reach an agreement.
- A general meeting can be used as a means to pass a resolution which would otherwise fail. As noted above (see paragraph 8.3.3), a resolution which is proposed as a written resolution will be passed if the necessary proportion of all the available votes are cast in favour of it, while a resolution which is proposed at a general meeting will be passed if the necessary proportion of all the votes which are actually cast are cast in favour of it. Consider the case of a company with several shareholders, one of whom holds a 40% stake. If that shareholder declines to participate in the company's affairs, the other shareholders will never be able to pass a special resolution by means of the written resolution procedure, because they will never be able to muster more than 60% of the available votes. They will, however, be able to pass a special resolution at a general meeting, because all that will be required is the support of 75% of the votes which are actually cast.

8.3.7.2 The procedure for passing a resolution at a general meeting is contained mainly in Chapter 3 of Part 13 of the Act. However, the statutory provisions are invariably supplemented by companies in their articles (see, for example, articles 37 to 47 of the model articles for private companies).

8.3.7.3 Although the precise details of the general meeting procedure for a particular company will, therefore, depend upon its articles, the key features of the procedure are set out below (articles 37 to 47 of the model articles are discussed in section 4.3.6).

- **A general meeting may be called either by the directors or by the shareholders.** The law in this area is similar to the law governing the proposal of a shareholders' written resolution, in that although it will normally be the directors who call a general meeting (s. 302), the Act gives the shareholders the power to force their hand (ss. 303 and 304). In fact, the back-up power given to shareholders in relation to general meetings is more extensive than it is in relation to written resolutions, in that in extreme cases they can actually call a meeting themselves (s. 305).

  The Act also confers on the court the power to order a meeting to be called (s. 306).

- **A general meeting is called by giving notice of it to the shareholders and the directors (s. 310).** The statutory requirement to give notice to the shareholders and the directors is expressed to be subject to the company's articles. Some companies may provide in their articles, for example, that shareholders who fail to provide the company with correct contact details cease to be entitled to receive notice (see, for example, article 80 of the model articles for public companies).

  Notice of a general meeting must also be sent to the company's auditor (s. 502(2)).

- **Although there is no prescribed format for a notice of a general meeting, the Act imposes certain requirements as to its contents and as to accompanying documentation.** The notice must state the time, date and place of the meeting (s. 311(1)).

  If the meeting's business is to include the consideration of a proposed special resolution, the notice must contain the text of the proposed special resolution and specify that it is intended that it will be proposed as a special resolution (s. 283(6)). In fact, it is good practice also to include in the notice the full text of any proposed ordinary resolutions.

  The notice must state 'the general nature of the business' which is to be conducted at the meeting (s. 311(2). The statutory requirement is expressed to be subject to the company's articles, but most companies' articles are silent on this point). It will generally suffice simply to state that the meeting will consider the proposed resolutions.

  The notice must contain a statement setting out the shareholders' statutory right to appoint one or more persons (known as 'proxies') to attend, speak and vote at the general meeting on their behalf (ss. 324 and 325) and will normally be accompanied by a proxy appointment form. The Act addresses in a limited fashion the timing of the delivery of a proxy appointment form to the company (s. 327), but does not prescribe its content or format. However, most companies' articles will fill this gap in the statutory framework. Article 45 of the model articles for private companies, for example, requires an appointment to be made in writing and lists the information which it must contain.

Depending upon the type of resolution which is being proposed, the notice may need to contain additional information and/or be accompanied (or followed) by additional documentation. For example, when an ordinary resolution to remove a director under s. 168 is being proposed, the notice will need to refer to any representations made by the director, and the company will have to send the shareholders a copy of the representations (s. 169(3)).

In certain circumstances, shareholders have the right to require the company to circulate a statement concerning any of the business which is to be conducted at the meeting (ss. 314 and 315).

In some cases, documents will need to be made available at the meeting itself. For example, if the meeting is to consider a proposed ordinary resolution to approve a directors' long-term service contract, a memorandum setting out the proposed contract will need to be made available for inspection by the shareholders (s. 188(5)).

- **The notice must normally be given to the shareholders and the directors at least 14 days before the general meeting is held (s. 307(1)).** This general rule merely establishes a default position. A company is free to impose a longer notice period in its articles (s. 307(3)), and, on the other hand, the shareholders can elect to hold a meeting on short notice (s. 307(4) to (6)).

  The concept of 'special notice' is referred to in relation to certain types of resolution, including an ordinary resolution to remove a director under s. 168. Where special notice of a resolution is required, notice of the resolution must be given to *the company* at least 28 days before the general meeting in question, and the company in turn must inform the shareholders of the proposed resolution (s. 312). (The company will normally comply with its obligation to inform the shareholders by incorporating the proposed resolution into the notice of the general meeting.) The fact that special notice is required of a particular resolution does not alter the fact that the shareholders and the directors must normally be given at least 14 days' notice of the general meeting itself; the two requirements are quite distinct.

- **A quorum must be in attendance at the general meeting.** The Act sets the quorum at two, unless the company has just one shareholder, in which case it sets the quorum at one (s. 318). The former threshold is expressed to be subject to the company's articles, and in fact it is common for companies to adapt the quorum requirement to suit their needs. If the company's shares are distributed among three families, for example, it might be appropriate for the articles to state that the quorum is three, and that at least one shareholder from each family must be in attendance.

- **Resolutions are voted on either by a show of hands or on a poll. (When a vote is taken 'on a poll', every vote held by every shareholder is counted.)** The articles will usually state that votes are to be taken on a show of hands unless a poll is demanded, and will list the persons who are entitled to demand a poll (see, for example, articles 42 and 44 of the model articles for private companies. These provisions are discussed in section 4.3.6).

The Act provides that every shareholder has one vote on a show of hands, and one vote per share on a poll (s. 284). This rule is, however, expressed to be subject to the company's articles, and it is not uncommon for shares to carry weighted voting rights or, indeed, no voting rights.

8.3.7.4 It has to be said that the law governing general meetings is far more complex than it needs to be. In this respect, a contrast may be drawn with the law governing shareholders' written resolutions, which is set out concisely and in a logical fashion. Be that as it may, it will be apparent from the preceding paragraphs that in essence, at least, the general meeting procedure is quite straightforward.

8.3.7.5 Similarly, the documentation requirements associated with the procedure are not excessive (although certainly the procedure places more of an administrative burden on companies than the shareholders' written resolution procedure or the s. 357 procedure). The key documents which will be required in order to call and hold a general meeting are as follows:

- a directors' written resolution or board minutes approving the notice of the general meeting;
- the notice of the general meeting (and any documents which are to accompany it);
- a proxy appointment form;
- minutes of the general meeting. (Under s. 355, companies are required to keep minutes of proceedings at general meetings (and to retain them for at least 10 years).)

8.3.8 The unanimous consent rule

8.3.8.1 A properly advised company will ensure that its shareholders take decisions in accordance with one of the statutory procedures described above. Many small companies, though, do not have the benefit of regular legal advice, and the shareholders of such companies may be aware neither of the precise situations in which a formal decision is needed, nor of the detail of the procedures governing the taking of such decisions. If, therefore, the company law regime insisted on a scrupulous adherence to the formal decision-making procedures, many (perhaps most) decisions taken by private companies would be invalid, and this in turn would threaten any actions which flowed from them.

8.3.8.2 In fact, the regime does not adopt an overly strict approach to decision-making, for the courts have developed the rule that an informal decision of the shareholders is valid as long as it is taken unanimously. This rule is known as the unanimous consent rule or, colloquially, as the Duomatic principle, after an early case in which its scope was delineated. The common law rule is preserved by s. 281(4) of the Act. Although that subsection does not refer to the rule in so many words, paragraph 523 of CA2006 Explanatory Notes confirms that it does, indeed, preserve the rule.

8.3.8.3 In *Re Duomatic Ltd* [1969] 2 Ch 365, the High Court considered various payments which had been made by a company to two of its directors. Although the company's articles provided for directors' remuneration to be decided upon by the shareholders in general meeting, no shareholders' resolutions on directors' pay were ever passed. In respect of payments made during a particular financial year, however, the court noted that the directors at the time, who were also the only voting shareholders at the time, had approved the company's accounts for that year, and that the company's auditor had explained to them that the accounts reflected the payments in question. Buckley J. felt that, in the circumstances, the shareholders must be taken to have approved the payments, despite the fact that they had not passed a formal resolution to that effect. He summarised the law on unanimous consent as follows:

> 'In other words, I proceed upon the basis that where it can be shown that all shareholders who have a right to attend and vote at a general meeting of the company assent to some matter which a general meeting of the company could carry into effect, that assent is as binding as a resolution in general meeting would be.' ([1969] 2 Ch 365, at 373C)

8.3.8.4 The unanimous consent rule may fairly be described as having a broad scope. In *Re Duomatic Ltd*, it was held to apply where the decision in question was required by a provision of the company's articles, but it is clear that it applies equally in respect of a decision which is required by statute. In *Re Oxted Motor Co, Ltd* [1921] 3 KB 32, the court applied the rule where shareholders passed a resolution pursuant to the Companies (Consolidation) Act 1908 to wind up the company without complying with all the formalities associated with such a resolution. It is also clear from the case law that the requirement for the 'assent' of all the shareholders will not be narrowly construed. In *Schofield v Schofield* ([2011] EWCA Civ 154, at [32]) the Court of Appeal noted that assent 'could be express or by implication, verbal or by conduct, given at the time or later'. Certainly, express assent is not required; it will suffice if the shareholders acquiesced in the decision.

8.3.8.5 However, the rule has its limits. For instance, it will not be applied unless there is evidence from which a court can objectively establish the shareholders' assent (*Schofield v Schofield* [2011] EWCA Civ 154, at [32]). That is to say, a decision which is not expressed outwardly in any way does not constitute assent for these purposes. Furthermore, the rule will not be applied so as to allow shareholders to, in effect, waive compliance with requirements which are designed to protect other parties. Thus, in *Bonham-Carter v Situ Ventures Ltd* [2012] EWHC 230 (Ch) (the case subsequently went to appeal, but the Court of Appeal's decision did not deal with the matters under discussion in this paragraph), the High Court was of the view that the rule could not be used to pass a resolution under s. 168 to remove a director, on the basis that the provisions in s. 169 are designed, at least in part, to protect directors, and so are not susceptible to waiver by the shareholders. It will by no means always be obvious whose interests particular formalities are designed to protect; ultimately, this is a matter to be determined by the courts.

8.3.8.6 The unanimous consent rule should not be regarded as an alternative to the three formal decision-making procedures, to be relied upon as a matter of course. This is partly because of the uncertainty, outlined in the paragraph above, as to the situations in which an informal decision will be effective, but primarily because of the importance to the smooth running of a company that full, written records are kept of all decisions taken by the shareholders. Well-advised shareholders will take the time to familiarise themselves both with the circumstances in which they are likely to need to pass a formal resolution and with the formal decision-making procedures, and will regard the unanimous consent rule as nothing more than a safety net, which in exceptional cases may be deployed in order to rescue a flawed decision.

8.4 Minority shareholder protection

8.4.1 As has been noted, shareholder decisions do not need to be unanimous. An ordinary resolution requires the support of a bare majority of the shareholders, and a special resolution requires the support of three-quarters of the shareholders.

8.4.2 This majority rule approach makes sense from an efficiency perspective, since a requirement for unanimity would in many cases inhibit the shareholders' ability to act swiftly and decisively. It is also only fair that the majority, who, by definition, have put more money into the company than the minority, should have a greater say in its affairs. The approach creates the risk, however, that the majority will act against the interests of the minority. If investors perceive that risk to be too great, they will be reluctant to take small stakes in companies, and this in turn will reduce the effectiveness of the company as a vehicle for doing business. In an effort to address this problem, the company law regime incorporates a number of measures which are designed to prevent majority shareholders from acting oppressively. It may be said, in fact, that the desire to protect minority shareholders from majority shareholders is one of the themes which runs through the regime.

8.4.3 Any consideration of the law on minority shareholder protection must, however, begin by recognising that, in general, the majority shareholders will get what they want. In other words, the majority do not normally have to consider the wishes or interests of the minority when they make their decisions.

8.4.4 Take the case of a manufacturing company with two shareholders, a majority shareholder who has no other business interests and a minority shareholder who owns a French company which manufactures similar products. If, pursuant to the articles, the shareholders are invited by the board to consider a proposal to expand the company's business into France, the majority shareholder will, in most cases, be perfectly entitled to vote in favour of the expansion even though he knows that it will damage the prospects of the minority shareholder's French company.

8.4.5 The following discussion of the means by which the regime seeks to protect minority shareholders must, therefore, be seen in its proper perspective. As important as some of the measures are, the balance of power is very much in favour of majority shareholders.

8.4.6 An overview of the minority shareholder protection measures

8.4.6.1 Some minority shareholders are in a position to take steps to protect their interests at the outset of their relationship with the company. An investor who is willing to invest in a struggling company by buying a small parcel of new shares, say, may well be able to drive a hard bargain with the existing shareholders. He might, for example, insist that the articles provide for his shares to carry weighted voting rights in relation to certain types of decisions or for him to have a seat on the board for as long as he retains his stake. He might also insist on entering into a separate agreement with the shareholders. Such an agreement (known as a 'shareholders' agreement') might provide, for example, that the shareholders will not vote in favour of any significant changes to the company's business unless they are all in favour of the proposal.

8.4.6.2 In practice, however, many minority shareholders are not in a position to force the majority to offer them bespoke protection. Their only protection, therefore, lies in the general law applicable to all shareholders. Chief among those aspects of the company law regime which are designed to protect minority shareholders are the following:

- The common law rule that the majority shareholders must, when they amend the articles, be acting in what they believe to be the company's interests, and not with the intention of oppressing the minority (this rule is discussed in section 4.4.1).

- CA2006 s. 25, which provides that an amendment to the articles which imposes on a shareholder a financial obligation to the company will not be binding unless he agrees to be bound by it (s. 25 is discussed in section 4.4.1).
- CA2006 s. 33, the effect of which is that the articles constitute a statutory contract, such that a shareholder can, in certain circumstances, bring proceedings to enforce his rights under them (s. 33 is discussed in sections 4.5.1 and 4.5.2).
- CA2006 ss. 260 to 264, under which a shareholder can bring a claim against a director on behalf of the company in respect of an alleged breach of duty (a so-called 'derivative claim') (the derivative claim is discussed in section 8.4.8).
- CA2006 s. 630, which requires the consent of shareholders of a class of shares to be obtained before the rights attached to their shares are varied (the law on varying class rights is discussed in section 4.4.1 and paragraph 9.2.5.9).
- CA2006 ss. 994 and 996, which provide that the court has the power to give such relief as it sees fit to a shareholder who can show that the company has been run in a manner which is unfairly prejudicial to his interests (the unfair prejudice remedy is discussed in section 8.4.7).
- Insolvency Act 1986 s. 122(1)(g), which gives a shareholder the right to ask the court to wind up the company on what is known as the 'just and equitable ground'.

A company's shareholders can decide to wind it up (i.e. to initiate the process of dissolving it) by passing a special resolution (Insolvency Act 1986 s. 84(1)(b)). In some cases, a minority shareholder may wish to wind the company up in order to end his relationship with the other shareholders and recover his investment, but the majority may be content for the company to continue its operations, thus effectively trapping the minority shareholder. Under s. 122(1)(g), the court has the power to order a company to be wound up if it 'is of the opinion that it is just and equitable that the company should be wound up', and individual shareholders have the right to apply to the court to invite it to exercise that power.

CA2006 does not define the phrase 'just and equitable', but although the courts, too, have refrained from providing an exhaustive definition, a good deal of guidance as to its meaning can be gleaned from the case law. It may, for example, be just and equitable to wind a company up if the parties are deadlocked (*Re Yenidje Tobacco Co, Ltd* [1916] 2 Ch 426, at 435 (per Warrington LJ)), if the relationship between them has deteriorated due to 'a lack of probity in the conduct of the company's affairs' (*Loch v John Blackwood, Ltd* [1924] AC 783, at 788) or if the company has served the purpose for which it was formed (*Re Kitson & Co Ltd* [1946] 1 All ER 435).

A minority shareholder's right to make an application under s. 122(1)(g) is a potentially useful means by which he can defend his interests, but a court will not order a company to be wound up lightly. The Insolvency Act 1986 s. 125(2) provides as follows:

'If the [winding-up] petition is presented by members of the company as contributories on the ground that it is just and equitable that the company should be wound up, the court, if it is of opinion –
(a) that the petitioners are entitled to relief either by winding up the company or by some other means, and
(b) that in the absence of any other remedy it would be just and equitable that the company should be wound up,
shall make a winding-up order; but this does not apply if the court is also of the opinion both that some other remedy is available to the petitioners and that they are acting unreasonably in seeking to have the company wound up instead of pursuing that other remedy.'

If, therefore, a minority shareholder has a suitable alternative remedy, in the shape of an unfair prejudice petition under s. 994, for example, or an offer from the majority shareholders to buy his shares at a fair price (*Re a Company (No. 002567 of 1982)* [1983] 1 WLR 927), he will be expected to pursue that option instead of applying to have the company wound up. A petition under s. 122(1)(g) should, in short, normally be regarded as a minority shareholder's last resort.

8.4.7 The unfair prejudice remedy

8.4.7.1 The statutory unfair prejudice remedy is regarded as the most powerful weapon in the armoury of an aggrieved minority shareholder. The courts have had occasion to consider the scope of the remedy many times over the years, and have shown themselves to be willing to come to the aid of such shareholders in appropriate cases. A quotation from a recent Court of Appeal decision serves to illustrate the courts' view of the nature of the remedy, as well as its purpose:

'The dominant characteristic of the unfair prejudice remedy, both in statute and case law, is its adaptability. This enables the courts to produce a just remedy where minority shareholders can show wrongdoing that prejudices their interests. It also makes the unfair prejudice remedy important as a means of encouraging proper corporate behaviour in the management of smaller companies and building up the confidence of investors in them.' (*Re Tobian Properties Ltd* [2012] EWCA Civ 998, at [28] (per Arden LJ))

8.4.7.2 Although there is no doubt that the remedy is potentially wide in scope, a minority shareholder who is considering whether he may have grounds for applying to the court for an unfair prejudice order should not fall into the trap of assuming that it cures all ills. The key to understanding the remedy is to appreciate that its incorporation of the concept of unfairness does *not* mean that courts have licence to do whatever they feel is just in all the circumstances. A shareholder will, instead, have to base his claim of unfairness on the breach of an agreement or understanding with the other parties.

8.4.7.3 The grounds on which a shareholder may apply to the court for an unfair prejudice order are contained in s. 994, and the court's power to grant relief is contained in s. 996. The text of the sections is set out in full in Figure 8.4.

Figure 8.4 Text of CA2006 ss. 994 and 996

Section 994 – Petition by company member

'(1) A member of a company may apply to the court by petition for an order under this Part on the ground –
  (a) that the company's affairs are being or have been conducted in a manner that is unfairly prejudicial to the interests of members generally or of some part of its members (including at least himself), or
  (b) that an actual or proposed act or omission of the company (including an act or omission on its behalf) is or would be so prejudicial.

(1A) For the purposes of subsection (1)(a), a removal of the company's auditor from office –
  (a) on grounds of divergence of opinions on accounting treatments or audit procedures, or
  (b) on any other improper grounds,
  shall be treated as being unfairly prejudicial to the interests of some part of the company's members.

(2) The provisions of this Part apply to a person who is not a member of a company but to whom shares in the company have been transferred or transmitted by operation of law as they apply to a member of a company.

(3) In this section, and so far as applicable for the purposes of this section in the other provisions of this Part, 'company' means –
  (a) a company within the meaning of this Act, or
  (b) a company that is not such a company but is a statutory water company within the meaning of the Statutory Water Companies Act 1991 (c. 58).'

Section 996 – Powers of the court under this Part

'(1) If the court is satisfied that a petition under this Part is well founded, it may make such order as it thinks fit for giving relief in respect of the matters complained of.

(2) Without prejudice to the generality of subsection (1), the court's order may –
  (a) regulate the conduct of the company's affairs in the future;
  (b) require the company –
    (i) to refrain from doing or continuing an act complained of, or
    (ii) to do an act that the petitioner has complained it has omitted to do;

(c) authorise civil proceedings to be brought in the name and on behalf of the company by such person or persons and on such terms as the court may direct;
(d) require the company not to make any, or any specified, alterations in its articles without the leave of the court;
(e) provide for the purchase of the shares of any members of the company by other members or by the company itself and, in the case of a purchase by the company itself, the reduction of the company's capital accordingly.'

8.4.7.4 There is a large body of decisions on the unfair prejudice remedy, and as a result this area of the law is not without its complexities. The remedy's key features can, however, be described in fairly straightforward terms.

- **The shareholder's complaint must concern the conduct of the company's affairs or an act or omission of the company (s. 994(1)).** The courts have given this aspect of the statutory wording a generous interpretation. In *Re City Branch Group Ltd [2004] EWCA Civ 815*, for example, the Court of Appeal was of the view that, in appropriate circumstances, the conduct of a subsidiary's affairs could constitute the conduct of the parent company's affairs.

    The point may be made that the unfair prejudice remedy does not require the shareholder to show a course of unfairly prejudicial conduct. It will suffice to found a claim that the shareholder can point to a single act (such as his removal from office as a director) which is, on the facts, unfairly prejudicial.

- **The shareholder's interests must have been prejudiced (s. 994(1)).** This is a broadly-drawn requirement. It is not confined to rights (such as rights under the company's articles), but extends to mere interests (such as a shareholder's interest in ensuring that the value of his shares does not fall), and the 'prejudice' need not involve financial loss (*Re Coroin Ltd* [2013] EWCA Civ 781, at [16]). Although the courts have stressed that the prejudice must be suffered by the shareholder in his capacity as a shareholder, this is, in practice, a less substantial qualification than one might expect: in the leading case on unfair prejudice, *O'Neill v Phillips* [1999] BCC 600, at 612H, Lord Hoffmann noted that 'the requirement that prejudice must be suffered as a member should not be too narrowly or technically construed'. Thus, a shareholder who is also a director may be said, in certain circumstances, to have suffered prejudice in his capacity as a shareholder if he is removed from the board, and the courts have gone so far as to hold that a shareholder's interests can extend to his interests as a creditor of the company (*Gamlestaden Fastigheter AB v Baltic Partners Ltd* [2007] UKPC 26, at [30]).

- **The prejudice suffered by the shareholder must have been unfair (s. 994(1)).** The concept of fairness is at the heart of the unfair prejudice remedy, but the

courts have taken the view that the statute does not confer on judges an unfettered discretion to decide what sort of behaviour is unfair (*O'Neill v Phillips* [1999] BCC 600, at 606F). Instead, a finding of unfairness will normally be based on a breach of an agreement between the parties. The agreement in question may, however, be implied and need not necessarily be enforceable. Thus, unfairness may consist of the following:
- a breach of the company's articles (*Re Tobian Properties Ltd* [2012] EWCA Civ 998, at [22]) or a shareholders' agreement – clearly, the articles and any shareholders' agreement form the primary agreement between the parties;
- a breach of the statutory directors' duties (*Re Tobian Properties Ltd* [2012] EWCA Civ 998, at [22]) – the parties will be taken to have impliedly agreed that any of their number who are directors will comply with their duties as such;
- a breach of any rights conferred by statute (*Re Tobian Properties Ltd* [2012] EWCA Civ 998, at [22]);
- in the case of a company which is a 'quasi-partnership' (in the sense that the parties to it have a personal relationship of trust), a breach of an informal understanding between the parties (*O'Neill v Phillips* [1999] BCC 600). Take the case of a group of friends who form a company in order to exploit an invention which they designed together. Although it is understood by all of them that the company will have no other purpose than to seek to make a profit from the invention, it does not occur to them to enter into a shareholders' agreement to that effect. If the company subsequently abandons its work on the invention and enters a new field of business, a court might well consider that the breach of the informal understanding as to the nature of the company's activities suffices to establish unfairness.

- **The court has a broad discretion to grant relief.** Section 996(1) gives the court the power to grant such relief as it sees fit, and s. 996(2) sets out a non-exhaustive list of possible orders which it may make. In practice, a minority shareholder will often feel that his relationship with the other parties is broken beyond repair, and will therefore be seeking an order that they buy his stake at a fair price, thus allowing him to wash his hands of the company (whereas a disgruntled shareholder in a listed company should be able to sell his shares on the open market without difficulty, a disgruntled shareholder in a small private company may well be unable to find a buyer for his shares).

  The crucial question of the valuation of the minority shareholder's stake has been the subject of a great deal of judicial analysis, and here, too, the flexible nature of the unfair prejudice remedy is evident. In *Profinance Trust SA v Gladstone* [2001] EWCA Civ 1031, the Court of Appeal held that there was an 'overriding requirement that the valuation should be fair on the facts of the particular case'. Thus, although the minority shareholder's stake will normally be valued as at the date on which the buy-out order is made, it may be valued as at an earlier date if, say, its value has been adversely affected by the majority shareholders' unfair conduct.

8.4.8 The derivative claim

8.4.8.1 It is a fundamental rule of company law that if a wrong is done to a company, it is for the company – and the company alone – to bring proceedings in respect of it. This is often referred to as 'the rule in *Foss v Harbottle*', after a nineteenth-century case in which, in the course of holding that two shareholders were not entitled to bring proceedings in respect of an alleged wrong done to a company, the court described it as 'the rule which, *primâ facie*, would require that the corporation should sue in its own name and in its corporate character, or in the name of someone whom the law has appointed to be its representative' (*Foss v Harbottle* (1843) 2 Hare 461, at 491)'.

8.4.8.2 In relation to directors' duties, the effect of the rule is that, since a breach of duty is a wrong done to the company (directors owe their duties to the company (s. 170(1)), and not to individual shareholders or anyone else), only the company is entitled to bring proceedings in respect of it. In most companies, the power to initiate legal proceedings is conferred on the board as part of the broad delegation of management power by the shareholders, so the decision as to whether to pursue a director in respect of an alleged breach is one for his fellow directors to take.

8.4.8.3 If the board decides not to initiate proceedings in a particular instance, but the majority of the shareholders disagree with that decision, the rule in *Foss v Harbottle* will prevent them from taking action on their own account, but they will have tools at their disposal either to overrule the board or to try to persuade it to think again (see paragraph 7.4.2.3). For example, they may threaten to remove from office those directors who voted against taking action. If, however, it is only a minority shareholder who feels that proceedings should be initiated, the position is rather different. A minority shareholder is not only barred from taking action on his own account, but has no means of forcing or encouraging the board to take action.

8.4.8.4 The minority shareholder's predicament can be justified on the grounds of both principle and practicality. As far as the former is concerned, the rule in *Foss v Harbottle* reflects the company's separate identity and respects its internal arrangements as to the division of power between the shareholders and the directors. As far as the latter is concerned, it prevents multiple actions being brought by individual shareholders in respect of the same cause of action.

8.4.8.5 If the board and the majority shareholders decline to act in respect of an alleged breach of duty for improper reasons, however, the strict application of the rule would lead to injustice. Consider the case of a company with three shareholders, two of whom together hold 90% of the company's shares and are the company's only directors. If the directors breach their duty to avoid a situation of conflict under s. 175, clearly they will not act against themselves, either in their capacity as directors or in their capacity as majority shareholders, and the effect of the rule is that the minority shareholder is in a very unfortunate position: he has suffered as a result of the majority shareholders' wrongdoing, but is powerless to hold them to account.

8.4.8.6 In response to this problem, the company law regime has devised an exception to the rule in *Foss v Harbottle*, under which a minority shareholder *can*, in certain very limited circumstances, initiate proceedings against a director for breach of duty on the company's behalf. The 'derivative claim', as it is known, was an invention of the courts, but the law in this area is now to be found in CA2006 Part 11, comprising ss. 260 to 269. The most important provisions are CA2006 ss. 260, 261 and 263, the full text of which is set out in Figure 8.5.

Figure 8.5 Text of CA2006 ss. 260, 261 and 263

Section 260 – Derivative claims

'(1) This Chapter applies to proceedings in England and Wales or Northern Ireland by a member of a company –
  (a) in respect of a cause of action vested in the company, and
  (b) seeking relief on behalf of the company.
  This is referred to in this Chapter as a 'derivative claim'.

(2) A derivative claim may only be brought –
  (a) under this Chapter, or
  (b) in pursuance of an order of the court in proceedings under section 994 (proceedings for protection of members against unfair prejudice).

(3) A derivative claim under this Chapter may be brought only in respect of a cause of action arising from an actual or proposed act or omission involving negligence, default, breach of duty or breach of trust by a director of the company.
  The cause of action may be against the director or another person (or both).

(4) It is immaterial whether the cause of action arose before or after the person seeking to bring or continue the derivative claim became a member of the company.

(5) For the purposes of this Chapter –
  (a) 'director' includes a former director;
  (b) a shadow director is treated as a director; and

(c) references to a member of a company include a person who is not a member but to whom shares in the company have been transferred or transmitted by operation of law.'

Section 261 – Application for permission to continue derivative claim
'(1) A member of a company who brings a derivative claim under this Chapter must apply to the court for permission (in Northern Ireland, leave) to continue it.
(2) If it appears to the court that the application and the evidence filed by the applicant in support of it do not disclose a prima facie case for giving permission (or leave), the court –
   (a) must dismiss the application, and
   (b) may make any consequential order it considers appropriate.
(3) If the application is not dismissed under subsection (2), the court –
   (a) may give directions as to the evidence to be provided by the company, and
   (b) may adjourn the proceedings to enable the evidence to be obtained.
(4) On hearing the application, the court may –
   (a) give permission (or leave) to continue the claim on such terms as it thinks fit,
   (b) refuse permission (or leave) and dismiss the claim, or
   (c) adjourn the proceedings on the application and give such directions as it thinks fit.'

Section 263 – Whether permission to be given
'(1) The following provisions have effect where a member of a company applies for permission (in Northern Ireland, leave) under section 261 or 262.
(2) Permission (or leave) must be refused if the court is satisfied –
   (a) that a person acting in accordance with section 172 (duty to promote the success of the company) would not seek to continue the claim, or
   (b) where the cause of action arises from an act or omission that is yet to occur, that the act or omission has been authorised by the company, or
   (c) where the cause of action arises from an act or omission that has already occurred, that the act or omission –
      (i) was authorised by the company before it occurred, or
      (ii) has been ratified by the company since it occurred.
(3) In considering whether to give permission (or leave) the court must take into account, in particular –

(a) whether the member is acting in good faith in seeking to continue the claim;
(b) the importance that a person acting in accordance with section 172 (duty to promote the success of the company) would attach to continuing it;
(c) where the cause of action results from an act or omission that is yet to occur, whether the act or omission could be, and in the circumstances would be likely to be –
   (i) authorised by the company before it occurs, or
   (ii) ratified by the company after it occurs;
(d) where the cause of action arises from an act or omission that has already occurred, whether the act or omission could be, and in the circumstances would be likely to be, ratified by the company;
(e) whether the company has decided not to pursue the claim;
(f) whether the act or omission in respect of which the claim is brought gives rise to a cause of action that the member could pursue in his own right rather than on behalf of the company.

(4) In considering whether to give permission (or leave) the court shall have particular regard to any evidence before it as to the views of members of the company who have no personal interest, direct or indirect, in the matter.

(5) The Secretary of State may by regulations –
(a) amend subsection (2) so as to alter or add to the circumstances in which permission (or leave) is to be refused;
(b) amend subsection (3) so as to alter or add to the matters that the court is required to take into account in considering whether to give permission (or leave).

(6) Before making any such regulations the Secretary of State shall consult such persons as he considers appropriate.

(7) Regulations under this section are subject to affirmative resolution procedure.'

8.4.8.7 At common law, derivative claims were permitted only in exceptional situations, and there was some uncertainty as to precisely what those situations were. The Act has not made it significantly easier to bring a derivative claim, but the scope and nature of the mechanism is now clearly defined.

8.4.8.8 The main features of the statutory derivative claim are as follows:

- **A derivative claim may be brought by any shareholder, regardless of how few shares he owns (s. 260(1)).**

- **A derivative claim may be brought only in respect of an alleged breach of duty by a director (s. 260(3)).**

A derivative claim will, therefore, normally lie only against a director, although a claim may be brought against a third party if it relates to an alleged breach of duty by a director (for example, if the third party assisted in the breach). The discussion of derivative claims in this chapter concerns derivative claims under Part 11 of the Act. In fact, although derivative claims are, indeed, dealt with primarily under Part 11, the court has a separate power to allow a derivative claim to be brought as part of its broad discretion to grant relief on an unfair prejudice petition (s. 996(2)(c)). Of interest for present purposes is the fact that whereas a derivative claim against a third party under Part 11 must relate to a breach of duty, it appears that a court has the power under s. 996 to authorise a derivative claim against a third party which does not arise from a breach of duty (*Iesini v Westrip Holdings Ltd* [2009] EWHC 2526 (Ch), at [82]).

- **Any relief which is awarded in respect of a derivative claim (damages in respect of a director's breach of his duty of care under 174, for example) is awarded to the company (s. 260(1)(b)).** Since the claim is brought on behalf of the company, it follows that any remedy must be awarded to the company rather than to the shareholder who brings the claim. By contrast, relief in respect of an unfair prejudice petition normally takes the form of personal relief granted to the shareholder. Thus, when an aggrieved minority shareholder is trying to decide whether his interests would be served better by a derivative claim or an unfair prejudice petition, the first question he should ask himself is whether he is seeking corporate relief or personal relief.
- **In order to bring a derivative claim, a shareholder must first obtain the permission of the court (s. 261(1)).** The Act establishes a two-stage procedure for seeking permission.

   At the first stage, the court considers whether, on the face of it, the company has a good case (and whether, as required, the case relates to a director's breach of duty) (*Iesini v Westrip Holdings Ltd* [2009] EWHC 2526 (Ch), at [78]). This stage is designed to weed out frivolous claims, and the court will therefore normally reach its decision solely on the basis of the evidence presented by the shareholder who is seeking permission to bring the claim.

   If the court concludes that the company does, on the face of it, have a good case, a full hearing will be held. The court will hear from both the shareholder and the company, and will decide whether to grant permission for the derivative claim to be brought. If the court finds that no director acting with the company's best interests in mind would pursue the claim, or that the breach of duty has been authorised or ratified, it must refuse permission (s. 263(2)). If there is no such mandatory bar to bringing the claim, it is up to the court to decide whether or not to grant permission. In exercising its discretion, it will take into account the factors listed in s. 260(3) and (4); among other things, it will consider whether the shareholder is acting in good faith, whether he has a suitable alternative remedy and whether the breach of duty is likely to be authorised or ratified. Essentially, the question which it will be addressing is: is the company's cause of action against the director worth pursuing?

8.4.8.9 It will be apparent from the last bullet point above that whereas the unfair prejudice remedy is regarded as a flexible and adaptable means of protecting minority shareholders, the derivative claim is to be used much more sparingly. This is no doubt because it operates as an exception to a rule which, as was noted in paragraph 8.4.8.4, is based on principles that go to the heart of company law: the separate identity of the company and the right of shareholders to decide for themselves how to divide up power within their company.

8.4.8.10 Certainly, there will be cases in which an aggrieved shareholder can make use of the statutory mechanism. In *Parry v Bartlett* [2011] EWHC 3146 (Ch) the court considered a request for permission to bring a derivative claim by a shareholder who felt that the company's only other shareholder had misappropriated the company's assets. Each of the shareholders held a 50% stake, and they were also the company's only directors. Taking the view that there was 'a strong prima facie case of breach of duty', that a director acting with the company's best interests in mind would consider the claim worth pursuing, that the alleged breach had been neither authorised nor ratified and that the shareholder did not have a suitable alternative remedy, the court granted permission for the derivative claim to be brought.

8.4.8.11 However, the courts will not grant permission lightly. Their reluctance to interfere in companies' internal affairs is illustrated by the decision in *Kleanthous v Paphitis* [2011] EWHC 2287 (Ch), a case in which a minority shareholder sought permission to bring a derivative claim against a director who was also the majority shareholder. The claim centred on an alleged breach of duty in the form of the diversion of a business opportunity which, it was suggested, had eventually yielded very substantial profits. The court felt that the chances of the company's claim succeeding were considerably less than 50%, but accepted that a successful claim could potentially result in the recovery of a substantial sum. However, having noted that a committee of directors who had not been involved in the alleged diversion had concluded that the claim would damage the company's commercial interests, and having decided that, on the facts, an unfair prejudice petition offered the shareholder a suitable alternative remedy, it refused permission for the derivative claim to be brought.

8.4.8.12 In practical terms, the most unhelpful feature of the statutory derivative claim from the perspective of an aggrieved minority shareholder is that it largely respects the will of the majority shareholders. Thus, the effect of s. 163(2)(b) and

(c) is that a derivative claim will not be available if the breach of duty:

(a) is susceptible to authorisation or ratification (ie is not an unratifiable breach) (the concept of unratifiable breaches is discussed in paragraph 7.4.3.6); and

(b) has, in fact, been authorised or ratified.

More generally, the statutory framework is clearly not designed to make it easy for minority shareholders to bring derivative claims, and the courts have shown no inclination to assist their cause by pushing the boundaries of the wording of the Act. It would be going too far to describe the derivative claim as a weapon of last resort for a minority shareholder who feels that he has been treated unfairly, but certainly in most cases it will be a less effective weapon than an unfair prejudice petition.

9

Shares

> **Summary**
> - Directors of a private company with only one class of shares may allot new shares of the same class unless the articles say otherwise. In all other cases, shareholder authorisation must be obtained before the directors can allot new shares.
> - Shares may be paid for in cash, but companies can agree to accept other forms of consideration, such as the transfer of a business to the company or the provision by the subscriber of services to the company.
> - The capital maintenance doctrine states that a company must not normally return capital to its shareholders. The doctrine underpins the various mechanisms by which shareholders can take money out of the company. Those mechanisms include a dividend, a share buy-back and a formal reduction of capital.

9.1 Introduction

9.1.1 The most important aspects of the law governing shares are set out in CA2006 Parts 17, 18 and 23.

- Part 17 is entitled 'A company's share capital'. It comprises ss. 540 to 657, and deals with matters such as the allotment of shares, the statutory pre-emption right, payment for shares, class rights and reductions of capital.
- Part 18 is entitled 'Acquisition by limited company of its own shares'. It comprises ss. 658 to 737, and deals with matters such as share buy-backs, redeemable shares and the financial assistance prohibition.
- Part 23 is entitled 'Distributions'. It comprises ss. 829 to 853, and deals with dividends and other distributions to shareholders.

These Parts adopt a prescriptive, rules-based approach, which means that anyone who is dealing with the law in this area will need to become familiar themself with the detail of the statutory provisions.

9.1.2 This chapter contains an introduction not only to the most important rules, but also to the principles which underpin them. It does this by considering how shares are used to put money into a company and how they are used to take money out of a company.

9.1.3 In relation to the use of shares to put money into a company, it addresses the following questions:

- How are shares allotted, and what is the statutory pre-emption right?
- Can a company issue shares which carry different rights?
- What are the rules governing payment for shares?
- What does 'capital' mean?
- What is the financial assistance prohibition?

9.1.4 In relation to the use of shares to take money out of the company, it addresses the following questions:

- What is the capital maintenance doctrine?
- In what circumstances can a company pay its shareholders a dividend?
- In what circumstances can a company acquire its own shares from a shareholder?
- What is a reduction of capital?

9.2 Putting money into a company

9.2.1 The law relating to the use of shares to invest in a company engages two of the most important principles of company law: the need to protect shareholders (who have handed over management power to the board) and the need to protect creditors (whose interests are compromised because shareholders are able to limit their liability for the company's debts).

9.2.2 Thus, although the Act recognises that it should be for the directors, who are best placed to determine the company's funding needs, to allot new shares in order to raise money, it also recognises that to give the directors complete freedom in this regard would be to give them an undue amount of power over the shareholders. The law on allotting shares therefore treads a fine line between giving directors freedom to act and ensuring that the shareholders have overall control of the company's activities in this sphere.

9.2.3 Similarly, the law concerning capital, including the requirement that a share must have a nominal value and the rule that any amount paid over and above that nominal value is treated as capital, is designed to ensure (in conjunction with the capital maintenance doctrine) that a company has a clearly defined pool of funds which is available for creditors to draw upon in the event of its failure.

9.2.4 Allotting shares

9.2.4.1 A company has the power to allot new shares (s. 617(2)(a)), and it is the directors who exercise that power (ss. 550 and 551).

9.2.4.2 Since a company allots shares in order to raise money, it makes sense for the directors, who are normally in charge of managing the company's business and who therefore have an intimate understanding of its financial condition and funding needs, to be fully involved in the process.

9.2.4.3 From a shareholder's perspective, however, a regime which gave the directors an unfettered power to allot new shares would be unsatisfactory, because when shares are issued to new investors the existing shareholders' financial stake in, and control of, the company is diluted. Take the case of a company with five shareholders, each of whom holds 20 shares. Each of the shareholders has a 20% stake in the company and any three of them acting together can pass an ordinary resolution. If the directors allot 20 shares each to five new investors, the stake held by each original shareholder falls to 10% (i.e. they still hold 20 shares, but the total number of shares has risen from 100 to 200) and they will not be able to pass an ordinary resolution without the support of at least one of the new investors.

9.2.4.4 The regime does not, therefore, give the directors an unfettered power to act. First, they will in certain cases need specific authorisation from the shareholders before they allot shares. Second, shareholders have a default 'pre-emption right', which entitles them to be offered the right to buy any new shares before they are offered to outside investors.

Shareholder authorisation

9.2.4.5 The law on shareholder authorisation divides companies into two categories:

- **Private companies with only one class of shares, which wish to issue further shares of that class.** Section 550 provides that directors of a private company with only one class of shares may allot new shares of the same class unless the company's articles say otherwise. In other words, they may, subject to the articles, allot such shares without prior shareholder approval. In practice, the articles of many companies whose directors can take advantage of s. 550 are silent on this point (as, indeed, are the model articles for private companies); in many such companies, the directors and the shareholders are the same people, and there is therefore nothing to be gained by restricting the directors' freedom. If, however, the directors and the shareholders are not identical, the shareholders may well want to include a provision in the articles requiring the directors to seek their approval in advance of any allotment.

- **All other companies.** Section 551 provides that the directors of any company other than a private company with only one class of shares which wishes to issue further shares of that class must obtain shareholder authorisation before allotting any new shares. The requirement for prior authorisation thus applies not only to a private company which has more than one class of shares before the allotment, but also to a private company which will have more than one class of shares after the allotment (the requirement for prior authorisation also applies to any allotment by a public company).

    The authorisation must be contained in the company's articles or in an ordinary resolution. (In fact, s. 551(1) states that authorisation may be given in the company's articles or 'by resolution of the company'. According to s. 281(3), the latter expression is to be read as a reference to an ordinary resolution unless the company's articles require a resolution of that type to be supported by more than a bare majority of the shareholders. In practice, many companies' articles are silent on this point.) It must state the maximum amount of shares which the directors are authorised to allot and the date on which the authorisation will expire (provided that an authorisation may not be given for a period of more than five years).

Statutory pre-emption right

9.2.4.6 The law on shareholder authorisation is supplemented by a statutory pre-emption right. Section 561(1) provides as follows:

> 'A company must not allot equity securities to a person on any terms unless –
> (a) it has made an offer to each person who holds ordinary shares in the company to allot to him on the same or more favourable terms a proportion of those securities that is as nearly as practicable equal to the proportion in nominal value held by him of the ordinary share capital of the company, and
> (b) the period during which any such offer may be accepted has expired or the company has received notice of the acceptance or refusal of every offer so made.'

9.2.4.7 The effect of this provision is that even if the directors either have been authorised to allot new shares or, pursuant to s. 550, do not require authorisation, they cannot proceed with an allotment until they have offered the shares to the existing shareholders in proportion to their respective holdings in the company.

9.2.4.8 By way of illustration of the impact of s. 561(1), consider the example of a company which has five shareholders, each of whom owns 20 ordinary shares. If the directors wish to raise money by issuing a further 100 ordinary shares to new investors, they will not need prior shareholder authorisation, because the case falls within the scope of s. 550, but pursuant to s. 561(1) they will be required to offer the new shares to the existing shareholders. Since each of the existing shareholders has a 20% stake in the company, they will each have to be offered 20% of the new shares (i.e. 20 shares). Only if they choose not to take up the offer, whether because they are eager to bring new investors into the company or because they do not have the funds to buy the additional shares, can the directors proceed to allot the shares to the new investors.

9.2.4.9 Given that the statutory pre-emption right is designed to protect shareholders, it is perhaps not surprising that they are free either to strengthen it or to dispense with it.

- **Companies are free to supplement the statutory right in their articles.** The statutory right is subject to several exceptions, the most important of which is that it does not apply if the new shares are to be paid for wholly or partly in non-cash consideration (s. 565). If, for example, the new investor intends to pay for his shares by transferring his business to the company, the shares are not covered by the statutory right and so will not need to be offered to the existing shareholders. One way to supplement the statutory right, therefore, is to provide in the articles that existing shareholders have a pre-emption right in respect of new shares which are to be paid for otherwise than in cash.
- **The Act gives shareholders the power to disapply the statutory right on a temporary basis or exclude it altogether.** In some instances, shareholders may feel that the statutory right is an unnecessary administrative burden. This might be the case if they are also the company's only directors, for example, or if their personal circumstances are such that they will not be able to meet any further funding requests. In recognition of this fact, the Act contains several provisions under which the shareholders can opt to waive the right.

The provisions in question are ss. 567, 569, 570, 571 and 573. Although they are perhaps a little more confusing on first reading than they need to be, they are all based on the notion that a three-quarters majority of the shareholders should be able to waive the statutory right either in relation to a specific allotment or more generally. For example, s. 567 provides that the articles of a private company may exclude the statutory right altogether, although s. 571 provides for the shareholders of a private company or a public company to disapply the right in relation to a specified allotment by means of a special resolution.

9.2.5 Rights attached to shares

9.2.5.1 When a company allots new shares, both the directors and the new shareholder need to know what rights are attached to those shares.

9.2.5.2 Any discussion of the nature of the rights a particular share carries is, however, complicated by the fact that it is for individual companies to decide what rights are attached to their shares.

9.2.5.3 The company law regime provides, by way of a default position, that a share carries the following rights:

- a right to vote on shareholders' resolutions, whether they are presented in the form of a written resolution or at a general meeting (s. 284);
- a right to participate in any dividend that the company chooses to declare (Article 30 of the model articles for private companies); and
- a right, in the event of the company's winding up (and after the company's creditors have been paid), to a return of capital and a share of any surplus assets (*Birch v Cropper, Re The Bridgewater Navigation Co Ltd* (1889) 14 App Cas 525, at 543 (per Lord Macnaghten)).

9.2.5.4 It is by no means uncommon for companies to be content with this default arrangement. Equally, however, many companies adjust and/or supplement these rights in order to meet the needs of their shareholder base. For example, a shareholder who is proposing to take a minority stake in a company which has fallen on hard times might insist that his shares carry enhanced voting rights in respect of a resolution to appoint or remove a director, or that they give him a right to receive a fixed dividend before any dividend is paid to the other shareholders. There are no restrictions on a company's freedom to devise such bespoke arrangements for its shares as it sees fit.

9.2.5.5 In some cases, a company's articles will give it the power to set out the rights attached to different types of shares in an ordinary resolution (see, for example, article 22 of the model articles for private companies). In practice, many companies set out the rights in the articles themselves. (It might be thought that the former option has the advantage of enabling the company to keep this aspect of its internal affairs out of the public eye, given that ordinary resolutions generally do not have to be filed at Companies House. However, this is not the case, because whenever a company allots new shares it is required to send a 'statement of capital' containing details of the rights attached to them to the registrar (s. 555(4)(c)(i) and article 2, Companies (Shares and Share Capital) Order 2009 (SI 2009/388).)

9.2.5.6 Shares which carry the same rights are said to form a class (s. 629) and a company is, again, free to create as many classes of shares as it sees fit.

9.2.5.7 The name of a class of shares may give some indication of the rights which the shares carry. For example, an 'ordinary share' will generally carry the default rights listed in paragraph 9.2.5.3, namely a right to vote, a right to a dividend and, in the event of the company's winding up, a right to a return of capital and a share of any surplus assets, while a 'preference share' will generally confer a right to a fixed dividend, paid before any dividend is paid to the ordinary shareholders, but not a right to vote. However, since even these common names are not defined (save that a broad definition of 'ordinary shares' for the purposes of the provisions on the statutory pre-emption right is included in s. 560(1)), the specific rights attached to a particular company's shares can be identified only by referring to that company's articles or to the resolution of its shareholders in which they are set out. It is perfectly possible, for example, for a company to have preference shares which carry voting rights, or to have two classes of ordinary shares, one of which carries no voting rights.

9.2.5.8 Shareholders of a particular class of shares face the risk that the other shareholders may be able to alter the rights attached to their shares against their will. Consider the case of a company with a class of ordinary shares which confer a right to vote and a class of preference shares which do not. If the preference shareholders' right to a fixed dividend, say, could be altered simply by amending the articles by means of a special resolution in accordance with s. 21, the preference shareholders would be in a very vulnerable position: since they have no right to vote, the ordinary shareholders would be free to adjust their rights at any time.

9.2.5.9 The Act addresses this risk by providing in s. 630 that rights attached to a class of shares may be varied only in accordance with any procedure in the company's articles for effecting such a variation or, if there is no such procedure, with (broadly) the consent of three-quarters of the shareholders of the class in question. Two points may be made about the law dealing with the variation of class rights.

- **Section 630 deals with 'the variation of the rights attached to a class of shares'.** The meaning of the phrase 'rights attached to a class of shares' has been given a wide interpretation by the courts, such that it includes not only rights which are attached to specific shares, but also rights which, though not attached to specific shares, are given to a shareholder in his capacity as a shareholder (*Cumbrian Newspapers Group Ltd v Cumberland & Westmorland Herald Newspaper & Printing Co Ltd* [1987] Ch 1). It would, therefore, encompass not only a right to a dividend which is conferred by a particular share, but also a right given to a named shareholder, as long as he remains a shareholder, to appoint a director.
- **Whether the applicable procedure for the variation of class rights is that contained in a company's articles or that contained in s. 630, it will apply only if there has, indeed, been a variation of such *rights*.** In other words, a procedure for the variation of class rights will not be triggered simply because the company's actions, while leaving the rights intact, have adversely affected the shareholders' enjoyment of them (*White v Bristol Aeroplane Co Ld* [1953] Ch 65). An issue of new shares of a particular class, for example, might reduce the voting power of the existing holders of such shares in that they might find themselves out-voted by the holders of the new shares, but it does not vary their right to vote. From the perspective of investors who are proposing to take

shares of a particular class, the solution to this problem is to seek to ensure that the articles provide for their consent to be obtained in as wide a variety of circumstances as possible. They might, for example, provide for consent to be obtained not only for any action which would vary the rights attached to the class, but also for any action which would affect 'the result of exercising those rights' (see *White v Bristol Aeroplane Co Ltd* [1953] Ch 65, at 82 (per Romer LJ)).

9.2.6 Payment for shares

9.2.6.1 When a company allots new shares, the price to be paid per share is a matter to be agreed between the directors and the subscriber. (Although a share is required to have a fixed nominal value, that value does not necessarily bear any relation to the price which the subscriber actually pays). The concept of nominal value is discussed in paragraph 9.2.7.4.

9.2.6.2 There is no requirement that the agreed price must be paid in cash (s. 583 contains a rather broad definition of 'cash consideration'). On the contrary, the Act specifies that shares 'may be paid up in money or money's worth (including goodwill and know-how)' (s. 582(1)). Thus, it is, again, for the directors and the subscribers to decide the form which the payment is to take.

9.2.6.3 Non-cash consideration can, in theory, take any form. It might constitute an asset (such as a vehicle or a business), but equally it might constitute services (such as an agreement by the subscriber to provide consultancy services to the company). Some types of non-cash consideration are not particularly easy to value, and so the directors' power to accept payment otherwise than in cash carries the risk that they might accept consideration which does not properly reflect the value of the shares. Consider the example of a subscriber who has expertise in public relations matters. What is the value of a promise by such a subscriber to 'be on call' for any public relations queries the company might have for a period of 12 months?

9.2.6.4 Given the obvious interest which both shareholders and, albeit perhaps to a lesser extent, creditors have in ensuring that any non-cash consideration is adequate, it might be assumed that the Act imposes restrictions on the circumstances in which companies can accept payment in such a form, and it does, indeed, contain a number of such restrictions as far as allotments by public companies are concerned. For example, public companies are prohibited from accepting certain types of non-cash consideration (such as an undertaking to do work for the company) (s. 585) and, in any case, any non-cash consideration which a public company accepts must be independently valued (s. 593). It does not, however, contain any such restrictions in relation to allotments by private companies.

9.2.6.5 The courts, too, have taken a laissez-faire attitude to this matter. In *Re Wragg, Ltd* [1897] 1 Ch 796 a company's liquidator argued that shares which had been issued as fully paid as part of the company's purchase of a business should not have been so issued, on the basis that the directors (two of whom were also the sellers of the business) had valued the business at considerably more than it was really worth. The suggestion, in other words, was that the directors had accepted non-cash consideration which did not reflect the true value of the shares. The Court of Appeal rejected the liquidator's claim, holding that a court would not enquire into the adequacy of non-cash consideration unless it was plainly illusory. As Lindley LJ put it: 'It has ... never yet been decided that a limited company cannot buy property or pay for services at any price it thinks proper, and pay for them in fully paid-up shares. Provided a limited company does so honestly and not colourably, and provided that it has not been so imposed upon as to be entitled to be relieved from its bargain, it appears to be settled ... that agreements by limited companies to pay for property or services in paid-up shares are valid and binding on the companies and their creditors' ([1897] 1 Ch 796, at 830).

9.2.6.6 In practice, then, if directors of a private company believe, in good faith and on reasonable grounds, that non-cash consideration offered to the company in exchange for an allotment of new shares is adequate, their decision to accept it is unlikely to be susceptible to challenge.

9.2.7 The meaning of 'capital'

9.2.7.1 This section of the handbook considers the meaning of 'capital' as the word is used in connection with the capital maintenance doctrine.

9.2.7.2 The word 'capital' is, in fact, used in a variety of different contexts. References are made, for example, to a company's 'working capital', 'debt capital' and 'share capital'. These expressions have quite different meanings, and 'capital' in the context of the capital maintenance doctrine is *not* an umbrella term which refers to their aggregate.

9.2.7.3 In relation to capital maintenance, 'capital' refers to sums (whether in the form of cash or otherwise) paid to a company in exchange for its new shares.

9.2.7.4 It was noted in paragraph 9.2.6.1 that it is for the directors and the subscriber to agree the price which the latter will pay for new shares in the company. That price may include two components: a sum in respect of the nominal value of the shares and a sum by way of premium.

- **The Act requires every share to have a 'fixed nominal value' (s. 542(1)).** This means that a company must assign a theoretical value to its shares. It is entirely up to a company to decide what that value should be. Some companies opt for a low nominal value (say, £10, £1 or even 1p), while others prefer a much higher value (say, £100 or £1,000).

Whatever the nominal value of a particular company's shares, they must not be allotted at a discount to that value (s. 580(1)). In other words, if a company's shares have a nominal value of, say, £10, the company cannot accept £4 as full payment, in effect writing off the outstanding £6. (It can, however, accept £4 as part payment, on the basis that the shareholder will pay the outstanding £6 in the future.) Partly paid shares are relatively uncommon, and in fact many companies' articles contain a prohibition on issuing shares on a partly paid basis (see, for example, article 21(1) of the model articles for private companies). If a company's articles contain such a prohibition, they will, of course, need to be amended if the company wishes to issue partly paid shares).

If a company allots shares at their nominal value (if, for example, it receives £10 for a share with a nominal value of £10), it is said to be allotting the shares 'at par'.

The aggregate sum received from a company in respect of the nominal value of its issued shares is known as 'share capital'.

- **If the price paid for a share is more than its nominal value, the sum paid over and above the nominal value is known as 'premium'.** Thus, if a share with a nominal value of £10 is allotted for £15, the shareholder is said to pay £10 in respect of the share's nominal value and £5 by way of premium. The fact that the nominal value of a share is fixed means that its nominal value is not affected by its actual value. Thus, in this example, the share's nominal value remains £10.

By way of illustration of the reasons why shares may be allotted at a premium, consider the case of a company which issued 300 shares at their nominal value of £10 each when it was formed in 2010, and assume that the company's business has been successful over the past few years, such that at present it is worth £1 million. If the directors are planning to raise funds through an allotment of shares to a new shareholder on the basis that he will take a 25% stake in the company, they will need to allot 100 shares to him. If they allot those shares to him at par, he will pay just £1000 for a 25% stake in a £1 million business. Although it will be a matter for the directors' discretion as to whether, in all the circumstances, it is appropriate to charge a premium (*Hilder v Dexter* [1902] AC 474, at 480 (per Lord Davey)), in this example it is almost inconceivable that they will agree to allot the shares at par. Instead, their negotiations with the subscriber will probably start from the proposition that he should pay £250,000 for the stake, or £2,500 per share, representing a premium of £2,490 per share.

9.2.7.5 In summary, for these purposes a company's capital consists of the sum of its share capital and any amounts paid to it by way of share premium.

9.2.7.6 It will be apparent from this definition that a loan extended to a company does not affect its capital. Equally, the consideration received by a shareholder who sells his shares to a third party does not affect the company's capital.

9.2.8 The financial assistance prohibition

9.2.8.1 Public companies are subject to a wide-ranging statutory prohibition on giving financial assistance to a person in connection with his acquisition of their shares. The prohibition applies not only to a person who is acquiring the shares, but also to a person who is proposing to do so or has already done so. It is contained in s. 678, subsections (1) and (3) of which provide as follows:

'(1) Where a person is acquiring or proposing to acquire shares in a public company, it is not lawful for that company, or a company that is a subsidiary of that company, to give financial assistance directly or indirectly for the purpose of the acquisition before or at the same time as the acquisition takes place.'

'(3) Where –
  (a) a person has acquired shares in a company, and
  (b) a liability has been incurred (by that or another person) for the purpose of the acquisition,
  it is not lawful for that company, or a company that is a subsidiary of that company, to give financial assistance directly or indirectly for the purpose of reducing or discharging the liability if, at the time the assistance is given, the company in which the shares were acquired is a public company.'

9.2.8.2 In practice, the prohibition has little impact on the activities of private companies. It does, however, prevent:

- a public company which is a subsidiary of a private company from giving financial assistance to a person who acquires shares in the private company (s. 679(1) and (3)); and
- a private company which is a subsidiary of a public company from giving financial assistance to a person who acquires shares in the public company (ss. 678(1) and (3)).

9.2.8.3 The first of these bullet points is relevant to the present discussion of the law governing the allotment of new shares by a private company. Although the prohibition is often discussed in the context of assistance provided to a person who is buying existing shares from a shareholder, it applies equally to an acquisition of new shares from the company (*Re Uniq plc* [2011] EWHC 749 (Ch)), and so it prevents a public company which is a subsidiary of a private company from giving financial assistance to a person who subscribes for new shares in the private company.

9.2.8.4 The statutory provisions are concise, but they are by no means straightforward, and the extensive judicial scrutiny which this area has received over the years has not resulted in a great deal of clarity in the law. As a result, it will not always be obvious whether a planned course of action will breach the prohibition.

9.2.8.5 The consequences of committing a breach are, however, potentially very serious. In the first place, the arrangement which constitutes the giving of assistance will be invalid (*Re Hill & Tyler Ltd (in administration)* [2004] EWHC 1261 (Ch), at [66] and [70]). The Act also imposes a criminal sanction on the company which gives the assistance (in this case, the public company subsidiary) and on any of its directors who are involved in the breach (s. 680). Finally, the directors of both companies may, by implementing the arrangement, have contravened their statutory directors' duties.

9.2.8.6 If directors suspect that the prohibition may be relevant in connection with any allotment of new shares, they should, therefore, be prepared to take legal advice on the matter.

9.3 Taking money out of a company

9.3.1 In the commercial sphere, a shareholder's interest in his company is primarily financial in nature. One way in which he can make money from the company is to sell his shares to a third party. Another way is to extract money from the company itself, and there are various means by which he can do so:

- his shares may confer a right to a portion of the company's profits, in the form of a dividend;
- he can arrange with the company for it to buy his shares – such an arrangement will involve either a share buy-back or the use of redeemable shares;
- the company can reduce its capital in such a way as to return money to him; or
- he can undertake paid work for the company – in smaller companies, in particular, it is common for the shareholders also to be directors, and to withdraw money from the company in the form of directors' remuneration.

9.3.2 The statutory rules which deal with the extraction of money from a company are notoriously elaborate, and anyone who works in this area will need to become familiar with the minutiae of the relevant provisions of the Act. In order to appreciate their scope, however, it is helpful to consider the policy rationale which underpins them. While in part they certainly seek to ensure that shareholders' interests are protected, their overriding aim is to afford creditors a degree of protection. In particular, they have been developed in accordance with the capital maintenance doctrine, which restricts shareholders' freedom to take money out of the company.

9.3.3 The capital maintenance doctrine

9.3.3.1 The capital maintenance doctrine states that a company must not normally return capital to its shareholders. In this context, 'capital' refers to sums (whether in the form of cash or otherwise) paid to a company in exchange for its new shares, whether in respect of their nominal value or by way of a premium (the meaning of 'capital' in the context of the capital maintenance doctrine is discussed in section 9.2.7).

9.3.3.2 What is the impact of the doctrine in practical terms? Consider the case of a company with a single shareholder, who bought 100,000 ordinary shares of £1 each at par upon the company's formation. Since he paid £100,000 to the company in exchange for its new shares, the company's capital is £100,000. If the company's business prospers, such that it makes a profit of £400,000 and so has £500,000 in the bank, the effect of the doctrine is that the shareholder is not normally permitted to take more than £400,000 out of the company. If, on the other hand, the business encounters difficulties, such that it makes a loss of £40,000, leaving it with just £60,000 in the bank, the effect of the doctrine is that the shareholder is not normally permitted to take any money at all out of the company.

9.3.3.3 The rationale for the doctrine can be traced back to the fact that shareholders have the power to limit their liability for the company's debts. Recognising that the principle of limited liability exposes creditors to risk in the event of the company's failure, the company law regime contains various measures designed to afford them a degree of protection, some of which are based on the notion that a company's capital should be regarded as a fund from which creditors can draw if the company cannot pay its debts. Of particular interest for present purposes is the rule that, upon a company's liquidation, its creditors are paid before any assets are distributed to its shareholders (Insolvency Act 1986 ss. 107 and 143), for the capital maintenance doctrine seeks to supplement that rule by ensuring that shareholders are not permitted to deplete the company's capital fund during its lifetime.

9.3.3.4 The doctrine is of long standing, and the following quotations from two well-known cases dating back to the nineteenth century express the courts' view that it forms a cornerstone of the regime's efforts to protect creditors.

> '... there is a statement that the capital shall be applied for the purposes of the business, and on the faith of that statement, which is sometimes said to be an implied contract with creditors, people dealing with the company give it credit. The creditor has no debtor but that impalpable thing the corporation, which has no property except the assets of the business. The creditor, therefore, I may say, gives credit to that capital, gives credit to the company on the faith of the representation that the capital shall be applied only for the purposes of the business, and he has therefore a right to say that the corporation

shall keep its capital and not return it to the shareholders ...' (*Re Exchange Banking Co, Flitcroft's Case* (1882) 21 ChD 519, at 533 (per Jessel MR))

'Paid-up capital may be diminished or lost in the course of the company's trading; that is a result which no legislation can prevent; but persons who deal with, and give credit to a limited company, naturally rely upon the fact that the company is trading with a certain amount of capital already paid, as well as upon the responsibility of its members for the capital remaining at call; and they are entitled to assume that no part of the capital which has been paid into the coffers of the company has been subsequently paid out, except in the legitimate course of its business.' (*Trevor v Whitworth* (1887) 12 App Cas 409, at 423 (per Lord Watson))

9.3.3.5 The doctrine does not place an absolute prohibition on the return of capital to shareholders. While CA2006 does, indeed, ensure that a company may not dip into its capital in order to pay a dividend, it allows private companies to acquire their shares from their shareholders using capital and gives both private and public companies the option of paying out capital to shareholders by means of a formal reduction of capital. In relation both to acquisitions by companies of their own shares and capital reductions, however, the impact of the doctrine is to be found in procedural mechanisms which protect creditors. If a private company wishes to use capital in order to carry out a share buy-back, for example, its directors will generally be required to confirm that, in their view, the company will be able to pay its debts as they fall due over the course of the following year (s. 714).

9.3.4 Dividends

9.3.4.1 The usual means by which shareholders take money out of their company is by arranging for it to pay them a dividend, which is simply a share in its profits.

9.3.4.2 The Act's provisions governing the payment of dividends do not, in fact, use the term 'dividend'. Instead, they refer to a 'distribution', which is defined as, subject to certain exceptions, 'every description of distribution of a company's assets to its members, whether in cash or otherwise' (s. 829(1)), and therefore encompasses, but is not confined to, a dividend.

9.3.4.3 There are various issues to consider in relation to dividends and distributions.

- **Are there are any restrictions on the funds out of which a dividend may be paid?** There is, indeed, a significant restriction, in that the Act provides, in accordance with the capital maintenance doctrine, that a dividend may be paid only out of profits. In other words, a dividend may not be paid out of capital. The relevant statutory provisions as far as private companies are concerned are s. 830(1) and (2) (public companies are subject not only to s. 830, but also to s. 831, which imposes a further restriction on their freedom to pay a dividend, based on the amount of their net assets):

'(1) A company may only make a distribution out of profits available for the purpose.

(2) A company's profits available for distribution are its accumulated, realised profits, so far as not previously utilised by distribution or capitalisation, less its accumulated, realised losses, so far as not previously written off in a reduction or reorganisation of capital duly made.'

The Act specifies that the question as to whether the company has profits which are available for distribution must normally be answered by reference to the company's most recent annual accounts (s. 836(2)). Those accounts should, however, be regarded merely as the starting point in the process of determining whether the company is permitted to pay a dividend. On the one hand, if the accounts would justify the payment of a dividend but the company's financial position has subsequently deteriorated, a dividend may be rendered unlawful by virtue of the underlying common law rule which prohibits the return of capital to shareholders (the common law rule, as outlined by Jessel MR in *Re Exchange Banking Co, Flitcroft's Case* (1882) 21 ChD 519 (see the extract from his judgment in paragraph 9.3.3.4), is preserved by s. 851). On the other hand, if the accounts would not justify the payment of a dividend but the company's financial position has subsequently improved, it will be permitted to pay a dividend if interim accounts show that it has profits available for distribution (ss. 836(2)(a) and 838(1)).

- **Who decides whether a dividend should be paid?** Companies are not obliged to pay a dividend simply because they have distributable profits. Of course, shareholders will normally expect to partake in their company's success if its business is thriving. In *Re a Company (No. 00370 of 1987), ex parte Glossop*, the judge commented as follows: '... it is important to remember that a company is simply a vehicle for carrying on a business for the benefit of all members. One of the major benefits to shareholders, i.e. members, in a company is, or ought to be, the payment of dividends' ([1988] 1 WLR 1068, at 1075D). Indeed, an ongoing failure to pay dividends might even form the basis for an unfair prejudice petition (*Re McCarthy Surfacing Ltd* [2008] EWHC 2279 (Ch), at [83]). There may, nevertheless, be good reasons why, in any given year, a company may decide against paying a dividend. A company which is about to embark upon a major expansion, for example, may well wish to plough its profits back into the business.

The Act does not specify which organ of the company decides whether profits should be distributed, so it is for companies to set out in their articles a framework that meets their needs. In practice, most private companies adopt the relevant provisions in the model articles for private companies (see articles

30 to 35), which place primary responsibility for the payment of dividends in the hands of the board. Specifically, they provide for the decision to pay a dividend to be taken either:
- by the directors themselves, in which case the dividend is known as an 'interim dividend' and must be paid in cash; or
- by the shareholders, who can choose to pay the dividend otherwise than in cash (a dividend paid otherwise than in cash is known as a 'dividend in specie' or a 'distribution in kind'), but have no power to act unless the directors have first made a recommendation as to the amount of the dividend.

- **Can a dividend which was wrongly paid out be recovered?** If a company pays a dividend otherwise than out of distributable profits, it will want to recover the money paid out, either from those who received it (i.e. the shareholders) or from the directors.

Shareholders may be liable to repay a dividend at common law (see *Precision Dippings Ltd v Precision Dippings Marketing Ltd* [1986] Ch 447, at 457–458; a brief analysis of the position at common law can be found in Arden LJ's judgment in *It's a Wrap (UK) Ltd (in liquidation) v Gula* [2006] EWCA Civ 544, at [11]–[12], or under the Act. As far as the latter is concerned, s. 847 provides that a shareholder must repay a dividend if he knows, or has reasonable grounds to believe, that it was paid in contravention of the statutory provisions. Section 847(1) and (2) reads as follows:

'(1) This section applies where a distribution, or part of one, made by a company to one of its members is made in contravention of this Part.

(2) If at the time of the distribution the member knows or has reasonable grounds for believing that it is so made, he is liable –
   (a) to repay it (or that part of it, as the case may be) to the company, or
   (b) in the case of a distribution made otherwise than in cash, to pay the company a sum equal to the value of the distribution (or part) at that time.'

It may be thought, on the basis of the wording of s. 847(1) and (2), that the liability to repay arises only if the shareholder is aware that there has been a breach of the Act, but the courts have taken the view that it is sufficient that the shareholder knows the underlying facts which constitute the breach (*It's a Wrap (UK) Ltd (in liquidation) v Gula* [2006] EWCA Civ 544). In other words, a shareholder who receives a dividend in circumstances in which he knows that the company has no profits will fall within s. 847, even if he does not know that the Act prohibits the payment of a dividend otherwise than out of distributable profits.

A director who participates in the payment of an unlawful dividend is likely to be in breach of his statutory duties. He is also likely to be liable at common law. In *Re Exchange Banking Co, Flitcroft's Case* (1882) 21 ChD

519, the company's directors presented the shareholders with accounts which wrongly showed that the company had distributable profits, and the shareholders proceeded to declare dividends on the basis of those accounts. The Court of Appeal held that the directors were liable not only in respect of the sums which they had received in their capacity as shareholders, but also in respect of the sums which had been paid to the other shareholders. According to Cotton LJ: '... directors are in the position of trustees, and are liable not only for what they put into their own pockets, but for what they in breach of trust pay to others'.

There is no doubt that liability under the common law attaches to a director who knowingly or negligently causes his company to pay an unlawful dividend. Although there is some room for debate as to the position of a director who neither knew of the unlawful nature of the dividend nor was negligent in the matter, the correct analysis seems to be that such a director, too, is liable, although he may be excused under s. 1157 of the Act, which gives the court the power to grant relief in respect of liability for a breach of trust if it feels that the director acted honestly and reasonably (*Holland v Commissioners for Her Majesty's Revenue and Customs* [2010] UKSC 51, at [45]–[47] (per Lord Hope)). In practice, an honest director who participates in the payment of an unlawful dividend will, save in exceptional circumstances, probably find it difficult to persuade a court that he acted with due care.

- **Does every payment made by a company to a shareholder constitute a distribution?** In the context of private companies, it is common for shareholders also to have a seat on the board and to take money out of the company in the form of remuneration for their work as a director. This is unobjectionable in principle and, if the amount of the remuneration reflects the work which the director has undertaken, it will not be regarded as a distribution. Similarly, it is perfectly acceptable for a company to enter into transactions with its shareholders in the ordinary course of its business. A shareholder may, for example, sell a property or a business to the company and, if the amount paid by the company reflects the value of the property or business, the payment will not be regarded as a distribution. (Transactions between a company and a shareholder who is also a director must comply with Chapter 4 of Part 10 of the Act, which specifies that certain types of transactions or arrangements with directors require the prior approval of the shareholders in the form of an ordinary resolution. A 'substantial property transaction' with a director, for example, requires such authorisation (s. 190). Chapter 4 of Part 10 is discussed in paragraph 7.3.15.8.

  What, though, is the position if the company appears to have paid more for the shareholder's goods or services than they are worth? Consider, for example, a scenario in which the company buys stock from a shareholder for £100,000 and then sells it on to customers a few weeks later for just £40,000. Is the £60,000 overpayment regarded as a gratuitous disposition of the company's assets, so as to constitute what is usually described as a 'disguised distribution'?

- The courts have generally adopted a sensible and pragmatic approach to this question, in that they will normally ask themselves whether the transaction in question was an arm's-length agreement in which the parties made a genuine attempt to fix an appropriate price for the goods or services. If it was, they will conclude that the overpayment simply represents a bad bargain on the part of the company and does not constitute a disguised distribution.
- The position may be different in relation to agreements concerning directors' pay, for the Supreme Court has indicated that any element of overpayment in that context will be regarded as a disguised distribution, and so will be unlawful unless it is paid out of distributable profits (*Progress Property Company Ltd v Moorgarth Group Ltd* [2010] UKSC 55, at [28] (per Lord Walker)). Whether or not this approach is sound in principle (it is unclear why, as a matter of principle, arrangements concerning directors' remuneration should be treated any differently from other arrangements with shareholders), it should, on the face of it, concern companies. In practice, however, the courts' instinctive reluctance to interfere in commercial decisions is such that it is very unlikely that any genuine attempt to set a director's pay at a sensible level will be disturbed.

The impact of the rules in this difficult area of the law may be illustrated by reference to the decisions in three well-known cases.
- In *Re Halt Garage (1964) Ltd* [1982] 3 All ER 1016, the High Court held that a portion of the remuneration paid to a shareholder in her capacity as a director was a disguised distribution. She was too ill to participate in the management of the company's business, and the judge felt that, in setting the level of her pay, the company had been seeking not genuinely to reward her for services which she rendered as a director, but rather to distribute money to her in her capacity as a co-owner of the business.
- In *Aveling Barford Ltd v Perion Ltd* (1989) 5 BCC 677, the facts, broadly, were that a company sold a property to its shareholder for £350,000 in February 1987 and the shareholder sold the property to a third party for £1.5 million six months later. The High Court concluded that the sale to the shareholder was known and intended to be at an undervalue, and was therefore a disguised distribution.
- In *Progress Property Company Ltd v Moorgarth Group Ltd* [2010] UKSC 55, a company sold shares to (in effect) a shareholder for a sum which may have represented a considerable undervalue. This scenario bears a superficial resemblance to the scenario in *Aveling Barford Ltd v Perion Ltd*, but the crucial difference between the two cases is that the sale in *Progress Property Company Ltd v Moorgarth Group Ltd* was found to be 'a genuine commercial sale' which, the parties believed, reflected the market value of the shares. As a result, according to the Supreme Court, it did not fall to be characterised as a disguised distribution.

9.3.5 Acquisition by a company of its own shares

9.3.5.1 It was noted earlier in this chapter that one means by which a shareholder can realise his investment in a company is to sell his shares to a third party. However, whereas a shareholder in a listed company will generally find a ready market for any shares which he wishes to sell, a shareholder in a private company is likely to be in a very different position. An investor who wishes to divest himself of a small stake in a local business, for example, may well struggle to find a buyer, whether from among his fellow shareholders or from among his family, friends and business contacts.

9.3.5.2 One solution to this problem is to allow a company to buy its own shares from its shareholders, and the Act does, indeed, permit it to do so in certain circumstances. The mechanisms by which such an acquisition can be effected are shaped by the capital maintenance doctrine, in that they ensure either that the acquisition does not materially affect the company's capital or, if the company's capital is affected, that creditors' interests are protected.

9.3.5.3 Under the Act, a company can acquire its own shares in two ways: by redeeming them or by purchasing them. A purchase by a company of its own shares is known as a share buy-back.

9.3.5.4 The conceptual difference between a redemption and a buy-back is that whereas a redemption involves the acquisition of shares which the parties contemplated at the outset would eventually be returned to the company (in that they were issued as redeemable shares), a buy-back involves an acquisition which is agreed upon by the parties at some date after the issue of the shares. It may be said, therefore, that a redemption involves a pre-planned acquisition by the company, while a buy-back involves an acquisition on an ad hoc basis.

9.3.5.5 The law on share redemptions and buy-backs is set out mainly in the Act. The core provisions, which are contained in Chapters 3, 4 and 5 of Part 18 (comprising ss. 684 to 723), are detailed and prescriptive, but it is vital that they are adhered to strictly, for a failure to comply with them not only renders the acquisition void, but also constitutes a criminal offence on the part of the company and on any director who was in default (s. 658).

9.3.5.6 The Act treats private companies and public companies differently in certain important respects. The following discussion considers the position of private companies.

Redeemable shares

9.3.5.7 A private company is permitted to issue redeemable shares unless its articles say otherwise (s. 684(1) and (2). For these purposes, a 'redeemable share' is a share which either:

- will be redeemed; or
- may be redeemed at the option of the company or the shareholder (s. 684(1)).

9.3.5.8 The terms, conditions and manner of redemption of the shares must be set out in the company's articles or, if they are authorised to do so by the articles or a shareholders' resolution, determined by the directors (s. 685).

A private company is permitted to finance a redemption out of:

- **Distributable profits (s. 687(2)(a)).** Once the shares have been redeemed, they are treated as cancelled (s. 688). Although the cancellation of the shares necessarily reduces the company's capital, the company is required to compensate for the reduction by transferring an equivalent amount to a 'capital redemption reserve', which is treated as capital (s. 733(2) and (6). The effect, therefore, of redeeming shares out of distributable profits is that the company's capital remains intact, in accordance with the spirit of the capital maintenance doctrine.
- **The proceeds of a fresh issue of shares (s. 687(2)(b).** Here, again, the shares, once they have been redeemed, are treated as cancelled (s. 688). However, since they have been replaced by new shares, the level of the company's capital has not been affected unless the capital represented by the new shares is, in fact, less than the capital represented by the redeemed shares, in which case the amount of the difference must be transferred to the capital redemption reserve (unless that amount is made up by a payment out of capital) (s. 733(3)). In either case, the end result is that, in effect, the company's capital remains intact.
- **Out of capital (s. 687(1) and 709(1)).** Unless its articles say otherwise, a private company can use capital to fund all or part of a redemption (s. 709(1)), provided that it must first apply towards the redemption payment any available distributable profits and the proceeds of any fresh issue of shares (s. 710(1)).

  A payment out of capital (described in the Act as a 'permissible capital payment') (s. 710(2)) may be made only if certain stringent conditions designed to protect the interests of shareholders and creditors are met (s. 713). The conditions are that:

  (a) The directors must make a statement setting out the proposed amount of the permissible capital payment and expressing their opinion that the company will be able to pay its debts as they fall due over the course of the following year (s. 714).

The statement, which must be signed by each of the directors (article 5, Companies (Shares and Share Capital) Order 2009 (SI 2009/388)) and accompanied by an auditor's report, must not be given lightly. If the directors' opinion as to the company's ability to pay its debts is not based on reasonable grounds, they commit a criminal offence (s. 715) and may have to contribute to the company's assets in the event that it is wound up within a year of the date of the payment out of capital (Insolvency Act 1986 s. 76).

The statement and the auditor's report must be made available for inspection by the company's shareholders and creditors (s. 720).

(b) The shareholders must, within a week of the date of the directors' statement, approve the payment out of capital by means of a special resolution (s. 716).

(c) The company must, within a week of the date of the special resolution approving the payment out of capital, publish a notice of the proposed payment in the *Gazette* (The *Gazette* is the official public record of statutory notices; its website, which provides details of the means by which a notice may be published in it, is www.thegazette.co.uk) and either also publish a notice in an appropriate newspaper or send a notice to each of its creditors (s. 719).

The notice must contain details of the proposed payment, state where the directors' statement and auditor's report may be inspected and alert the company's creditors to their right to apply to the court to prevent the payment.

The creditors' right to apply to the court is contained in s. 721. (It is also open to any shareholder who did not support the special resolution to apply to the court under that section.)

Assuming the conditions are met, the payment out of capital must be made in a specified window, namely the period between five and seven weeks after the date of the special resolution (s. 723). Once the shares have been redeemed, they are treated as cancelled (s. 688).

Not surprisingly, the Act does not require an amount corresponding to the reduction of the company's capital caused by the cancellation of the shares to be transferred to the capital redemption reserve (unless the sum of the permissible capital payment and the proceeds of any fresh issue of shares is less than the capital represented by the redeemed shares, in which case the amount of the difference must be transferred to the reserve) (s. 734). The rationale for allowing the capital maintenance doctrine to be compromised in this way is that the statutory procedure is designed to ensure that creditors' interests are adequately protected.

Share buy-backs

9.3.5.9 The rules governing share buy-backs are modified in relation to a buy-back which is carried out in connection with an employees' share scheme. An examination of the modified rules is beyond the scope of this handbook.

9.3.5.10 A private company may carry out a share buy-back if its articles do not say otherwise (s. 690) and if the terms of the purchase have been approved in advance by its shareholders in the form of an ordinary resolution (ss. 693 and 694).

9.3.5.11 The following discussion of the means by which a private company may finance a buy-back reflects minor amendments to the law in this area which were introduced by the Companies Act 2006 (Amendment of Part 18) Regulations 2015 (SI 2015/532) with effect from 6 April 2015.

9.3.5.12 A private company is permitted to finance a buy-back out of:

- **Distributable profits (s. 692(2)(a)(i)).** Once the shares have been purchased, they are treated as cancelled (s. 706(b)) (unless the company opts to hold them in treasury). (If a company funds a buy-back out of distributable profits, it can elect to hold the shares in question itself, in which case they are not treated as cancelled. Shares which are held in this way are said to be held 'in treasury'. If the company anticipates that it will need to issue shares in the near future, it may be more efficient to hold shares which have been bought back in treasury than to cancel them and issue new shares in due course. Treasury shares are dealt with in Chapter 6 of Part 18 (ss. 724 to 732).) Although the cancellation of the shares necessarily reduces the company's capital, the company is required to compensate for the reduction by transferring an equivalent amount to the capital redemption reserve, which is treated as capital (s. 733(2) and (6). The effect, therefore, of purchasing shares out of distributable profits is that the company's capital remains intact, in accordance with the spirit of the capital maintenance doctrine.
- **The proceeds of a fresh issue of shares (s. 692(2)(a)(ii)).** Once the shares have been purchased, they are treated as cancelled (s. 706(b)). Since they have been replaced by new shares, the level of the company's capital has not been affected unless the capital represented by the new shares is, in fact, less than the capital represented by the purchased shares, in which case the amount of the difference must be transferred to the capital redemption reserve (unless that amount is made up by a payment out of capital) (s. 733(3)). In either case, the end result is that, in effect, the company's capital remains intact.
- **Out of capital (ss. 682(1)and (1ZA) and 709)).** A private company may finance a buy-back out of capital under s. 692(1ZA) or under Chapter 5 of Part 18.

  Under s. 692(1ZA), a private company can carry out a small buy-back out of capital if its articles so provide. Although a company cannot pay out more than the lower of £15,000 and the nominal value of 5% of its share capital under this section, the advantage of using this procedure is that the stringent creditor protection mechanisms imposed in relation to a buy-back out of capital under Chapter 5 do not apply. Of course, the directors will, as always, need to ensure that they are acting in accordance with their statutory duties, and, in particular, will need to bear in mind that they have a specific obligation to act in creditors' interests if the company is approaching insolvency (s. 172(3). This aspect of the statutory duties is discussed in paragraph 7.3.4.21).

All but the smallest buy-backs out of capital will need to be carried out in accordance with Chapter 5. Under that chapter, a private company can, unless its articles say otherwise, use capital to fund all or part of a buy-back (s. 709(1)), provided that it must first apply towards the buy-back payment any available distributable profits and the proceeds of any fresh issue of shares (s. 710(1)) and that it must comply with certain conditions designed to protect the interests of shareholders and creditors (s. 713). A payment out of capital under Chapter 5 is described as a 'permissible capital payment' (s. 710(2)).

The conditions designed to protect shareholders and creditors are as follows:

(a) The directors must make a statement setting out the proposed amount of the permissible capital payment and expressing their opinion that the company will be able to pay its debts as they fall due over the course of the following year (s. 714).

The statement, which must be signed by each of the directors (article 5, Companies (Shares and Share Capital) Order 2009 (SI 2009/388)) and accompanied by an auditor's report, must not be given lightly. If the directors' opinion as to the company's ability to pay its debts is not based on reasonable grounds, they commit a criminal offence (s. 715) and may have to contribute to the company's assets in the event that it is wound up within a year of the date of the payment out of capital (Insolvency Act 1986 s. 76).

The statement and the auditor's report must be made available for inspection by the company's shareholders and creditors (s. 720).

(b) The shareholders must, within a week of the date of the directors' statement, approve the payment out of capital by means of a special resolution (s. 716).

(c) The company must, within a week of the date of the special resolution approving the payment out of capital, publish a notice of the proposed payment in the *Gazette* (The *Gazette* is the official public record of statutory notices; its website, which provides details of the means by which a notice may be published in it, is www.thegazette.co.uk) and either also publish a notice in an appropriate newspaper or send a notice to each of its creditors (s. 719).

The notice must contain details of the proposed payment, state where the directors' statement and auditor's report may be inspected and alert the company's creditors to their right to apply to the court to prevent the payment.

The creditors' right to apply to the court is contained in s. 721. (It is also open to any shareholder who did not support the special resolution to apply to the court under that section.)

Assuming the conditions are met, the payment out of capital must be made in a specified window, namely the period between five and seven weeks after the date of the special resolution (s. 723).

Whether the payment out of capital is made under s. 692(1ZA) or Chapter 5, the shares are treated as cancelled once they have been purchased (s. 706(b)). The Act does not require an amount corresponding to the reduction of the company's capital caused by the cancellation to be transferred to the capital redemption reserve (unless the sum of the payment out of capital and the proceeds of any fresh issue of shares is less than the capital represented by the shares which have been purchased, in which case the amount of the difference must be transferred to the reserve) (s. 734), and a payment out of capital therefore contravenes the capital maintenance doctrine. As has been noted, however, the interests of creditors are protected to a considerable extent by a combination of the general law and the creditor protection mechanisms in Chapter 5.

9.3.6 Reduction of capital

9.3.6.1 The Act contains a mechanism by means of which a company can reduce its capital.

9.3.6.2 The main provisions are in Chapter 10 of Part 17, which comprises ss. 641 to 653, and the essence of the procedure is to be found in s. 641, which is set out in full in Figure 9.1.

Figure 9.1 Text of CA2006 s. 641

Section 641 – Circumstances in which a company may reduce its share capital

'(1) A limited company having a share capital may reduce its share capital –
  (a) in the case of a private company limited by shares, by special resolution supported by a solvency statement (see sections 642 to 644);
  (b) in any case, by special resolution confirmed by the court (see sections 645 to 651).
(2) A company may not reduce its capital under subsection (1)(a) if as a result of the reduction there would no longer be any member of the company holding shares other than redeemable shares.

(3) Subject to that, a company may reduce its share capital under this section in any way.
(4) In particular, a company may –
   (a) extinguish or reduce the liability on any of its shares in respect of share capital not paid up, or
   (b) either with or without extinguishing or reducing liability on any of its shares –
      (i) cancel any paid-up share capital that is lost or unrepresented by available assets, or
      (ii) repay any paid-up share capital in excess of the company's wants.
(5) A special resolution under this section may not provide for a reduction of share capital to take effect later than the date on which the resolution has effect in accordance with this Chapter.
(6) This Chapter (apart from subsection (5) above) has effect subject to any provision of the company's articles restricting or prohibiting the reduction of the company's share capital.
(7) In subsection (1)(b), section 91(5)(b)(iii), sections 645 to 651 (except in the phrase 'sanctioned by the court under Part 26') and 653(1) 'the court' means, in England and Wales, the High Court.'

9.3.6.3 Under Chapter 10, a company may, unless its articles say otherwise (s. 641(6)), reduce its capital 'in any way' (s. 641(3)). Section 641(4) identifies several methods by which a company might choose to reduce its capital – for example, by reducing the shareholders' liability on unpaid shares or returning to shareholders capital which is surplus to its requirements – but the list is non-exhaustive.

9.3.6.4 It will be apparent from the two examples cited above that a capital reduction does not necessarily involve a transfer of funds from a company to its shareholders, but that it can be used to effect such a transfer. By way of an illustration of its utility as a means of taking money out of a company, consider the case of a company which divests itself of surplus cash by cancelling shares or reducing its share premium account and paying the amount by which the capital has thereby been reduced to its shareholders. The use of a capital reduction in this way clearly derogates from the notion that a company must not return capital to its shareholders. As was the case in relation to payments out of capital to fund share redemptions or share buy-backs, however, this contravention of the capital maintenance doctrine is tolerated because the regime incorporates safeguards which seek to protect creditors' interests.

Procedure

9.3.6.5 A private company seeking to carry out a reduction of capital has two options: it can pass a special resolution on the basis of a directors' solvency statement or it can pass a special resolution and then apply for confirmation of the reduction from the court (s. 641(1)). (A public company, by contrast, does not have any choice in terms of the procedure for effecting a reduction. Pursuant to s. 641(1), it may only reduce its capital by passing a special resolution and then applying for confirmation of the reduction from the court.)

- **Solvency statement procedure.** This procedure consists of three steps.
  First, the directors must make a statement of the company's solvency, in which they report, essentially, that, in their opinion, the company will be able to pay its debts as they fall due over the course of the following year (s. 643(1)). The statement, which must be signed by each of the directors (Article 2, Companies (Reduction of Share Capital) Order 2008 (SI 2008/1915)), must not be given lightly, because the directors commit a criminal offence if their opinion is not based on reasonable grounds (s. 643(4)).
  Second, the shareholders must, within 15 days after the date of the directors' solvency statement, pass a special resolution reducing the company's capital (s. 642(1)(a)).
  Third, the company must file the special resolution, the directors' solvency statement and a statement of capital containing certain prescribed information with the registrar within 15 days after the date of the special resolution (ss. 29, 30 and 644(1)). This final step, which might appear to be purely administrative in nature, is, in fact, extremely important, for the reduction will not take effect until the registrar has registered the documents (s. 644(4)). The company has a separate, but related, obligation to file a statement by the directors confirming that their solvency statement was made no more than 15 days before the date of the special resolution (s. 644(5)).
  Although the solvency statement procedure does not provide for any dissenting shareholders or concerned creditors to apply to the court to prevent the reduction, the latter are protected to some extent by the fact that, as noted above, the directors must not make the solvency statement unless they have reason to believe that the company will be able to pay its debts, and both constituencies are protected by the directors' underlying obligation to comply with their general statutory duties.
- **Court confirmation procedure.** In *British and American Trustee and Finance Corporation, Ltd v Couper* [1894] AC 399, a case dating back to the end of the nineteenth century, Lord Macnaghten noted that under the Companies Act 1867 companies had the power to reduce their capital, and proceeded to outline the nature of the court confirmation procedure as follows:
  'The exercise of the power is fenced round by safeguards which are calculated to protect the interests of creditors, the interests of shareholders, and the

interests of the public. Creditors are protected by express provisions. Their consent must be procured or their claims must be satisfied. The public, the shareholders, and every class of shareholders individually and collectively, are protected by the necessary publicity of the proceedings and by the discretion which is entrusted to the Court. Until confirmed by the Court the proposed reduction is not to take effect, though all the creditors have been satisfied.'

The two main aims of the nineteenth century procedure – namely to protect creditors and to protect shareholders – are reflected faithfully in its modern equivalent, which, like the solvency statement procedure, consists of three steps.

First, the shareholders must pass a special resolution reducing the company's capital (s. 645(1)).

Second, the company must apply to the court for an order confirming the reduction (s. 645(1)). When considering whether to make the order, the court will consider the position of both the company's creditors and its shareholders. Creditor protection is built into the statutory procedure, in that the Act provides that the court must not confirm the reduction unless it is satisfied that the debt of every creditor who is likely to be prejudiced by it has been discharged or secured, or that every such creditor has consented to the reduction (s. 648(2)). Shareholder protection is addressed by the common law rule that the court will only confirm a reduction if its treatment of shareholders of the same class (*British and American Trustee and Finance Corporation, Ltd v Couper* [1894] AC 399, at 406 (per Lord Herschell, LC)) and shareholders of different classes (*Scottish Insurance Corporation, Ltd v Wilsons & Clyde Coal Company Ltd* [1949] AC 462, at 486 (per Lord Simonds)) is fair and equitable.

Third, the company must file the special resolution, a copy of the court order confirming the reduction and a statement of capital containing certain prescribed information with the registrar (ss. 29, 30 and 649(1)). The reduction will normally take effect when the registrar registers the court order and the statement of capital (s. 649(3)(b)).

9.3.6.6 It is for the directors to decide whether, in any given case, the company should follow the solvency statement procedure or the court confirmation procedure. From a purely personal perspective, directors may be concerned that they run the risk of committing a criminal offence if they make a solvency statement. On the other hand, they will need to ensure that if they opt for the court confirmation procedure, which is likely to be comparatively expensive and time-consuming, they are not thereby breaching their statutory duties. In particular, they will need to be acting not in their own interests, but in those of the company.

Appendix 1

Prescribed form of memorandum of association

Schedule 1, Companies (Registration) Regulations 2008 (SI 2008/3014)

2008/3014 COMPANIES (REGISTRATION) REGULATIONS 2008

COMPANIES	
Made	*20th November 2008*
Coming into force	*1st October 2009*

The Secretary of State makes the following Regulations in exercise of the powers conferred by sections 8(2), 10(3), 11(2), 103(2)(a), 110(2)(a), 1167 and 1292(1)(a) of CA2006.

1 Citation, commencement and interpretation

(1) These Regulations may be cited as the Companies (Registration) Regulations 2008 and come into force on 1st October 2009.
(2) In these Regulations "the Act" means the Companies Act 2006.

2 Memorandum of association

For the purposes of section 8 of the Act–
(a) the memorandum of association of a company having a share capital shall be in the form set out in Schedule 1; and
(b) the memorandum of association of a company not having a share capital shall be in the form set out in Schedule 2.

Commencement:
1 October 2009 (reg 1(1))

3 Statement of capital and initial shareholdings

For the purposes of section 10(3) of the Act, the statement of capital and initial shareholdings shall contain the name and address of each subscriber to the memorandum of association.

Commencement:
1 October 2009 (reg 1(1))

4 Statement of guarantee

For the purposes of section 11(2) of the Act, the statement of guarantee shall contain the name and address of each subscriber to the memorandum of association.

Commencement:
1 October 2009 (reg 1(1))

5 Form of assent for re-registration of private limited company as unlimited

The form set out in Schedule 3 is the form prescribed for the purposes of section 103(2)(a) of the Act.

Commencement:
1 October 2009 (reg 1(1))

6 Form of assent for re-registration of public company as private and unlimited

The form set out in Schedule 4 is the form prescribed for the purposes of section 110(2)(a) of the Act.

Commencement:
1 October 2009 (reg 1(1))

SCHEDULE 1 COMPANY HAVING A SHARE CAPITAL

Regulation 2(a)
Click here to view a PDF version of this Form.

Commencement:
1 October 2009 (reg 1(1))

SCHEDULE 2 COMPANY NOT HAVING A SHARE CAPITAL

Regulation 2(b)
Click here to view a PDF version of this Form.

Commencement:
1 October 2009 (reg 1(1))

APPENDIX 1

SCHEDULE 3 FORM OF ASSENT FOR RE-REGISTRATION OF PRIVATE LIMITED COMPANY AS UNLIMITED

Regulation 5
Click here to view a PDF version of this Form.

Commencement:
1 October 2009 (reg 1(1))

SCHEDULE 4 FORM OF ASSENT FOR RE-REGISTRATION OF PUBLIC COMPANY AS PRIVATE AND UNLIMITED

Regulation 6
Click here to view a PDF version of this Form.

Commencement:
1 October 2009 (reg 1(1))

EXPLANATORY NOTE

(This note is not part of the Regulations)

The Companies Act 2006 (c.46) makes changes to the form of a company's constitutional documents. The Companies Act 1985 (c.6) and the Companies (Northern Ireland) Order 1986 (S.I. 1986/1032 (N.I. 6)) both require a company to include a substantial amount of information in its memorandum of association and allow a company's constitutional rules to be divided between its memorandum and articles of association. Under the Companies Act 2006 all the constitutional rules will be contained in the articles of association; the memorandum of association will be a much shorter document.

Regulation 2 prescribes the form of the memorandum of association required under the Companies Act 2006. The forms in Schedules 1 and 2 serve the limited purpose of providing evidence of the intention of each subscriber to form a company and become a member of that company and, in the case of a company that is to have a share capital on formation, to take at least one share.

Regulations 3 and 4 prescribe the information required to be contained in the statement of capital and the statement of guarantee to identify each subscriber to the memorandum of association. This is the name and address of each subscriber.

Regulations 5 and 6 prescribe the forms of assent for re-registration of a private limited company as an unlimited company and re-registration of a public company as a private and unlimited company.

Appendix 2

Companies House Form IN01 – Application to register a company (current version as of February 2015)

In accordance with Section 9 of the Companies Act 2006.

IN01
Application to register a company

Companies House

A fee is payable with this form.
Please see 'How to pay' on the last page.

✓ **What this form is for**
You may use this form to register a private or public company.

✗ **What this form is NOT for**
You cannot use this form to register a limited liability partnership. To do this, please use form LL IN01.

For further information, please refer to our guidance at www.companieshouse.gov.uk

Part 1 — Company details

A1 Company name

To check if a company name is available use our WebCHeck service and select the 'Company Name Availability Search' option:

www.companieshouse.gov.uk/info

Please show the proposed company name below.

Proposed company name in full ❶

For official use

→ **Filling in this form**
Please complete in typescript or in bold black capitals.

All fields are mandatory unless specified or indicated by *

❶ **Duplicate names**
Duplicate names are not permitted. A list of registered names can be found on our website. There are various rules that may affect your choice of name. More information on this is available in our guidance booklet GP1 at: www.companieshouse.gov.uk

A2 Company name restrictions ❷

Please tick the box only if the proposed company name contains sensitive or restricted words or expressions that require you to seek comments of a government department or other specified body.

☐ I confirm that the proposed company name contains sensitive or restricted words or expressions and that approval, where appropriate, has been sought of a government department or other specified body and I attach a copy of their response.

❷ **Company name restrictions**
A list of sensitive or restricted words or expressions that require consent can be found in our guidance booklet GP1 at: www.companieshouse.gov.uk

A3 Exemption from name ending with 'Limited' or 'Cyfyngedig' ❸

Please tick the box if you wish to apply for exemption from the requirement to have the name ending with 'Limited', Cyfyngedig' or permitted alternative.

☐ I confirm that the above proposed company meets the conditions for exemption from the requirement to have a name ending with 'Limited', 'Cyfyngedig' or permitted alternative.

❸ **Name ending exemption**
Only private companies that are limited by guarantee and meet other specific requirements are eligible to apply for this. For more details, please go to our website: www.companieshouse.gov.uk

A4 Company type ❹

Please tick the box that describes the proposed company type and members' liability (only one box must be ticked):

☐ Public limited by shares
☐ Private limited by shares
☐ Private limited by guarantee
☐ Private unlimited with share capital
☐ Private unlimited without share capital

❹ **Company type**
If you are unsure of your company's type, please go to our website: www.companieshouse.gov.uk

CHFP000
05/12 Version 5.0

APPENDIX 2

IN01
Application to register a company

A5	**Situation of registered office** ❶	
	Please tick the appropriate box below that describes the situation of the proposed registered office (only one box must be ticked): ☐ England and Wales ☐ Wales ☐ Scotland ☐ Northern Ireland	❶ **Registered office** Every company must have a registered office and this is the address to which the Registrar will send correspondence. For England and Wales companies, the address must be in England or Wales. For Welsh, Scottish or Northern Ireland companies, the address must be in Wales, Scotland or Northern Ireland respectively.

A6	**Registered office address** ❷	
	Please give the registered office address of your company.	❷ **Registered office address** You must ensure that the address shown in this section is consistent with the situation indicated in section A5. You must provide an address in England or Wales for companies to be registered in England and Wales. You must provide an address in Wales, Scotland or Northern Ireland for companies to be registered in Wales, Scotland or Northern Ireland respectively.
Building name/number		
Street		
Post town		
County/Region		
Postcode		

A7	**Articles of association** ❸	
	Please choose one option only and tick one box only.	❸ For details of which company type can adopt which model articles, please go to our website: www.companieshouse.gov.uk
Option 1	I wish to adopt one of the following model articles in its entirety. Please tick only **one** box. ☐ Private limited by shares ☐ Private limited by guarantee ☐ Public company	
Option 2	I wish to adopt the following model articles with additional and/or amended provisions. I attach a copy of the additional and/or amended provision(s). Please tick only **one** box. ☐ Private limited by shares ☐ Private limited by guarantee ☐ Public company	
Option 3	☐ I wish to adopt entirely bespoke articles. I attach a copy of the bespoke articles to this application.	

A8	**Restricted company articles** ❹	
	Please tick the box below if the company's articles are restricted. ☐	❹ **Restricted company articles** Restricted company articles are those containing provision for entrenchment. For more details, please go to our website: www.companieshouse.gov.uk

CHFP000
05/12 Version 5.0

IN01
Application to register a company

Part 2 Proposed officers

For private companies the appointment of a secretary is optional, however, if you do decide to appoint a company secretary you must provide the relevant details. Public companies are required to appoint at least one secretary.

Private companies must appoint at least one director who is an individual. Public companies must appoint at least two directors, one of which must be an individual.

For a secretary who is an individual, go to Section B1; For a corporate secretary, go to Section C1; For a director who is an individual, go to Section D1; For a corporate director, go to Section E1.

Secretary

B1 Secretary appointments ❶

Please use this section to list all the secretary appointments taken on formation.
For a corporate secretary, complete Sections C1-C5.

Title*	
Full forename(s)	
Surname	
Former name(s) ❷	

❶ **Corporate appointments**
For corporate secretary appointments, please complete section C1-C5 instead of section B.

Additional appointments
If you wish to appoint more than one secretary, please use the 'Secretary appointments' continuation page.

❷ **Former name(s)**
Please provide any previous names which have been used for business purposes in the last 20 years. Married women do not need to give former names unless previously used for business purposes.

B2 Secretary's service address ❸

Building name/number	
Street	
Post town	
County/Region	
Postcode	
Country	

❸ **Service address**
This is the address that will appear on the public record. This does not have to be your usual residential address.

Please state 'The Company's Registered Office' if your service address will be recorded in the proposed company's register of secretaries as the company's registered office.

If you provide your residential address here it will appear on the public record.

B3 Signature ❹

I consent to act as secretary of the proposed company named in **Section A1**.

Signature

Signature
X   X

❹ **Signature**
The person named above consents to act as secretary of the proposed company.

CHFP000
05/12 Version 5.0

APPENDIX 2

IN01
Application to register a company

Corporate secretary

C1 Corporate secretary appointments ❶

Please use this section to list all the corporate secretary appointments taken on formation.

Name of corporate body/firm

Building name/number

Street

Post town

County/Region

Postcode

Country

❶ Additional appointments
If you wish to appoint more than one corporate secretary, please use the 'Corporate secretary appointments' continuation page.

Registered or principal address
This is the address that will appear on the public record. This address must be a physical location for the delivery of documents. It cannot be a PO box number (unless contained within a full address), DX number or LP (Legal Post in Scotland) number.

C2 Location of the registry of the corporate body or firm

Is the corporate secretary registered within the European Economic Area (EEA)?
→ Yes Complete **Section C3 only**
→ No Complete **Section C4 only**

C3 EEA companies ❷

Please give details of the register where the company file is kept (including the relevant state) and the registration number in that register.

Where the company/firm is registered ❸

Registration number

❷ EEA
A full list of countries of the EEA can be found in our guidance:
www.companieshouse.gov.uk

❸ This is the register mentioned in Article 3 of the First Company Law Directive (68/151/EEC).

C4 Non-EEA companies

Please give details of the legal form of the corporate body or firm and the law by which it is governed. If applicable, please also give details of the register in which it is entered (including the state) and its registration number in that register.

Legal form of the corporate body or firm

Governing law

If applicable, where the company/firm is registered ❹

Registration number

❹ Non-EEA
Where you have provided details of the register (including state) where the company or firm is registered, you must also provide its number in that register.

C5 Signature ❺

I consent to act as secretary of the proposed company named in **Section A1**.

Signature

Signature
X   X

❺ Signature
The person named above consents to act as corporate secretary of the proposed company.

CHFP000
05/12 Version 5.0

IN01
Application to register a company

Director

D1 Director appointments ❶

Please use this section to list all the director appointments taken on formation. For a corporate director, complete Sections E1-E5.

Title*	
Full forename(s)	
Surname	
Former name(s) ❷	
Country/State of residence ❸	
Nationality	
Date of birth	d d m m y y y y
Business occupation (if any) ❹	

❶ Appointments
Private companies must appoint at least one director who is an individual. Public companies must appoint at least two directors, one of which must be an individual.

❷ Former name(s)
Please provide any previous names which have been used for business purposes in the last 20 years. Married women do not need to give former names unless previously used for business purposes.

❸ Country/State of residence
This is in respect of your usual residential address as stated in section D4

❹ Business occupation
If you have a business occupation, please enter here. If you do not, please leave blank.

Additional appointments
If you wish to appoint more than one director, please use the 'Director appointments' continuation page.

D2 Director's service address ❺

Please complete the service address below. You must also fill in the director's usual residential address in **Section D4**.

Building name/number	
Street	
Post town	
County/Region	
Postcode	
Country	

❺ Service address
This is the address that will appear on the public record. This does not have to be your usual residential address.

Please state 'The Company's Registered Office' if your service address will be recorded in the proposed company's register of directors as the company's registered office.

If you provide your residential address here it will appear on the public record.

D3 Signature ❻

I consent to act as director of the proposed company named in **Section A1**.

Signature: X   X

❻ Signature
The person named above consents to act as director of the proposed company.

CHFP000
05/12 Version 5.0

APPENDIX 2

IN01
Application to register a company

X

This page is not shown on the public record

Do not cover this barcode

D4 Director's usual residential address ❶

Please complete your usual residential address below.

Building name/number	
Street	
Post town	
County/Region	
Postcode	
Country	

❶ **New director's usual residential address**
Please state 'Same as service address' in this section if your usual residential address is recorded in the company's proposed register of director's residential addresses as 'Same as service address'.

You cannot state 'Same as service address' if your service address has been stated in Section D2 as 'The Company's Registered Office'. You will need to complete the address in full.

This address cannot be a PO Box, DX or LP (Legal Post in Scotland) number.

Section 243 of Companies Act 2006

Section 243 exemption ❷

Only tick the box below if you are in the process of applying for, or have been granted, exemption by the Registrar from disclosing your usual residential address to credit reference agencies under section 243 of the Companies Act 2006.

☐

Different postal address:
If you are applying for, or have been granted, a section 243 exemption, please post this whole form to the different postal address below:
The Registrar of Companies, PO Box 4082, Cardiff, CF14 3WE.

Where you are applying for a section 243 exemption with this notice, the application and this form must be posted together.

❷ If you are currently in the process of applying for, or have been granted, a section 243 exemption, you may wish to check you have not entered your usual residential address in Section D2 as this will appear on the public record.

X

CHFP000
05/12 Version 5.0

IN01
Application to register a company

Director

D1 Director appointments ❶

Please use this section to list all the director appointments taken on formation. For a corporate director, complete Sections E1-E5.

Title*	
Full forename(s)	
Surname	
Former name(s) ❷	
Country/State of residence ❸	
Nationality	
Date of birth	d d m m y y y y
Business occupation (if any) ❹	

❶ Appointments
Private companies must appoint at least one director who is an individual. Public companies must appoint at least two directors, one of which must be an individual.

❷ Former name(s)
Please provide any previous names which have been used for business purposes in the last 20 years. Married women do not need to give former names unless previously used for business purposes.

❸ Country/State of residence
This is in respect of your usual residential address as stated in Section D4

❹ Business occupation
If you have a business occupation, please enter here. If you do not, please leave blank.

Additional appointments
If you wish to appoint more than one director, please use the 'Director appointments' continuation page.

D2 Director's service address ❺

Please complete the service address below. You must also fill in the director's usual residential address in **Section D4**.

Building name/number	
Street	
Post town	
County/Region	
Postcode	
Country	

❺ Service address
This is the address that will appear on the public record. This does not have to be your usual residential address.

Please state 'The Company's Registered Office' if your service address will be recorded in the proposed company's register of directors as the company's registered office.

If you provide your residential address here it will appear on the public record.

D3 Signature ❻

I consent to act as director of the proposed company named in **Section A1**.

Signature | Signature
X | X

❻ Signature
The person named above consents to act as director of the proposed company.

CHFP000
05/12 Version 5.0

APPENDIX 2

IN01
Application to register a company

☒

This page is not shown on the public record

|||||||||||||||||||||

Do not cover this barcode

D4   **Director's usual residential address** ❶

Please complete your usual residential address below.

Building name/number	
Street	
Post town	
County/Region	
Postcode	
Country	

❶ **New director's usual residential address**
Please state 'Same as service address' in this section if your usual residential address is recorded in the company's proposed register of director's residential addresses as 'Same as service address'.

You cannot state 'Same as service address' if your service address has been stated in section D2 as 'The Company's Registered Office'. You will need to complete the address in full.

This address cannot be a PO Box, DX or LP (Legal Post in Scotland) number.

Section 243 of Companies Act 2006

Section 243 exemption ❷

Only tick the box below if you are in the process of applying for, or have been granted, exemption by the Registrar from disclosing your usual residential address to credit reference agencies under section 243 of the Companies Act 2006.

☐

Different postal address:
If you are applying for, or have been granted, a section 243 exemption, please post this whole form to the different postal address below:
The Registrar of Companies, PO Box 4082, Cardiff, CF14 3WE.

Where you are applying for a section 243 exemption with this notice, the application and this form must be posted together.

❷ If you are currently in the process of applying for, or have been granted, a section 243 exemption, you may wish to check you have not entered your usual residential address in Section D2 as this will appear on the public record.

☒

CHFP000
05/12 Version 5.0

IN01
Application to register a company

Corporate director

E1 **Corporate director appointments** ❶

Please use this section to list all the corporate directors taken on formation.

Name of corporate body or firm	
Building name/number	
Street	
Post town	
County/Region	
Postcode	
Country	

❶ **Additional appointments**
If you wish to appoint more than one corporate director, please use the 'Corporate director appointments' continuation page.

Registered or principal address
This is the address that will appear on the public record. This address must be a physical location for the delivery of documents. It cannot be a PO box number (unless contained within a full address), DX number or LP (Legal Post in Scotland) number.

E2 **Location of the registry of the corporate body or firm**

Is the corporate director registered within the European Economic Area (EEA)?
→ Yes Complete **Section E3 only**
→ No Complete **Section E4 only**

E3 **EEA companies** ❷

Please give details of the register where the company file is kept (including the relevant state) and the registration number in that register.

Where the company/firm is registered ❸	
Registration number	

❷ **EEA**
A full list of countries of the EEA can be found in our guidance:
www.companieshouse.gov.uk

❸ This is the register mentioned in Article 3 of the First Company Law Directive (68/151/EEC).

E4 **Non-EEA companies**

Please give details of the legal form of the corporate body or firm and the law by which it is governed. If applicable, please also give details of the register in which it is entered (including the state) and its registration number in that register.

Legal form of the corporate body or firm	
Governing law	
If applicable, where the company/firm is registered ❹	
If applicable, the registration number	

❹ **Non-EEA**
Where you have provided details of the register (including state) where the company or firm is registered, you must also provide its number in that register.

E5 **Signature** ❺

I consent to act as director of the proposed company named in **Section A1**.

Signature	Signature
Signature	X X

❺ **Signature**
The person named above consents to act as corporate director of the proposed company.

CHFP000
05/12 Version 5.0

APPENDIX 2

IN01
Application to register a company

Part 3   Statement of capital

Does your company have share capital?
→ **Yes** Complete the sections below.
→ **No** Go to **Part 4 (Statement of guarantee)**.

F1   Share capital in pound sterling (£)

Please complete the table below to show each class of shares held in pound sterling.
If all your issued capital is in sterling, only complete **Section F1** and then go to **Section F4**.

Class of shares (E.g. Ordinary/Preference etc.)	Amount paid up on each share ❶	Amount (if any) unpaid on each share ❶	Number of shares ❷	Aggregate nominal value ❸
				£
				£
				£
				£
			Totals	£

F2   Share capital in other currencies

Please complete the table below to show any class of shares held in other currencies.
Please complete a separate table for each currency.

Currency

Class of shares (E.g. Ordinary/Preference etc.)	Amount paid up on each share ❶	Amount (if any) unpaid on each share ❶	Number of shares ❷	Aggregate nominal value ❸
			Totals	

Currency

Class of shares (E.g. Ordinary/Preference etc.)	Amount paid up on each share ❶	Amount (if any) unpaid on each share ❶	Number of shares ❷	Aggregate nominal value ❸
			Totals	

F3   Totals

Please give the total number of shares and total aggregate nominal value of issued share capital.

Total number of shares	
Total aggregate nominal value ❹	

❶ Including both the nominal value and any share premium.
❷ Total number of issued shares in this class.
❸ Number of shares issued multiplied by nominal value of each share.

❹ **Total aggregate nominal value**
Please list total aggregate values in different currencies separately. For example: £100 + €100 + $10 etc.

Continuation Pages
Please use a Statement of Capital continuation page if necessary.

CHFP000
05/12 Version 5.0

IN01
Application to register a company

F4 Statement of capital (Prescribed particulars of rights attached to shares)

Please give the prescribed particulars of rights attached to shares for each class of share shown in the statement of capital share tables in **Sections F1** and **F2**.

Class of share

Prescribed particulars ❶

❶ **Prescribed particulars of rights attached to shares**

The particulars are:
a. particulars of any voting rights, including rights that arise only in certain circumstances;
b. particulars of any rights, as respects dividends, to participate in a distribution;
c. particulars of any rights, as respects capital, to participate in a distribution (including on winding up); and
d. whether the shares are to be redeemed or are liable to be redeemed at the option of the company or the shareholder and any terms or conditions relating to redemption of these shares.

A separate table must be used for each class of share.

Continuation pages
Please use the next page or a 'Statement of Capital (Prescribed particulars of rights attached to shares)' continuation page if necessary.

CHFP000
05/12 Version 5.0

APPENDIX 2

IN01
Application to register a company

Class of share

Prescribed particulars ❶

❶ **Prescribed particulars of rights attached to shares**

The particulars are:
a. particulars of any voting rights, including rights that arise only in certain circumstances;
b. particulars of any rights, as respects dividends, to participate in a distribution;
c. particulars of any rights, as respects capital, to participate in a distribution (including on winding up); and
d. whether the shares are to be redeemed or are liable to be redeemed at the option of the company or the shareholder and any terms or conditions relating to redemption of these shares.

A separate table must be used for each class of share.

Continuation pages
Please use a 'Statement of capital (Prescribed particulars of rights attached to shares)' continuation page if necessary.

CHFP000
05/12 Version 5.0

IN01
Application to register a company

F5 **Initial shareholdings**

This section should only be completed by companies incorporating with share capital.

Please complete the details below for each subscriber.

The addresses will appear on the public record. These do not need to be the subscribers' usual residential address.

Initial shareholdings
Please list the company's subscribers in alphabetical order.

Please use an 'Initial shareholdings' continuation page if necessary.

Subscriber's details	Class of share	Number of shares	Currency	Nominal value of each share	Amount (if any) unpaid	Amount paid
Name						
Address						
Name						
Address						
Name						
Address						
Name						
Address						
Name						
Address						

CHFP000
05/12 Version 5.0

APPENDIX 2

IN01
Application to register a company

Part 4 — Statement of guarantee

Is your company limited by guarantee?
→ **Yes** Complete the sections below.
→ **No** Go to **Part 5** (Statement of compliance).

G1 Subscribers

Please complete this section if you are a subscriber of a company limited by guarantee. The following statement is being made by each and every person named below.

I confirm that if the company is wound up while I am a member, or within one year after I cease to be a member, I will contribute to the assets of the company by such amount as may be required for:
- payment of debts and liabilities of the company contracted before I cease to be a member;
- payment of costs, charges and expenses of winding up, and;
- adjustment of the rights of the contributors among ourselves, not exceeding the specified amount below.

❶ **Name**
Please use capital letters.

❷ **Address**
The addresses in this section will appear on the public record. They do not have to be the subscribers' usual residential address.

❸ **Amount guaranteed**
Any valid currency is permitted.

Continuation pages
Please use a 'Subscribers' continuation page if necessary.

Subscriber's details

Field	
Forename(s) ❶	
Surname ❶	
Address ❷	
Postcode	
Amount guaranteed ❸	

Subscriber's details

Field	
Forename(s) ❶	
Surname ❶	
Address ❷	
Postcode	
Amount guaranteed ❸	

Subscriber's details

Field	
Forename(s) ❶	
Surname ❶	
Address ❷	
Postcode	
Amount guaranteed ❸	

CHFP000
05/12 Version 5.0

IN01
Application to register a company

Subscriber's details

Forename(s)
Surname
Address

Postcode

Amount guaranteed

Subscriber's details

Forename(s)
Surname
Address

Postcode

Amount guaranteed

Subscriber's details

Forename(s)
Surname
Address

Postcode

Amount guaranteed

Subscriber's details

Forename(s)
Surname
Address

Postcode

Amount guaranteed

Subscriber's details

Forename(s)
Surname
Address

Postcode

Amount guaranteed

❶ Name
Please use capital letters.

❷ Address
The addresses in this section will appear on the public record. They do not have to be the subscribers' usual residential address.

❸ Amount guaranteed
Any valid currency is permitted.

Continuation pages
Please use a 'Subscribers' continuation page if necessary.

CHFP000
05/12 Version 5.0

APPENDIX 2

IN01
Application to register a company

Part 5 Statement of compliance

This section must be completed by all companies.

Is the application by an agent on behalf of all the subscribers?

→ **No** Go to **Section H1** (Statement of compliance delivered by the subscribers).
→ **Yes** Go to **Section H2** (Statement of compliance delivered by an agent).

H1 Statement of compliance delivered by the subscribers ❶

Please complete this section if the application is not delivered by an agent for the subscribers of the memorandum of association.

I confirm that the requirements of the Companies Act 2006 as to registration have been complied with.

❶ **Statement of compliance delivered by the subscribers**
Every subscriber to the memorandum of association must sign the statement of compliance.

Subscriber's signature — Signature ✗ ✗

Subscriber's signature — Signature ✗ ✗

Subscriber's signature — Signature ✗ ✗

Subscriber's signature — Signature ✗ ✗

Subscriber's signature — Signature ✗ ✗

Subscriber's signature — Signature ✗ ✗

Subscriber's signature — Signature ✗ ✗

Subscriber's signature — Signature ✗ ✗

CHFP000
05/12 Version 5.0

IN01
Application to register a company

Subscriber's signature	Signature ✗ ... ✗	**Continuation pages** Please use a 'Statement of compliance delivered by the subscribers' continuation page if more subscribers need to sign.
Subscriber's signature	Signature ✗ ... ✗	
Subscriber's signature	Signature ✗ ... ✗	
Subscriber's signature	Signature ✗ ... ✗	

H2 Statement of compliance delivered by an agent

Please complete this section if this application is delivered by an agent for the subscribers to the memorandum of association.

Agent's name	
Building name/number	
Street	
Post town	
County/Region	
Postcode	
Country	

I confirm that the requirements of the Companies Act 2006 as to registration have been complied with.

Agent's signature	Signature ✗ ... ✗

CHFP000
05/12 Version 5.0

IN01
Application to register a company

Presenter information

You do not have to give any contact information, but if you do it will help Companies House if there is a query on the form. The contact information you give will be visible to searchers of the public record.

Contact name

Company name

Address

Post town

County/Region

Postcode

Country

DX

Telephone

✓ Certificate

We will send your certificate to the presenters address (shown above) or if indicated to another address shown below:
- [ ] At the registered office address (Given in Section A6).
- [ ] At the agents address (Given in Section H2).

✓ Checklist

We may return forms completed incorrectly or with information missing.

Please make sure you have remembered the following:
- [ ] You have checked that the proposed company name is available as well as the various rules that may affect your choice of name. More information can be found in guidance on our website.
- [ ] If the name of the company is the same as one already on the register as permitted by The Company and Business Names (Miscellaneous Provisions) Regulations 2008, please attach consent.
- [ ] You have used the correct appointment sections.
- [ ] Any addresses given must be a physical location. They cannot be a PO Box number (unless part of a full service address), DX or LP (Legal Post in Scotland) number.
- [ ] The document has been signed, where indicated.
- [ ] All relevant attachments have been included.
- [ ] You have enclosed the Memorandum of Association.
- [ ] You have enclosed the correct fee.

! Important information

Please note that all information on this form will appear on the public record, apart from information relating to usual residential addresses.

£ How to pay

A fee is payable on this form.
Make cheques or postal orders payable to 'Companies House'. For information on fees, go to: www.companieshouse.gov.uk

✉ Where to send

You may return this form to any Companies House address, however for expediency we advise you to return it to the appropriate address below:

For companies registered in England and Wales:
The Registrar of Companies, Companies House,
Crown Way, Cardiff, Wales, CF14 3UZ.
DX 33050 Cardiff.

For companies registered in Scotland:
The Registrar of Companies, Companies House,
Fourth floor, Edinburgh Quay 2,
139 Fountainbridge, Edinburgh, Scotland, EH3 9FF.
DX ED235 Edinburgh 1
or LP - 4 Edinburgh 2 (Legal Post).

For companies registered in Northern Ireland:
The Registrar of Companies, Companies House,
Second Floor, The Linenhall, 32-38 Linenhall Street,
Belfast, Northern Ireland, BT2 8BG.
DX 481 N.R. Belfast 1.

Section 243 exemption
If you are applying for, or have been granted a section 243 exemption, please post this whole form to the different postal address below:
The Registrar of Companies, PO Box 4082,
Cardiff, CF14 3WE.

i Further information

For further information, please see the guidance notes on the website at www.companieshouse.gov.uk
or email enquiries@companieshouse.gov.uk

This form is available in an alternative format. Please visit the forms page on the website at www.companieshouse.gov.uk

This form has been provided free of charge by Companies House.

CHFP000
05/12 Version 5.0

Appendix 3

Model articles for private companies limited by shares and model articles for public companies

Schedules 1 and 3, Companies (Model Articles) Regulations 2008 (SI 2008/3229)

(Note: This appendix sets out the model articles in the form in which they were originally published. Article 18(e) of the model articles for private companies limited by shares and article 22(e) of the model articles for public companies were deleted by the Mental Health (Discrimination) Act 2013 with effect from 28 April 2013.)

STATUTORY INSTRUMENTS
2008 No. 3229
COMPANIES

The Companies (Model Articles) Regulations 2008

Made - - - -	16th December 2008
Laid before Parliament	17th December 2008
Coming into force - -	1st October 2009

The Secretary of State makes the following Regulations in exercise of the powers conferred by section 19 of CA2006(a)—

Citation and Commencement

1. These Regulations may be cited as the Companies (Model Articles) Regulations 2008 and come into force on 1st October 2009.

Model articles for private companies limited by shares

2. Schedule 1 to these Regulations prescribes the model articles of association for private companies limited by shares.

Model articles for private companies limited by guarantee

3. Schedule 2 to these Regulations prescribes the model articles of association for private companies limited by guarantee.

Model articles for public companies

4. Schedule 3 to these Regulations prescribes the model articles of association for public companies.

Ian Pearson
Economic and Business Minister,
16th December 2008   Department for Business, Enterprise and Regulatory Reform

APPENDIX 3

SCHEDULE 1   Regulation 2
MODEL ARTICLES FOR PRIVATE COMPANIES LIMITED BY SHARES

INDEX TO THE ARTICLES

PART 1
INTERPRETATION AND LIMITATION OF LIABILITY

1. Defined terms
2. Liability of members

PART 2
DIRECTORS
DIRECTORS' POWERS AND RESPONSIBILITIES

3. Directors' general authority
4. Shareholders' reserve power
5. Directors may delegate
6. Committees

DECISION-MAKING BY DIRECTORS

7. Directors to take decisions collectively
8. Unanimous decisions
9. Calling a directors' meeting
10. Participation in directors' meetings
11. Quorum for directors' meetings
12. Chairing of directors' meetings
13. Casting vote
14. Conflicts of interest
15. Records of decisions to be kept
16. Directors' discretion to make further rules

APPOINTMENT OF DIRECTORS

17. Methods of appointing directors
18. Termination of director's appointment
19. Directors' remuneration
20. Directors' expenses

PART 3
SHARES AND DISTRIBUTIONS
SHARES

21. All shares to be fully paid up
22. Powers to issue different classes of share
23. Company not bound by less than absolute interests
24. Share certificates
25. Replacement share certificates
26. Share transfers
27. Transmission of shares
28. Exercise of transmittees' rights
29. Transmittees bound by prior notices

DIVIDENDS AND OTHER DISTRIBUTIONS
30. Procedure for declaring dividends
31. Payment of dividends and other distributions
32. No interest on distributions
33. Unclaimed distributions
34. Non-cash distributions
35. Waiver of distributions

CAPITALISATION OF PROFITS
36. Authority to capitalise and appropriation of capitalised sums

PART 4
DECISION-MAKING BY SHAREHOLDERS
ORGANISATION OF GENERAL MEETINGS
37. Attendance and speaking at general meetings
38. Quorum for general meetings
39. Chairing general meetings
40. Attendance and speaking by directors and non-shareholders
41. Adjournment
42. Voting: general
43. Errors and disputes
44. Poll votes
45. Content of proxy notices
46. Delivery of proxy notices

VOTING AT GENERAL MEETINGS
47. Amendments to resolutions

PART 5
ADMINISTRATIVE ARRANGEMENTS
48. Means of communication to be used
49. Company seals
50. No right to inspect accounts and other records
51. Provision for employees on cessation of business

DIRECTORS' INDEMNITY AND INSURANCE
52. Indemnity
53. Insurance

PART 1
INTERPRETATION AND LIMITATION OF LIABILITY

Defined terms

1. In the articles, unless the context requires otherwise— "articles" means the company's articles of association;
"bankruptcy" includes individual insolvency proceedings in a jurisdiction other than England and Wales or Northern Ireland which have an effect similar to that of bankruptcy;
"chairman" has the meaning given in article 12;
"chairman of the meeting" has the meaning given in article 39;

"Companies Acts" means the Companies Acts (as defined in section 2 of CA2006), in so far as they apply to the company;
"director" means a director of the company, and includes any person occupying the position of director, by whatever name called;
"distribution recipient" has the meaning given in article 31;
"document" includes, unless otherwise specified, any document sent or supplied in electronic form;
"electronic form" has the meaning given in section 1168 of CA2006;
"fully paid" in relation to a share, means that the nominal value and any premium to be paid to the company in respect of that share have been paid to the company;
"hard copy form" has the meaning given in section 1168 of CA2006;
"holder" in relation to shares means the person whose name is entered in the register of members as the holder of the shares;
"instrument" means a document in hard copy form;
"ordinary resolution" has the meaning given in section 282 of CA2006; "paid" means paid or credited as paid;
"participate", in relation to a directors' meeting, has the meaning given in article 10;
"proxy notice" has the meaning given in article 45;
"shareholder" means a person who is the holder of a share; "shares" means shares in the company;
"special resolution" has the meaning given in section 283 of CA2006; "subsidiary" has the meaning given in section 1159 of CA2006;
"transmittee" means a person entitled to a share by reason of the death or bankruptcy of a shareholder or otherwise by operation of law; and
"writing" means the representation or reproduction of words, symbols or other information in a visible form by any method or combination of methods, whether sent or supplied in electronic form or otherwise.
Unless the context otherwise requires, other words or expressions contained in these articles bear the same meaning as in CA2006 as in force on the date when these articles become binding on the company.

Liability of members
2. The liability of the members is limited to the amount, if any, unpaid on the shares held by them.

PART 2
DIRECTORS
DIRECTORS' POWERS AND RESPONSIBILITIES

Directors' general authority
3. Subject to the articles, the directors are responsible for the management of the company's business, for which purpose they may exercise all the powers of the company.

Shareholders' reserve power
4.—(1) The shareholders may, by special resolution, direct the directors to take, or refrain from taking, specified action.

(2) No such special resolution invalidates anything which the directors have done before the passing of the resolution.

Directors may delegate
5.—(1) Subject to the articles, the directors may delegate any of the powers which are conferred on them under the articles—
   (a) to such person or committee;
   (b) by such means (including by power of attorney);
   (c) to such an extent;
   (d) in relation to such matters or territories; and
   (e) on such terms and conditions;
   as they think fit.
(2) If the directors so specify, any such delegation may authorise further delegation of the directors' powers by any person to whom they are delegated.
(3) The directors may revoke any delegation in whole or part, or alter its terms and conditions.

Committees
6.—(1) Committees to which the directors delegate any of their powers must follow procedures which are based as far as they are applicable on those provisions of the articles which govern the taking of decisions by directors.
(2) The directors may make rules of procedure for all or any committees, which prevail over rules derived from the articles if they are not consistent with them.

DECISION-MAKING BY DIRECTORS

Directors to take decisions collectively
7.—(1) The general rule about decision-making by directors is that any decision of the directors must be either a majority decision at a meeting or a decision taken in accordance with article 8.
(2) If—
   (a) the company only has one director, and
   (b) no provision of the articles requires it to have more than one director, the general rule does not apply, and the director may take decisions without regard to any of the provisions of the articles relating to directors' decision-making.

Unanimous decisions
8.—(1) A decision of the directors is taken in accordance with this article when all eligible directors indicate to each other by any means that they share a common view on a matter.
(2) Such a decision may take the form of a resolution in writing, copies of which have been signed by each eligible director or to which each eligible director has otherwise indicated agreement in writing.
(3) References in this article to eligible directors are to directors who would have been entitled to vote on the matter had it been proposed as a resolution at a directors' meeting.
(4) A decision may not be taken in accordance with this article if the eligible directors would not have formed a quorum at such a meeting.

Calling a directors' meeting

9.—(1) Any director may call a directors' meeting by giving notice of the meeting to the directors or by authorising the company secretary (if any) to give such notice.
  (2) Notice of any directors' meeting must indicate—
   (a) its proposed date and time;
   (b) where it is to take place; and
   (c) if it is anticipated that directors participating in the meeting will not be in the same place, how it is proposed that they should communicate with each other during the meeting.
  (3) Notice of a directors' meeting must be given to each director, but need not be in writing.
  (4) Notice of a directors' meeting need not be given to directors who waive their entitlement to notice of that meeting, by giving notice to that effect to the company not more than 7 days after the date on which the meeting is held. Where such notice is given after the meeting has been held, that does not affect the validity of the meeting, or of any business conducted at it.

Participation in directors' meetings

10.—(1) Subject to the articles, directors participate in a directors' meeting, or part of a directors' meeting, when—
   (a) the meeting has been called and takes place in accordance with the articles, and
   (b) they can each communicate to the others any information or opinions they have on any particular item of the business of the meeting.
  (2) In determining whether directors are participating in a directors' meeting, it is irrelevant where any director is or how they communicate with each other.
  (3) If all the directors participating in a meeting are not in the same place, they may decide that the meeting is to be treated as taking place wherever any of them is.

Quorum for directors' meetings

11.—(1) At a directors' meeting, unless a quorum is participating, no proposal is to be voted on, except a proposal to call another meeting.
  (2) The quorum for directors' meetings may be fixed from time to time by a decision of the directors, but it must never be less than two, and unless otherwise fixed it is two.
  (3) If the total number of directors for the time being is less than the quorum required, the directors must not take any decision other than a decision—
   (a) to appoint further directors, or
   (b) to call a general meeting so as to enable the shareholders to appoint further directors.

Chairing of directors' meetings

12.—(1) The directors may appoint a director to chair their meetings.
  (2) The person so appointed for the time being is known as the chairman.
  (3) The directors may terminate the chairman's appointment at any time.
  (4) If the chairman is not participating in a directors' meeting within ten minutes of the time at which it was to start, the participating directors must appoint one of themselves to chair it.

Casting vote

13.—(1) If the numbers of votes for and against a proposal are equal, the chairman or other director chairing the meeting has a casting vote.

(2) But this does not apply if, in accordance with the articles, the chairman or other director is not to be counted as participating in the decision-making process for quorum or voting purposes.

Conflicts of interest

14.—(1) If a proposed decision of the directors is concerned with an actual or proposed transaction or arrangement with the company in which a director is interested, that director is not to be counted as participating in the decision-making process for quorum or voting purposes.

(2) But if paragraph (3) applies, a director who is interested in an actual or proposed transaction or arrangement with the company is to be counted as participating in the decision-making process for quorum and voting purposes.

(3) This paragraph applies when—
  (a) the company by ordinary resolution disapplies the provision of the articles which would otherwise prevent a director from being counted as participating in the decision-making process;
  (b) the director's interest cannot reasonably be regarded as likely to give rise to a conflict of interest; or
  (c) the director's conflict of interest arises from a permitted cause.

(4) For the purposes of this article, the following are permitted causes—
  (a) a guarantee given, or to be given, by or to a director in respect of an obligation incurred by or on behalf of the company or any of its subsidiaries;
  (b) subscription, or an agreement to subscribe, for shares or other securities of the company or any of its subsidiaries, or to underwrite, sub-underwrite, or guarantee subscription for any such shares or securities; and
  (c) arrangements pursuant to which benefits are made available to employees and directors or former employees and directors of the company or any of its subsidiaries which do not provide special benefits for directors or former directors.

(5) For the purposes of this article, references to proposed decisions and decision-making processes include any directors' meeting or part of a directors' meeting.

(6) Subject to paragraph (7), if a question arises at a meeting of directors or of a committee of directors as to the right of a director to participate in the meeting (or part of the meeting) for voting or quorum purposes, the question may, before the conclusion of the meeting, be referred to the chairman whose ruling in relation to any director other than the chairman is to be final and conclusive.

(7) If any question as to the right to participate in the meeting (or part of the meeting) should arise in respect of the chairman, the question is to be decided by a decision of the directors at that meeting, for which purpose the chairman is not to be counted as participating in the meeting (or that part of the meeting) for voting or quorum purposes.

Records of decisions to be kept
15. The directors must ensure that the company keeps a record, in writing, for at least 10 years from the date of the decision recorded, of every unanimous or majority decision taken by the directors.

Directors' discretion to make further rules
16. Subject to the articles, the directors may make any rule which they think fit about how they take decisions, and about how such rules are to be recorded or communicated to directors.

APPOINTMENT OF DIRECTORS

Methods of appointing directors
17.—(1) Any person who is willing to act as a director, and is permitted by law to do so, may be appointed to be a director—
   (a) by ordinary resolution, or
   (b) by a decision of the directors.
(2) In any case where, as a result of death, the company has no shareholders and no directors, the personal representatives of the last shareholder to have died have the right, by notice in writing, to appoint a person to be a director.
(3) For the purposes of paragraph (2), where 2 or more shareholders die in circumstances rendering it uncertain who was the last to die, a younger shareholder is deemed to have survived an older shareholder.

Termination of director's appointment
18. A person ceases to be a director as soon as—
   (a) that person ceases to be a director by virtue of any provision of CA2006 or is prohibited from being a director by law;
   (b) a bankruptcy order is made against that person;
   (c) a composition is made with that person's creditors generally in satisfaction of that person's debts;
   (d) a registered medical practitioner who is treating that person gives a written opinion to the company stating that that person has become physically or mentally incapable of acting as a director and may remain so for more than three months;
   (e) by reason of that person's mental health, a court makes an order which wholly or partly prevents that person from personally exercising any powers or rights which that person would otherwise have;
   (f) notification is received by the company from the director that the director is resigning from office, and such resignation has taken effect in accordance with its terms.

Directors' remuneration
19.—(1) Directors may undertake any services for the company that the directors decide.
   (2) Directors are entitled to such remuneration as the directors determine—
      (a) for their services to the company as directors, and
      (b) for any other service which they undertake for the company.
   (3) Subject to the articles, a director's remuneration may—

(a) take any form, and
(b) include any arrangements in connection with the payment of a pension, allowance or gratuity, or any death, sickness or disability benefits, to or in respect of that director.

(4) Unless the directors decide otherwise, directors' remuneration accrues from day to day.

(5) Unless the directors decide otherwise, directors are not accountable to the company for any remuneration which they receive as directors or other officers or employees of the company's subsidiaries or of any other body corporate in which the company is interested.

Directors' expenses

20. The company may pay any reasonable expenses which the directors properly incur in connection with their attendance at—
    (a) meetings of directors or committees of directors,
    (b) general meetings, or
    (c) separate meetings of the holders of any class of shares or of debentures of the company, or otherwise in connection with the exercise of their powers and the discharge of their responsibilities in relation to the company.

PART 3
SHARES AND DISTRIBUTIONS
SHARES

All shares to be fully paid up

21.—(1) No share is to be issued for less than the aggregate of its nominal value and any premium to be paid to the company in consideration for its issue.

(2) This does not apply to shares taken on the formation of the company by the subscribers to the company's memorandum.

Powers to issue different classes of share

22.—(1) Subject to the articles, but without prejudice to the rights attached to any existing share, the company may issue shares with such rights or restrictions as may be determined by ordinary resolution.

(2) The company may issue shares which are to be redeemed, or are liable to be redeemed at the option of the company or the holder, and the directors may determine the terms, conditions and manner of redemption of any such shares.

Company not bound by less than absolute interests

23. Except as required by law, no person is to be recognised by the company as holding any share upon any trust, and except as otherwise required by law or the articles, the company is not in any way to be bound by or recognise any interest in a share other than the holder's absolute ownership of it and all the rights attaching to it.

Share certificates

24.—(1) The company must issue each shareholder, free of charge, with one or more certificates in respect of the shares which that shareholder holds.

(2) Every certificate must specify—
- (a) in respect of how many shares, of what class, it is issued;
- (b) the nominal value of those shares;
- (c) that the shares are fully paid; and
- (d) any distinguishing numbers assigned to them.

(3) No certificate may be issued in respect of shares of more than one class.

(4) If more than one person holds a share, only one certificate may be issued in respect of it.

(5) Certificates must—
- (a) have affixed to them the company's common seal, or
- (b) be otherwise executed in accordance with the Companies Acts.

Replacement share certificates

25.— (1) If a certificate issued in respect of a shareholder's shares is—
- (a) damaged or defaced, or
- (b) said to be lost, stolen or destroyed, that shareholder is entitled to be issued with a replacement certificate in respect of the same shares.

(2) A shareholder exercising the right to be issued with such a replacement certificate—
- (a) may at the same time exercise the right to be issued with a single certificate or separate certificates;
- (b) must return the certificate which is to be replaced to the company if it is damaged or defaced; and
- (c) must comply with such conditions as to evidence, indemnity and the payment of a reasonable fee as the directors decide.

Share transfers

26.— (1) Shares may be transferred by means of an instrument of transfer in any usual form or any other form approved by the directors, which is executed by or on behalf of the transferor.

(2) No fee may be charged for registering any instrument of transfer or other document relating to or affecting the title to any share.

(3) The company may retain any instrument of transfer which is registered.

(4) The transferor remains the holder of a share until the transferee's name is entered in the register of members as holder of it.

(5) The directors may refuse to register the transfer of a share, and if they do so, the instrument of transfer must be returned to the transferee with the notice of refusal unless they suspect that the proposed transfer may be fraudulent.

Transmission of shares

27.— (1) If title to a share passes to a transmittee, the company may only recognise the transmittee as having any title to that share.

(2) A transmittee who produces such evidence of entitlement to shares as the directors may properly require—
- (a) may, subject to the articles, choose either to become the holder of those shares or to have them transferred to another person, and
- (b) subject to the articles, and pending any transfer of the shares to another person, has the same rights as the holder had.

(3) But transmittees do not have the right to attend or vote at a general meeting, or agree to a proposed written resolution, in respect of shares to which they are entitled, by reason of the holder's death or bankruptcy or otherwise, unless they become the holders of those shares.

Exercise of transmittees' rights
28.—(1) Transmittees who wish to become the holders of shares to which they have become entitled must notify the company in writing of that wish.
  (2) If the transmittee wishes to have a share transferred to another person, the transmittee must execute an instrument of transfer in respect of it.
  (3) Any transfer made or executed under this article is to be treated as if it were made or executed by the person from whom the transmittee has derived rights in respect of the share, and as if the event which gave rise to the transmission had not occurred.

Transmittees bound by prior notices
29. If a notice is given to a shareholder in respect of shares and a transmittee is entitled to those shares, the transmittee is bound by the notice if it was given to the shareholder before the transmittee's name has been entered in the register of members.

DIVIDENDS AND OTHER DISTRIBUTIONS

Procedure for declaring dividends
30.—(1) The company may by ordinary resolution declare dividends, and the directors may decide to pay interim dividends.
  (2) A dividend must not be declared unless the directors have made a recommendation as to its amount. Such a dividend must not exceed the amount recommended by the directors.
  (3) No dividend may be declared or paid unless it is in accordance with shareholders' respective rights.
  (4) Unless the shareholders' resolution to declare or directors' decision to pay a dividend, or the terms on which shares are issued, specify otherwise, it must be paid by reference to each shareholder's holding of shares on the date of the resolution or decision to declare or pay it.
  (5) If the company's share capital is divided into different classes, no interim dividend may be paid on shares carrying deferred or non-preferred rights if, at the time of payment, any preferential dividend is in arrear.
  (6) The directors may pay at intervals any dividend payable at a fixed rate if it appears to them that the profits available for distribution justify the payment.
  (7) If the directors act in good faith, they do not incur any liability to the holders of shares conferring preferred rights for any loss they may suffer by the lawful payment of an interim dividend on shares with deferred or non-preferred rights.

Payment of dividends and other distributions
31.—(1) Where a dividend or other sum which is a distribution is payable in respect of a share, it must be paid by one or more of the following means—

(a) transfer to a bank or building society account specified by the distribution recipient either in writing or as the directors may otherwise decide;
(b) sending a cheque made payable to the distribution recipient by post to the distribution recipient at the distribution recipient's registered address (if the distribution recipient is a holder of the share), or (in any other case) to an address specified by the distribution recipient either in writing or as the directors may otherwise decide;
(c) sending a cheque made payable to such person by post to such person at such address as the distribution recipient has specified either in writing or as the directors may otherwise decide; or
(d) any other means of payment as the directors agree with the distribution recipient either in writing or by such other means as the directors decide.
(2) In the articles, "the distribution recipient" means, in respect of a share in respect of which a dividend or other sum is payable—
(a) the holder of the share; or
(b) if the share has two or more joint holders, whichever of them is named first in the register of members; or
(c) if the holder is no longer entitled to the share by reason of death or bankruptcy, or otherwise by operation of law, the transmittee.

No interest on distributions

32. The company may not pay interest on any dividend or other sum payable in respect of a share unless otherwise provided by—
(a) the terms on which the share was issued, or
(b) the provisions of another agreement between the holder of that share and the company.

Unclaimed distributions

33.—(1) All dividends or other sums which are—
(a) payable in respect of shares, and
(b) unclaimed after having been declared or become payable, may be invested or otherwise made use of by the directors for the benefit of the company until claimed.
(2) The payment of any such dividend or other sum into a separate account does not make the company a trustee in respect of it.
(3) If—
(a) twelve years have passed from the date on which a dividend or other sum became due for payment, and
(b) the distribution recipient has not claimed it, the distribution recipient is no longer entitled to that dividend or other sum and it ceases to remain owing by the company.

Non-cash distributions

34.—(1) Subject to the terms of issue of the share in question, the company may, by ordinary resolution on the recommendation of the directors, decide to pay all or part of a dividend or other distribution payable in respect of a share by transferring non-cash assets of equivalent value (including, without limitation, shares or other securities in any company).

(2) For the purposes of paying a non-cash distribution, the directors may make whatever arrangements they think fit, including, where any difficulty arises regarding the distribution—
(a) fixing the value of any assets;
(b) paying cash to any distribution recipient on the basis of that value in order to adjust the rights of recipients; and
(c) vesting any assets in trustees.

Waiver of distributions

35. Distribution recipients may waive their entitlement to a dividend or other distribution payable in respect of a share by giving the company notice in writing to that effect, but if—
(a) the share has more than one holder, or
(b) more than one person is entitled to the share, whether by reason of the death or bankruptcy of one or more joint holders, or otherwise, the notice is not effective unless it is expressed to be given, and signed, by all the holders or persons otherwise entitled to the share.

CAPITALISATION OF PROFITS

Authority to capitalise and appropriation of capitalised sums

36.— (1) Subject to the articles, the directors may, if they are so authorised by an ordinary resolution—
(a) decide to capitalise any profits of the company (whether or not they are available for distribution) which are not required for paying a preferential dividend, or any sum standing to the credit of the company's share premium account or capital redemption reserve; and
(b) appropriate any sum which they so decide to capitalise (a "capitalised sum") to the persons who would have been entitled to it if it were distributed by way of dividend (the "persons entitled") and in the same proportions.
(2) Capitalised sums must be applied—
(a) on behalf of the persons entitled, and
(b) in the same proportions as a dividend would have been distributed to them.
(3) Any capitalised sum may be applied in paying up new shares of a nominal amount equal to the capitalised sum which are then allotted credited as fully paid to the persons entitled or as they may direct.
(4) A capitalised sum which was appropriated from profits available for distribution may be applied in paying up new debentures of the company which are then allotted credited as fully paid to the persons entitled or as they may direct.
(5) Subject to the articles the directors may—
(a) apply capitalised sums in accordance with paragraphs (3) and (4) partly in one way and partly in another;
(b) make such arrangements as they think fit to deal with shares or debentures becoming distributable in fractions under this article (including the issuing of fractional certificates or the making of cash payments); and
(c) authorise any person to enter into an agreement with the company on behalf of all the persons entitled which is binding on them in respect of the allotment of shares and debentures to them under this article.

PART 4
DECISION-MAKING BY SHAREHOLDERS
ORGANISATION OF GENERAL MEETINGS

Attendance and speaking at general meetings

37.—(1) A person is able to exercise the right to speak at a general meeting when that person is in a position to communicate to all those attending the meeting, during the meeting, any information or opinions which that person has on the business of the meeting.
(2) A person is able to exercise the right to vote at a general meeting when—
  (a) that person is able to vote, during the meeting, on resolutions put to the vote at the meeting, and
  (b) that person's vote can be taken into account in determining whether or not such resolutions are passed at the same time as the votes of all the other persons attending the meeting.
(3) The directors may make whatever arrangements they consider appropriate to enable those attending a general meeting to exercise their rights to speak or vote at it.
(4) In determining attendance at a general meeting, it is immaterial whether any two or more members attending it are in the same place as each other.
(5) Two or more persons who are not in the same place as each other attend a general meeting if their circumstances are such that if they have (or were to have) rights to speak and vote at that meeting, they are (or would be) able to exercise them.

Quorum for general meetings

38. No business other than the appointment of the chairman of the meeting is to be transacted at a general meeting if the persons attending it do not constitute a quorum.

Chairing general meetings

39.—(1) If the directors have appointed a chairman, the chairman shall chair general meetings if present and willing to do so.
(2) If the directors have not appointed a chairman, or if the chairman is unwilling to chair the meeting or is not present within ten minutes of the time at which a meeting was due to start—
  (a) the directors present, or
  (b) (if no directors are present), the meeting, must appoint a director or shareholder to chair the meeting, and the appointment of the chairman of the meeting must be the first business of the meeting.
(3) The person chairing a meeting in accordance with this article is referred to as "the chairman of the meeting".

Attendance and speaking by directors and non-shareholders

40.—(1) Directors may attend and speak at general meetings, whether or not they are shareholders.
(2) The chairman of the meeting may permit other persons who are not—
  (a) shareholders of the company, or
  (b) otherwise entitled to exercise the rights of shareholders in relation to general meetings, to attend and speak at a general meeting.

Adjournment

41.—(1) If the persons attending a general meeting within half an hour of the time at which the meeting was due to start do not constitute a quorum, or if during a meeting a quorum ceases to be present, the chairman of the meeting must adjourn it.

(2) The chairman of the meeting may adjourn a general meeting at which a quorum is present if—

(a) the meeting consents to an adjournment, or

(b) it appears to the chairman of the meeting that an adjournment is necessary to protect the safety of any person attending the meeting or ensure that the business of the meeting is conducted in an orderly manner.

(3) The chairman of the meeting must adjourn a general meeting if directed to do so by the meeting.

(4) When adjourning a general meeting, the chairman of the meeting must—

(a) either specify the time and place to which it is adjourned or state that it is to continue at a time and place to be fixed by the directors, and

(b) have regard to any directions as to the time and place of any adjournment which have been given by the meeting.

(5) If the continuation of an adjourned meeting is to take place more than 14 days after it was adjourned, the company must give at least 7 clear days' notice of it (that is, excluding the day of the adjourned meeting and the day on which the notice is given)—

(a) to the same persons to whom notice of the company's general meetings is required to be given, and

(b) containing the same information which such notice is required to contain.

(6) No business may be transacted at an adjourned general meeting which could not properly have been transacted at the meeting if the adjournment had not taken place.

VOTING AT GENERAL MEETINGS

Voting: general

42. A resolution put to the vote of a general meeting must be decided on a show of hands unless a poll is duly demanded in accordance with the articles.

Errors and disputes

43.—(1) No objection may be raised to the qualification of any person voting at a general meeting except at the meeting or adjourned meeting at which the vote objected to is tendered, and every vote not disallowed at the meeting is valid.

(2) Any such objection must be referred to the chairman of the meeting, whose decision is final.

Poll votes

44.—(1) A poll on a resolution may be demanded—

(a) in advance of the general meeting where it is to be put to the vote, or

(b) at a general meeting, either before a show of hands on that resolution or immediately after the result of a show of hands on that resolution is declared.

(2) A poll may be demanded by—
- (a) the chairman of the meeting;
- (b) the directors;
- (c) two or more persons having the right to vote on the resolution; or
- (d) a person or persons representing not less than one tenth of the total voting rights of all the shareholders having the right to vote on the resolution.

(3) A demand for a poll may be withdrawn if—
- (a) the poll has not yet been taken, and
- (b) the chairman of the meeting consents to the withdrawal.

(4) Polls must be taken immediately and in such manner as the chairman of the meeting directs.

Content of proxy notices

45.— (1) Proxies may only validly be appointed by a notice in writing (a "proxy notice") which—
- (a) states the name and address of the shareholder appointing the proxy;
- (b) identifies the person appointed to be that shareholder's proxy and the general meeting in relation to which that person is appointed;
- (c) is signed by or on behalf of the shareholder appointing the proxy, or is authenticated in such manner as the directors may determine; and
- (d) is delivered to the company in accordance with the articles and any instructions contained in the notice of the general meeting to which they relate.

(2) The company may require proxy notices to be delivered in a particular form, and may specify different forms for different purposes.

(3) Proxy notices may specify how the proxy appointed under them is to vote (or that the proxy is to abstain from voting) on one or more resolutions.

(4) Unless a proxy notice indicates otherwise, it must be treated as—
- (a) allowing the person appointed under it as a proxy discretion as to how to vote on any ancillary or procedural resolutions put to the meeting, and
- (b) appointing that person as a proxy in relation to any adjournment of the general meeting to which it relates as well as the meeting itself.

Delivery of proxy notices

46.— (1) A person who is entitled to attend, speak or vote (either on a show of hands or on a poll) at a general meeting remains so entitled in respect of that meeting or any adjournment of it, even though a valid proxy notice has been delivered to the company by or on behalf of that person.

(2) An appointment under a proxy notice may be revoked by delivering to the company a notice in writing given by or on behalf of the person by whom or on whose behalf the proxy notice was given.

(3) A notice revoking a proxy appointment only takes effect if it is delivered before the start of the meeting or adjourned meeting to which it relates.

(4) If a proxy notice is not executed by the person appointing the proxy, it must be accompanied by written evidence of the authority of the person who executed it to execute it on the appointor's behalf.

Amendments to resolutions

47.—(1) An ordinary resolution to be proposed at a general meeting may be amended by ordinary resolution if—
  (a) notice of the proposed amendment is given to the company in writing by a person entitled to vote at the general meeting at which it is to be proposed not less than 48 hours before the meeting is to take place (or such later time as the chairman of the meeting may determine), and
  (b) the proposed amendment does not, in the reasonable opinion of the chairman of the meeting, materially alter the scope of the resolution.
(2) A special resolution to be proposed at a general meeting may be amended by ordinary resolution, if—
  (a) the chairman of the meeting proposes the amendment at the general meeting at which the resolution is to be proposed, and
  (b) the amendment does not go beyond what is necessary to correct a grammatical or other non-substantive error in the resolution.
(3) If the chairman of the meeting, acting in good faith, wrongly decides that an amendment to a resolution is out of order, the chairman's error does not invalidate the vote on that resolution.

PART 5
ADMINISTRATIVE ARRANGEMENTS

Means of communication to be used

48.—(1) Subject to the articles, anything sent or supplied by or to the company under the articles may be sent or supplied in any way in which CA2006 provides for documents or information which are authorised or required by any provision of that Act to be sent or supplied by or to the company.
(2) Subject to the articles, any notice or document to be sent or supplied to a director in connection with the taking of decisions by directors may also be sent or supplied by the means by which that director has asked to be sent or supplied with such notices or documents for the time being.
(3) A director may agree with the company that notices or documents sent to that director in a particular way are to be deemed to have been received within a specified time of their being sent, and for the specified time to be less than 48 hours.

Company seals

49.—(1) Any common seal may only be used by the authority of the directors.
(2) The directors may decide by what means and in what form any common seal is to be used.
(3) Unless otherwise decided by the directors, if the company has a common seal and it is affixed to a document, the document must also be signed by at least one authorised person in the presence of a witness who attests the signature.
(4) For the purposes of this article, an authorised person is—
  (a) any director of the company;
  (b) the company secretary (if any); or
  (c) any person authorised by the directors for the purpose of signing documents to which the common seal is applied.

APPENDIX 3

No right to inspect accounts and other records

50. Except as provided by law or authorised by the directors or an ordinary resolution of the company, no person is entitled to inspect any of the company's accounting or other records or documents merely by virtue of being a shareholder.

Provision for employees on cessation of business

51. The directors may decide to make provision for the benefit of persons employed or formerly employed by the company or any of its subsidiaries (other than a director or former director or shadow director) in connection with the cessation or transfer to any person of the whole or part of the undertaking of the company or that subsidiary.

DIRECTORS' INDEMNITY AND INSURANCE

Indemnity

52.—(1) Subject to paragraph (2), a relevant director of the company or an associated company may be indemnified out of the company's assets against—
  (a) any liability incurred by that director in connection with any negligence, default, breach of duty or breach of trust in relation to the company or an associated company,
  (b) any liability incurred by that director in connection with the activities of the company or an associated company in its capacity as a trustee of an occupational pension scheme (as defined in section 235(6) of CA2006),
  (c) any other liability incurred by that director as an officer of the company or an associated company.
 (2) This article does not authorise any indemnity which would be prohibited or rendered void by any provision of the Companies Acts or by any other provision of law.
 (3) In this article—
  (a) companies are associated if one is a subsidiary of the other or both are subsidiaries of the same body corporate, and
  (b) a "relevant director" means any director or former director of the company or an associated company.

Insurance

53.—(1) The directors may decide to purchase and maintain insurance, at the expense of the company, for the benefit of any relevant director in respect of any relevant loss.
 (2) In this article—
  (a) a "relevant director" means any director or former director of the company or an associated company,
  (b) a "relevant loss" means any loss or liability which has been or may be incurred by a relevant director in connection with that director's duties or powers in relation to the company, any associated company or any pension fund or employees' share scheme of the company or associated company, and
  (c) companies are associated if one is a subsidiary of the other or both are subsidiaries of the same body corporate.

SCHEDULE 3 Regulation 4
MODEL ARTICLES FOR PUBLIC COMPANIES

INDEX TO THE ARTICLES

PART 1
INTERPRETATION AND LIMITATION OF LIABILITY

1. Defined terms
2. Liability of members

PART 2
DIRECTORS
DIRECTORS' POWERS AND RESPONSIBILITIES

3. Directors' general authority
4. Members' reserve power
5. Directors may delegate
6. Committees

DECISION-MAKING BY DIRECTORS

7. Directors to take decisions collectively
8. Calling a directors' meeting
9. Participation in directors' meetings
10. Quorum for directors' meetings
11. Meetings where total number of directors less than quorum
12. Chairing directors' meetings
13. Voting at directors' meetings: general rules
14. Chairman's casting vote at directors' meetings
15. Alternates voting at directors' meetings
16. Conflicts of interest
17. Proposing directors' written resolutions
18. Adoption of directors' written resolutions
19. Directors' discretion to make further rules

APPOINTMENT OF DIRECTORS

20. Methods of appointing directors
21. Retirement of directors by rotation
22. Termination of director's appointment
23. Directors' remuneration
24. Directors' expenses

ALTERNATE DIRECTORS

25. Appointment and removal of alternates
26. Rights and responsibilities of alternate directors
27. Termination of alternate directorship

PART 3
DECISION-MAKING BY MEMBERS
ORGANISATION OF GENERAL MEETINGS
28. Members can call general meeting if not enough directors
29. Attendance and speaking at general meetings
30. Quorum for general meetings
31. Chairing general meetings
32. Attendance and speaking by directors and non-members
33. Adjournment
34. Voting: general
35. Errors and disputes
36. Demanding a poll
37. Procedure on a poll
38. Content of proxy notices
39. Delivery of proxy notices

VOTING AT GENERAL MEETINGS
40. Amendments to resolutions

RESTRICTIONS ON MEMBERS' RIGHTS
41. No voting of shares on which money owed to company

APPLICATION OF RULES TO CLASS MEETINGS
42. Class meetings

PART 4
SHARES AND DISTRIBUTIONS
ISSUE OF SHARES
43. Powers to issue different classes of share
44. Payment of commissions on subscription for shares

INTERESTS IN SHARES
45. Company not bound by less than absolute interests

SHARE CERTIFICATES
46. Certificates to be issued except in certain cases
47. Contents and execution of share certificates
48. Consolidated share certificates
49. Replacement share certificates

SHARES NOT HELD IN CERTIFICATED FORM
50. Uncertificated shares
51. Share warrants

PARTLY PAID SHARES
52. Company's lien over partly paid shares
53. Enforcement of the company's lien
54. Call notices
55. Liability to pay calls
56. When call notice need not be issued
57. Failure to comply with call notice: automatic consequences
58. Notice of intended forfeiture

59. Directors' power to forfeit shares
60. Effect of forfeiture
61. Procedure following forfeiture
62. Surrender of shares

TRANSFER AND TRANSMISSION OF SHARES

63. Transfers of certificated shares
64. Transfer of uncertificated shares
65. Transmission of shares
66. Transmittees' rights
67. Exercise of transmittees' rights
68. Transmittees bound by prior notices

CONSOLIDATION OF SHARES

69. Procedure for disposing of fractions of shares

DISTRIBUTIONS

70. Procedure for declaring dividends
71. Calculation of dividends
72. Payment of dividends and other distributions
73. Deductions from distributions in respect of sums owed to the company
74. No interest on distributions
75. Unclaimed distributions
76. Non-cash distributions
77. Waiver of distributions

CAPITALISATION OF PROFITS

78. Authority to capitalise and appropriation of capitalised sums

PART 5
MISCELLANEOUS PROVISIONS
COMMUNICATIONS

79. Means of communication to be used
80. Failure to notify contact details

ADMINISTRATIVE ARRANGEMENTS

81. Company seals
82. Destruction of documents
83. No right to inspect accounts and other records
84. Provision for employees on cessation of business

DIRECTORS' INDEMNITY AND INSURANCE

85. Indemnity
86. Insurance

PART 1
INTERPRETATION AND LIMITATION OF LIABILITY

Defined terms
1. In the articles , unless the context requires otherwise—
"alternate" or "alternate director" has the meaning given in article 25; "appointor" has the meaning given in article 25;
"articles" means the company's articles of association;
"bankruptcy" includes individual insolvency proceedings in a jurisdiction other than England and Wales or Northern Ireland which have an effect similar to that of bankruptcy;
"call" has the meaning given in article 54;
"call notice" has the meaning given in article 54;
"certificate" means a paper certificate (other than a share warrant) evidencing a person's title to specified shares or other securities;
"certificated" in relation to a share, means that it is not an uncertificated share or a share in respect of which a share warrant has been issued and is current;
"chairman" has the meaning given in article 12;
"chairman of the meeting" has the meaning given in article 31;
"Companies Acts" means the Companies Acts (as defined in section 2 of CA2006), in so far as they apply to the company; "company's lien" has the meaning given in article 52;
"director" means a director of the company, and includes any person occupying the position of director, by whatever name called;
"distribution recipient" has the meaning given in article 72;
"document" includes, unless otherwise specified, any document sent or supplied in electronic form;
"electronic form" has the meaning given in section 1168 of CA2006;
"fully paid" in relation to a share, means that the nominal value and any premium to be paid to the company in respect of that share have been paid to the company;
"hard copy form" has the meaning given in section 1168 of CA2006;
"holder" in relation to shares means the person whose name is entered in the register of members as the holder of the shares, or, in the case of a share in respect of which a share warrant has been issued (and not cancelled), the person in possession of that warrant;
"instrument" means a document in hard copy form;
"lien enforcement notice" has the meaning given in article 53;
"member" has the meaning given in section 112 of CA2006;
"ordinary resolution" has the meaning given in section 282 of CA2006; "paid" means paid or credited as paid;
"participate", in relation to a directors' meeting, has the meaning given in article 9;
"partly paid" in relation to a share means that part of that share's nominal value or any premium at which it was issued has not been paid to the company;
"proxy notice" has the meaning given in article 38;
"securities seal" has the meaning given in article 47;
"shares" means shares in the company;
"special resolution" has the meaning given in section 283 of CA2006; "subsidiary" has the meaning given in section 1159 of CA2006;

"transmittee" means a person entitled to a share by reason of the death or bankruptcy of a shareholder or otherwise by operation of law;

"uncertificated" in relation to a share means that, by virtue of legislation (other than section 778 of CA2006) permitting title to shares to be evidenced and transferred without a certificate, title to that share is evidenced and may be transferred without a certificate; and

"writing" means the representation or reproduction of words, symbols or other information in a visible form by any method or combination of methods, whether sent or supplied in electronic form or otherwise.

Unless the context otherwise requires, other words or expressions contained in these articles bear the same meaning as in CA2006 as in force on the date when these articles become binding on the company.

Liability of members

2. The liability of the members is limited to the amount, if any, unpaid on the shares held by them.

PART 2
DIRECTORS
DIRECTORS' POWERS AND RESPONSIBILITIES

Directors' general authority

3. Subject to the articles, the directors are responsible for the management of the company's business, for which purpose they may exercise all the powers of the company.

Members' reserve power

4.— (1) The members may, by special resolution, direct the directors to take, or refrain from taking, specified action.

(2) No such special resolution invalidates anything which the directors have done before the passing of the resolution.

Directors may delegate

5.— (1) Subject to the articles, the directors may delegate any of the powers which are conferred on them under the articles—
  (a) to such person or committee;
  (b) by such means (including by power of attorney);
  (c) to such an extent;
  (d) in relation to such matters or territories; and
  (e) on such terms and conditions;
    as they think fit.

(2) If the directors so specify, any such delegation may authorise further delegation of the directors' powers by any person to whom they are delegated.

(3) The directors may revoke any delegation in whole or part, or alter its terms and conditions.

Committees

6.— (1) Committees to which the directors delegate any of their powers must follow procedures which are based as far as they are applicable on those provisions of the articles which govern the taking of decisions by directors.

(2) The directors may make rules of procedure for all or any committees, which prevail over rules derived from the articles if they are not consistent with them.

DECISION-MAKING BY DIRECTORS

Directors to take decisions collectively

7. Decisions of the directors may be taken—
   (a) at a directors' meeting, or
   (b) in the form of a directors' written resolution.

Calling a directors' meeting

8. —(1) Any director may call a directors' meeting.
   (2) The company secretary must call a directors' meeting if a director so requests.
   (3) A directors' meeting is called by giving notice of the meeting to the directors.
   (4) Notice of any directors' meeting must indicate—
      (a) its proposed date and time;
      (b) where it is to take place; and
      (c) if it is anticipated that directors participating in the meeting will not be in the same place, how it is proposed that they should communicate with each other during the meeting.
   (5) Notice of a directors' meeting must be given to each director, but need not be in writing.
   (6) Notice of a directors' meeting need not be given to directors who waive their entitlement to notice of that meeting, by giving notice to that effect to the company not more than 7 days after the date on which the meeting is held. Where such notice is given after the meeting has been held, that does not affect the validity of the meeting, or of any business conducted at it.

Participation in directors' meetings

9.— (1) Subject to the articles, directors participate in a directors' meeting, or part of a directors' meeting, when—
      (a) the meeting has been called and takes place in accordance with the articles, and
      (b) they can each communicate to the others any information or opinions they have on any particular item of the business of the meeting.
   (2) In determining whether directors are participating in a directors' meeting, it is irrelevant where any director is or how they communicate with each other.
   (3) If all the directors participating in a meeting are not in the same place, they may decide that the meeting is to be treated as taking place wherever any of them is.

Quorum for directors' meetings

10.— (1) At a directors' meeting, unless a quorum is participating, no proposal is to be voted on, except a proposal to call another meeting.

(2) The quorum for directors' meetings may be fixed from time to time by a decision of the directors, but it must never be less than two, and unless otherwise fixed it is two.

Meetings where total number of directors less than quorum
11.— (1) This article applies where the total number of directors for the time being is less than the quorum for directors' meetings.
  (2) If there is only one director, that director may appoint sufficient directors to make up a quorum or call a general meeting to do so.
  (3) If there is more than one director—
    (a) a directors' meeting may take place, if it is called in accordance with the articles and at least two directors participate in it, with a view to appointing sufficient directors to make up a quorum or calling a general meeting to do so, and
    (b) if a directors' meeting is called but only one director attends at the appointed date and time to participate in it, that director may appoint sufficient directors to make up a quorum or call a general meeting to do so.

Chairing directors' meetings
12.— (1) The directors may appoint a director to chair their meetings.
  (2) The person so appointed for the time being is known as the chairman.
  (3) The directors may appoint other directors as deputy or assistant chairmen to chair directors' meetings in the chairman's absence.
  (4) The directors may terminate the appointment of the chairman, deputy or assistant chairman at any time.
  (5) If neither the chairman nor any director appointed generally to chair directors' meetings in the chairman's absence is participating in a meeting within ten minutes of the time at which it was to start, the participating directors must appoint one of themselves to chair it.

Voting at directors' meetings: general rules
13.— (1) Subject to the articles, a decision is taken at a directors' meeting by a majority of the votes of the participating directors.
  (2) Subject to the articles, each director participating in a directors' meeting has one vote.
  (3) Subject to the articles, if a director has an interest in an actual or proposed transaction or arrangement with the company—
    (a) that director and that director's alternate may not vote on any proposal relating to it, but
    (b) this does not preclude the alternate from voting in relation to that transaction or arrangement on behalf of another appointor who does not have such an interest.

Chairman's casting vote at directors' meetings
14.— (1) If the numbers of votes for and against a proposal are equal, the chairman or other director chairing the meeting has a casting vote.

(2) But this does not apply if, in accordance with the articles, the chairman or other director is not to be counted as participating in the decision-making process for quorum or voting purposes.

Alternates voting at directors' meetings
15. A director who is also an alternate director has an additional vote on behalf of each appointor who is—
    (a) not participating in a directors' meeting, and
    (b) would have been entitled to vote if they were participating in it.

Conflicts of interest
16.—(1) If a directors' meeting, or part of a directors' meeting, is concerned with an actual or proposed transaction or arrangement with the company in which a director is interested, that director is not to be counted as participating in that meeting, or part of a meeting, for quorum or voting purposes.
(2) But if paragraph (3) applies, a director who is interested in an actual or proposed transaction or arrangement with the company is to be counted as participating in a decision at a directors' meeting, or part of a directors' meeting, relating to it for quorum and voting purposes.
(3) This paragraph applies when—
   (a) the company by ordinary resolution disapplies the provision of the articles which would otherwise prevent a director from being counted as participating in, or voting at, a directors' meeting;
   (b) the director's interest cannot reasonably be regarded as likely to give rise to a conflict of interest; or
   (c) the director's conflict of interest arises from a permitted cause.
(4) For the purposes of this article, the following are permitted causes—
   (a) a guarantee given, or to be given, by or to a director in respect of an obligation incurred by or on behalf of the company or any of its subsidiaries;
   (b) subscription, or an agreement to subscribe, for shares or other securities of the company or any of its subsidiaries, or to underwrite, sub-underwrite, or guarantee subscription for any such shares or securities; and
   (c) arrangements pursuant to which benefits are made available to employees and directors or former employees and directors of the company or any of its subsidiaries which do not provide special benefits for directors or former directors.
(5) Subject to paragraph (6), if a question arises at a meeting of directors or of a committee of directors as to the right of a director to participate in the meeting (or part of the meeting) for voting or quorum purposes, the question may, before the conclusion of the meeting, be referred to the chairman whose ruling in relation to any director other than the chairman is to be final and conclusive.
(6) If any question as to the right to participate in the meeting (or part of the meeting) should arise in respect of the chairman, the question is to be decided by a decision of the directors at that meeting, for which purpose the chairman is not to be counted as participating in the meeting (or that part of the meeting) for voting or quorum purposes.

Proposing directors' written resolutions

17.—(1) Any director may propose a directors' written resolution.
  (2) The company secretary must propose a directors' written resolution if a director so requests.
  (3) A directors' written resolution is proposed by giving notice of the proposed resolution to the directors.
  (4) Notice of a proposed directors' written resolution must indicate—
    (a) the proposed resolution, and
    (b) the time by which it is proposed that the directors should adopt it.
  (5) Notice of a proposed directors' written resolution must be given in writing to each director.
  (6) Any decision which a person giving notice of a proposed directors' written resolution takes regarding the process of adopting that resolution must be taken reasonably in good faith.

Adoption of directors' written resolutions

18.—(1) A proposed directors' written resolution is adopted when all the directors who would have been entitled to vote on the resolution at a directors' meeting have signed one or more copies of it, provided that those directors would have formed a quorum at such a meeting.
  (2) It is immaterial whether any director signs the resolution before or after the time by which the notice proposed that it should be adopted.
  (3) Once a directors' written resolution has been adopted, it must be treated as if it had been a decision taken at a directors' meeting in accordance with the articles.
  (4) The company secretary must ensure that the company keeps a record, in writing, of all directors' written resolutions for at least ten years from the date of their adoption.

Directors' discretion to make further rules

19. Subject to the articles, the directors may make any rule which they think fit about how they take decisions, and about how such rules are to be recorded or communicated to directors.

APPOINTMENT OF DIRECTORS

Methods of appointing directors

20. Any person who is willing to act as a director, and is permitted by law to do so, may be appointed to be a director—
  (a) by ordinary resolution, or
  (b) by a decision of the directors.

Retirement of directors by rotation

21.—(1) At the first annual general meeting all the directors must retire from office.
  (2) At every subsequent annual general meeting any directors—
    (a) who have been appointed by the directors since the last annual general meeting, or
    (b) who were not appointed or reappointed at one of the preceding two annual general meetings, must retire from office and may offer themselves for reappointment by the members.

APPENDIX 3

Termination of director's appointment

22. A person ceases to be a director as soon as—
    (a) that person ceases to be a director by virtue of any provision of CA2006 or is prohibited from being a director by law;
    (b) a bankruptcy order is made against that person;
    (c) a composition is made with that person's creditors generally in satisfaction of that person's debts;
    (d) a registered medical practitioner who is treating that person gives a written opinion to the company stating that that person has become physically or mentally incapable of acting as a director and may remain so for more than three months;
    (e) by reason of that person's mental health, a court makes an order which wholly or partly prevents that person from personally exercising any powers or rights which that person would otherwise have;
    (f) notification is received by the company from the director that the director is resigning from office as director, and such resignation has taken effect in accordance with its terms.

Directors' remuneration

23.—(1) Directors may undertake any services for the company that the directors decide.
   (2) Directors are entitled to such remuneration as the directors determine—
       (a) for their services to the company as directors, and
       (b) for any other service which they undertake for the company.
   (3) Subject to the articles, a director's remuneration may—
       (a) take any form, and
       (b) include any arrangements in connection with the payment of a pension, allowance or gratuity, or any death, sickness or disability benefits, to or in respect of that director.
   (4) Unless the directors decide otherwise, directors' remuneration accrues from day to day.
   (5) Unless the directors decide otherwise, directors are not accountable to the company for any remuneration which they receive as directors or other officers or employees of the company's subsidiaries or of any other body corporate in which the company is interested.

Directors' expenses

24. The company may pay any reasonable expenses which the directors properly incur in connection with their attendance at—
    (a) meetings of directors or committees of directors,
    (b) general meetings, or
    (c) separate meetings of the holders of any class of shares or of debentures of the company, or otherwise in connection with the exercise of their powers and the discharge of their responsibilities in relation to the company.

ALTERNATE DIRECTORS

Appointment and removal of alternates

25.—(1) Any director (the "appointor") may appoint as an alternate any other director, or any other person approved by resolution of the directors, to—

(a) exercise that director's powers, and
(b) carry out that director's responsibilities, in relation to the taking of decisions by the directors in the absence of the alternate's appointor.

(2) Any appointment or removal of an alternate must be effected by notice in writing to the company signed by the appointor, or in any other manner approved by the directors.

(3) The notice must—
(a) identify the proposed alternate, and
(b) in the case of a notice of appointment, contain a statement signed by the proposed alternate that the proposed alternate is willing to act as the alternate of the director giving the notice.

Rights and responsibilities of alternate directors

26.—(1) An alternate director has the same rights, in relation to any directors' meeting or directors' written resolution, as the alternate's appointor.

(2) Except as the articles specify otherwise, alternate directors—
(a) are deemed for all purposes to be directors;
(b) are liable for their own acts and omissions;
(c) are subject to the same restrictions as their appointors; and
(d) are not deemed to be agents of or for their appointors.

(3) A person who is an alternate director but not a director—
(a) may be counted as participating for the purposes of determining whether a quorum is participating (but only if that person's appointor is not participating), and
(b) may sign a written resolution (but only if it is not signed or to be signed by that person's appointor).

No alternate may be counted as more than one director for such purposes.

(4) An alternate director is not entitled to receive any remuneration from the company for serving as an alternate director except such part of the alternate's appointor's remuneration as the appointor may direct by notice in writing made to the company.

Termination of alternate directorship

27. An alternate director's appointment as an alternate terminates—
(a) when the alternate's appointor revokes the appointment by notice to the company in writing specifying when it is to terminate;
(b) on the occurrence in relation to the alternate of any event which, if it occurred in relation to the alternate's appointor, would result in the termination of the appointor's appointment as a director;
(c) on the death of the alternate's appointor; or
(d) when the alternate's appointor's appointment as a director terminates, except that an alternate's appointment as an alternate does not terminate when the appointor retires by rotation at a general meeting and is then re-appointed as a director at the same general meeting.

PART 3
DECISION-MAKING BY MEMBERS
ORGANISATION OF GENERAL MEETINGS

Members can call general meeting if not enough directors

28. If—
   (a) the company has fewer than two directors, and
   (b) the director (if any) is unable or unwilling to appoint sufficient directors to make up a quorum or to call a general meeting to do so, then two or more members may call a general meeting (or instruct the company secretary to do so) for the purpose of appointing one or more directors.

Attendance and speaking at general meetings

29.—(1) A person is able to exercise the right to speak at a general meeting when that person is in a position to communicate to all those attending the meeting, during the meeting, any information or opinions which that person has on the business of the meeting.
   (2) A person is able to exercise the right to vote at a general meeting when—
      (a) that person is able to vote, during the meeting, on resolutions put to the vote at the meeting, and
      (b) that person's vote can be taken into account in determining whether or not such resolutions are passed at the same time as the votes of all the other persons attending the meeting.
   (3) The directors may make whatever arrangements they consider appropriate to enable those attending a general meeting to exercise their rights to speak or vote at it.
   (4) In determining attendance at a general meeting, it is immaterial whether any two or more members attending it are in the same place as each other.
   (5) Two or more persons who are not in the same place as each other attend a general meeting if their circumstances are such that if they have (or were to have) rights to speak and vote at that meeting, they are (or would be) able to exercise them.

Quorum for general meetings

30. No business other than the appointment of the chairman of the meeting is to be transacted at a general meeting if the persons attending it do not constitute a quorum.

Chairing general meetings

31.—(1) If the directors have appointed a chairman, the chairman shall chair general meetings if present and willing to do so.
   (2) If the directors have not appointed a chairman, or if the chairman is unwilling to chair the meeting or is not present within ten minutes of the time at which a meeting was due to start—
      (a) the directors present, or
      (b) (if no directors are present), the meeting, must appoint a director or member to chair the meeting, and the appointment of the chairman of the meeting must be the first business of the meeting.
   (3) The person chairing a meeting in accordance with this article is referred to as "the chairman of the meeting".

Attendance and speaking by directors and non-members

32.—(1) Directors may attend and speak at general meetings, whether or not they are members.

(2) The chairman of the meeting may permit other persons who are not—
  (a) members of the company, or
  (b) otherwise entitled to exercise the rights of members in relation to general meetings, to attend and speak at a general meeting.

Adjournment

33.—(1) If the persons attending a general meeting within half an hour of the time at which the meeting was due to start do not constitute a quorum, or if during a meeting a quorum ceases to be present, the chairman of the meeting must adjourn it.

(2) The chairman of the meeting may adjourn a general meeting at which a quorum is present if—
  (a) the meeting consents to an adjournment, or
  (b) it appears to the chairman of the meeting that an adjournment is necessary to protect the safety of any person attending the meeting or ensure that the business of the meeting is conducted in an orderly manner.

(3) The chairman of the meeting must adjourn a general meeting if directed to do so by the meeting.

(4) When adjourning a general meeting, the chairman of the meeting must—
  (a) either specify the time and place to which it is adjourned or state that it is to continue at a time and place to be fixed by the directors, and
  (b) have regard to any directions as to the time and place of any adjournment which have been given by the meeting.

(5) If the continuation of an adjourned meeting is to take place more than 14 days after it was adjourned, the company must give at least 7 clear days' notice of it (that is, excluding the day of the adjourned meeting and the day on which the notice is given)—
  (a) to the same persons to whom notice of the company's general meetings is required to be given, and
  (b) containing the same information which such notice is required to contain.

(6) No business may be transacted at an adjourned general meeting which could not properly have been transacted at the meeting if the adjournment had not taken place.

VOTING AT GENERAL MEETINGS

Voting: general

34. A resolution put to the vote of a general meeting must be decided on a show of hands unless a poll is duly demanded in accordance with the articles.

Errors and disputes

35.—(1) No objection may be raised to the qualification of any person voting at a general meeting except at the meeting or adjourned meeting at which the vote objected to is tendered, and every vote not disallowed at the meeting is valid.

APPENDIX 3

(2) Any such objection must be referred to the chairman of the meeting whose decision is final.

Demanding a poll
36.—(1) A poll on a resolution may be demanded—
    (a) in advance of the general meeting where it is to be put to the vote, or
    (b) at a general meeting, either before a show of hands on that resolution or immediately after the result of a show of hands on that resolution is declared.
(2) A poll may be demanded by—
    (a) the chairman of the meeting;
    (b) the directors;
    (c) two or more persons having the right to vote on the resolution; or
    (d) a person or persons representing not less than one tenth of the total voting rights of all the members having the right to vote on the resolution.
(3) A demand for a poll may be withdrawn if—
    (a) the poll has not yet been taken, and
    (b) the chairman of the meeting consents to the withdrawal.

Procedure on a poll
37.—(1) Subject to the articles, polls at general meetings must be taken when, where and in such manner as the chairman of the meeting directs.
(2) The chairman of the meeting may appoint scrutineers (who need not be members) and decide how and when the result of the poll is to be declared.
(3) The result of a poll shall be the decision of the meeting in respect of the resolution on which the poll was demanded.
(4) A poll on—
    (a) the election of the chairman of the meeting, or
    (b) a question of adjournment, must be taken immediately.
(5) Other polls must be taken within 30 days of their being demanded.
(6) A demand for a poll does not prevent a general meeting from continuing, except as regards the question on which the poll was demanded.
(7) No notice need be given of a poll not taken immediately if the time and place at which it is to be taken are announced at the meeting at which it is demanded.
(8) In any other case, at least 7 days' notice must be given specifying the time and place at which the poll is to be taken.

Content of proxy notices
38.—(1) Proxies may only validly be appointed by a notice in writing (a "proxy notice") which—
    (a) states the name and address of the member appointing the proxy;
    (b) identifies the person appointed to be that member's proxy and the general meeting in relation to which that person is appointed;
    (c) is signed by or on behalf of the member appointing the proxy, or is authenticated in such manner as the directors may determine; and
    (d) is delivered to the company in accordance with the articles and any instructions contained in the notice of the general meeting to which they relate.
(2) The company may require proxy notices to be delivered in a particular form, and may specify different forms for different purposes.

(3) Proxy notices may specify how the proxy appointed under them is to vote (or that the proxy is to abstain from voting) on one or more resolutions.
(4) Unless a proxy notice indicates otherwise, it must be treated as—
   (a) allowing the person appointed under it as a proxy discretion as to how to vote on any ancillary or procedural resolutions put to the meeting, and
   (b) appointing that person as a proxy in relation to any adjournment of the general meeting to which it relates as well as the meeting itself.

Delivery of proxy notices

39.— (1) Any notice of a general meeting must specify the address or addresses ("proxy notification address") at which the company or its agents will receive proxy notices relating to that meeting, or any adjournment of it, delivered in hard copy or electronic form.
(2) A person who is entitled to attend, speak or vote (either on a show of hands or on a poll) at a general meeting remains so entitled in respect of that meeting or any adjournment of it, even though a valid proxy notice has been delivered to the company by or on behalf of that person.
(3) Subject to paragraphs (4) and (5), a proxy notice must be delivered to a proxy notification address not less than 48 hours before the general meeting or adjourned meeting to which it relates.
(4) In the case of a poll taken more than 48 hours after it is demanded, the notice must be delivered to a proxy notification address not less than 24 hours before the time appointed for the taking of the poll.
(5) In the case of a poll not taken during the meeting but taken not more than 48 hours after it was demanded, the proxy notice must be delivered—
   (a) in accordance with paragraph (3), or
   (b) at the meeting at which the poll was demanded to the chairman, secretary or any director.
(6) An appointment under a proxy notice may be revoked by delivering a notice in writing given by or on behalf of the person by whom or on whose behalf the proxy notice was given to a proxy notification address.
(7) A notice revoking a proxy appointment only takes effect if it is delivered before—
   (a) the start of the meeting or adjourned meeting to which it relates, or
   (b) (in the case of a poll not taken on the same day as the meeting or adjourned meeting) the time appointed for taking the poll to which it relates.
(8) If a proxy notice is not signed by the person appointing the proxy, it must be accompanied by written evidence of the authority of the person who executed it to execute it on the appointor's behalf.

Amendments to resolutions

40.— (1) An ordinary resolution to be proposed at a general meeting may be amended by ordinary resolution if—
   (a) notice of the proposed amendment is given to the company secretary in writing by a person entitled to vote at the general meeting at which it is to be proposed not less than 48 hours before the meeting is to take place (or such later time as the chairman of the meeting may determine), and
   (b) the proposed amendment does not, in the reasonable opinion of the chairman of the meeting, materially alter the scope of the resolution.

(2) A special resolution to be proposed at a general meeting may be amended by ordinary resolution, if—
   (a) the chairman of the meeting proposes the amendment at the general meeting at which the resolution is to be proposed, and
   (b) the amendment does not go beyond what is necessary to correct a grammatical or other non-substantive error in the resolution.
(3) If the chairman of the meeting, acting in good faith, wrongly decides that an amendment to a resolution is out of order, the chairman's error does not invalidate the vote on that resolution.

RESTRICTIONS ON MEMBERS' RIGHTS

No voting of shares on which money owed to company
41. No voting rights attached to a share may be exercised at any general meeting, at any adjournment of it, or on any poll called at or in relation to it, unless all amounts payable to the company in respect of that share have been paid.

APPLICATION OF RULES TO CLASS MEETINGS

Class meetings
42. The provisions of the articles relating to general meetings apply, with any necessary modifications, to meetings of the holders of any class of shares.

PART 4
SHARES AND DISTRIBUTIONS
ISSUE OF SHARES

Powers to issue different classes of share
43.—(1) Subject to the articles, but without prejudice to the rights attached to any existing share, the company may issue shares with such rights or restrictions as may be determined by ordinary resolution.
   (2) The company may issue shares which are to be redeemed, or are liable to be redeemed at the option of the company or the holder, and the directors may determine the terms, conditions and manner of redemption of any such shares.

Payment of commissions on subscription for shares
44.—(1) The company may pay any person a commission in consideration for that person—
   (a) subscribing, or agreeing to subscribe, for shares, or
   (b) procuring, or agreeing to procure, subscriptions for shares.
   (2) Any such commission may be paid—
   (a) in cash, or in fully paid or partly paid shares or other securities, or partly in one way and partly in the other, and
   (b) in respect of a conditional or an absolute subscription.

INTERESTS IN SHARES

Company not bound by less than absolute interests

45. Except as required by law, no person is to be recognised by the company as holding any share upon any trust, and except as otherwise required by law or the articles, the company is not in any way to be bound by or recognise any interest in a share other than the holder's absolute ownership of it and all the rights attaching to it.

SHARE CERTIFICATES

Certificates to be issued except in certain cases

46.— (1) The company must issue each member with one or more certificates in respect of the shares which that member holds.
    (2) This article does not apply to—
        (a) uncertificated shares;
        (b) shares in respect of which a share warrant has been issued; or
        (c) shares in respect of which the Companies Acts permit the company not to issue a certificate.
    (3) Except as otherwise specified in the articles, all certificates must be issued free of charge.
    (4) No certificate may be issued in respect of shares of more than one class.
    (5) If more than one person holds a share, only one certificate may be issued in respect of it.

Contents and execution of share certificates

47.— (1) Every certificate must specify—
        (a) in respect of how many shares, of what class, it is issued;
        (b) the nominal value of those shares;
        (c) the amount paid up on them; and
        (d) any distinguishing numbers assigned to them.
    (2) Certificates must—
        (a) have affixed to them the company's common seal or an official seal which is a facsimile of the company's common seal with the addition on its face of the word "Securities" (a "securities seal"), or
        (b) be otherwise executed in accordance with the Companies Acts.

Consolidated share certificates

48.— (1) When a member's holding of shares of a particular class increases, the company may issue that member with—
        (a) a single, consolidated certificate in respect of all the shares of a particular class which that member holds, or
        (b) a separate certificate in respect of only those shares by which that member's holding has increased.
    (2) When a member's holding of shares of a particular class is reduced, the company must ensure that the member is issued with one or more certificates in respect of the number of shares held by the member after that reduction. But the company need not (in the absence of a request from the member) issue any new certificate if—

(a) all the shares which the member no longer holds as a result of the reduction, and
(b) none of the shares which the member retains following the reduction, were, immediately before the reduction, represented by the same certificate.
(3) A member may request the company, in writing, to replace—
(a) the member's separate certificates with a consolidated certificate, or
(b) the member's consolidated certificate with two or more separate certificates representing such proportion of the shares as the member may specify.
(4) When the company complies with such a request it may charge such reasonable fee as the directors may decide for doing so.
(5) A consolidated certificate must not be issued unless any certificates which it is to replace have first been returned to the company for cancellation.

Replacement share certificates
49.— (1) If a certificate issued in respect of a member's shares is—
(a) damaged or defaced, or
(b) said to be lost, stolen or destroyed, that member is entitled to be issued with a replacement certificate in respect of the same shares.
(2) A member exercising the right to be issued with such a replacement certificate—
(a) may at the same time exercise the right to be issued with a single certificate or separate certificates;
(b) must return the certificate which is to be replaced to the company if it is damaged or defaced; and
(c) must comply with such conditions as to evidence, indemnity and the payment of a reasonable fee as the directors decide.

SHARES NOT HELD IN CERTIFICATED FORM

Uncertificated shares
50.— (1) In this article, "the relevant rules" means—
(a) any applicable provision of the Companies Acts about the holding, evidencing of title to, or transfer of shares other than in certificated form, and
(b) any applicable legislation, rules or other arrangements made under or by virtue of such provision.
(2) The provisions of this article have effect subject to the relevant rules.
(3) Any provision of the articles which is inconsistent with the relevant rules must be disregarded, to the extent that it is inconsistent, whenever the relevant rules apply.
(4) Any share or class of shares of the company may be issued or held on such terms, or in such a way, that—
(a) title to it or them is not, or must not be, evidenced by a certificate, or
(b) it or they may or must be transferred wholly or partly without a certificate.
(5) The directors have power to take such steps as they think fit in relation to—
(a) the evidencing of and transfer of title to uncertificated shares (including in connection with the issue of such shares);
(b) any records relating to the holding of uncertificated shares;
(c) the conversion of certificated shares into uncertificated shares; or
(d) the conversion of uncertificated shares into certificated shares.

(6) The company may by notice to the holder of a share require that share—
- (a) if it is uncertificated, to be converted into certificated form, and
- (b) if it is certificated, to be converted into uncertificated form, to enable it to be dealt with in accordance with the articles.

(7) If—
- (a) the articles give the directors power to take action, or require other persons to take action, in order to sell, transfer or otherwise dispose of shares, and
- (b) uncertificated shares are subject to that power, but the power is expressed in terms which assume the use of a certificate or other written instrument, the directors may take such action as is necessary or expedient to achieve the same results when exercising that power in relation to uncertificated shares.

(8) In particular, the directors may take such action as they consider appropriate to achieve the sale, transfer, disposal, forfeiture, re-allotment or surrender of an uncertificated share or otherwise to enforce a lien in respect of it.

(9) Unless the directors otherwise determine, shares which a member holds in uncertificated form must be treated as separate holdings from any shares which that member holds in certificated form.

(10) A class of shares must not be treated as two classes simply because some shares of that class are held in certificated form and others are held in uncertificated form.

Share warrants

51.—(1) The directors may issue a share warrant in respect of any fully paid share.

(2) Share warrants must be—
- (a) issued in such form, and
- (b) executed in such manner, as the directors decide.

(3) A share represented by a share warrant may be transferred by delivery of the warrant representing it.

(4) The directors may make provision for the payment of dividends in respect of any share represented by a share warrant.

(5) Subject to the articles, the directors may decide the conditions on which any share warrant is issued. In particular, they may—
- (a) decide the conditions on which new warrants are to be issued in place of warrants which are damaged or defaced, or said to have been lost, stolen or destroyed;
- (b) decide the conditions on which bearers of warrants are entitled to attend and vote at general meetings;
- (c) decide the conditions subject to which bearers of warrants may surrender their warrant so as to hold their shares in certificated or uncertificated form instead; and
- (d) vary the conditions of issue of any warrant from time to time, and the bearer of a warrant is subject to the conditions and procedures in force in relation to it, whether or not they were decided or specified before the warrant was issued.

(6) Subject to the conditions on which the warrants are issued from time to time, bearers of share warrants have the same rights and privileges as they would if their names had been included in the register as holders of the shares represented by their warrants.

(7) The company must not in any way be bound by or recognise any interest in a share represented by a share warrant other than the absolute right of the bearer of that warrant to that warrant.

PARTLY PAID SHARES

Company's lien over partly paid shares

52.— (1) The company has a lien ("the company's lien") over every share which is partly paid for any part of—
- (a) that share's nominal value, and
- (b) any premium at which it was issued, which has not been paid to the company, and which is payable immediately or at some time in the future, whether or not a call notice has been sent in respect of it.

(2) The company's lien over a share—
- (a) takes priority over any third party's interest in that share, and
- (b) extends to any dividend or other money payable by the company in respect of that share and (if the lien is enforced and the share is sold by the company) the proceeds of sale of that share.

(3) The directors may at any time decide that a share which is or would otherwise be subject to the company's lien shall not be subject to it, either wholly or in part.

Enforcement of the company's lien

53.— (1) Subject to the provisions of this article, if—
- (a) a lien enforcement notice has been given in respect of a share, and
- (b) the person to whom the notice was given has failed to comply with it, the company may sell that share in such manner as the directors decide.

(2) A lien enforcement notice—
- (a) may only be given in respect of a share which is subject to the company's lien, in respect of which a sum is payable and the due date for payment of that sum has passed;
- (b) must specify the share concerned;
- (c) must require payment of the sum payable within 14 days of the notice;
- (d) must be addressed either to the holder of the share or to a person entitled to it by reason of the holder's death, bankruptcy or otherwise; and
- (e) must state the company's intention to sell the share if the notice is not complied with.

(3) Where shares are sold under this article—
- (a) the directors may authorise any person to execute an instrument of transfer of the shares to the purchaser or a person nominated by the purchaser, and
- (b) the transferee is not bound to see to the application of the consideration, and the transferee's title is not affected by any irregularity in or invalidity of the process leading to the sale.

(4) The net proceeds of any such sale (after payment of the costs of sale and any other costs of enforcing the lien) must be applied—
- (a) first, in payment of so much of the sum for which the lien exists as was payable at the date of the lien enforcement notice,

(b) second, to the person entitled to the shares at the date of the sale, but only after the certificate for the shares sold has been surrendered to the company for cancellation or a suitable indemnity has been given for any lost certificates, and subject to a lien equivalent to the company's lien over the shares before the sale for any money payable in respect of the shares after the date of the lien enforcement notice.

(5) A statutory declaration by a director or the company secretary that the declarant is a director or the company secretary and that a share has been sold to satisfy the company's lien on a specified date—
  (a) is conclusive evidence of the facts stated in it as against all persons claiming to be entitled to the share, and
  (b) subject to compliance with any other formalities of transfer required by the articles or by law, constitutes a good title to the share.

Call notices

54.—(1) Subject to the articles and the terms on which shares are allotted, the directors may send a notice (a "call notice") to a member requiring the member to pay the company a specified sum of money (a "call") which is payable in respect of shares which that member holds at the date when the directors decide to send the call notice.

(2) A call notice—
  (a) may not require a member to pay a call which exceeds the total sum unpaid on that member's shares (whether as to the share's nominal value or any amount payable to the company by way of premium);
  (b) must state when and how any call to which it relates it is to be paid; and
  (c) may permit or require the call to be paid by instalments.

(3) A member must comply with the requirements of a call notice, but no member is obliged to pay any call before 14 days have passed since the notice was sent.

(4) Before the company has received any call due under a call notice the directors may—
  (a) revoke it wholly or in part, or
  (b) specify a later time for payment than is specified in the notice, by a further notice in writing to the member in respect of whose shares the call is made.

Liability to pay calls

55.—(1) Liability to pay a call is not extinguished or transferred by transferring the shares in respect of which it is required to be paid.

(2) Joint holders of a share are jointly and severally liable to pay all calls in respect of that share.

(3) Subject to the terms on which shares are allotted, the directors may, when issuing shares, provide that call notices sent to the holders of those shares may require them—
  (a) to pay calls which are not the same, or
  (b) to pay calls at different times.

When call notice need not be issued

56.—(1) A call notice need not be issued in respect of sums which are specified, in the terms on which a share is issued, as being payable to the company in respect of that share (whether in respect of nominal value or premium)—

(a) on allotment;
(b) on the occurrence of a particular event; or
(c) on a date fixed by or in accordance with the terms of issue.

(2) But if the due date for payment of such a sum has passed and it has not been paid, the holder of the share concerned is treated in all respects as having failed to comply with a call notice in respect of that sum, and is liable to the same consequences as regards the payment of interest and forfeiture.

Failure to comply with call notice: automatic consequences

57.— (1) If a person is liable to pay a call and fails to do so by the call payment date—
(a) the directors may issue a notice of intended forfeiture to that person, and
(b) until the call is paid, that person must pay the company interest on the call from the call payment date at the relevant rate.

(2) For the purposes of this article—
(a) the "call payment date" is the time when the call notice states that a call is payable, unless the directors give a notice specifying a later date, in which case the "call payment date" is that later date;
(b) the "relevant rate" is—
    (i) the rate fixed by the terms on which the share in respect of which the call is due was allotted;
    (ii) such other rate as was fixed in the call notice which required payment of the call, or has otherwise been determined by the directors; or
    (iii) if no rate is fixed in either of these ways, 5 per cent per annum.

(3) The relevant rate must not exceed by more than 5 percentage points the base lending rate most recently set by the Monetary Policy Committee of the Bank of England in connection with its responsibilities under Part 2 of the Bank of England Act 1998(a).

(4) The directors may waive any obligation to pay interest on a call wholly or in part.

Notice of intended forfeiture

58. A notice of intended forfeiture—
(a) may be sent in respect of any share in respect of which a call has not been paid as required by a call notice;
(b) must be sent to the holder of that share or to a person entitled to it by reason of the holder's death, bankruptcy or otherwise;
(c) must require payment of the call and any accrued interest by a date which is not less than 14 days after the date of the notice;
(d) must state how the payment is to be made; and
(e) must state that if the notice is not complied with, the shares in respect of which the call is payable will be liable to be forfeited.

Directors' power to forfeit shares

59. If a notice of intended forfeiture is not complied with before the date by which payment of the call is required in the notice of intended forfeiture, the directors may decide that any share in respect of which it was given is forfeited, and the forfeiture is to include all dividends or other moneys payable in respect of the forfeited shares and not paid before the forfeiture.

Effect of forfeiture

60.— (1) Subject to the articles, the forfeiture of a share extinguishes—
    (a) all interests in that share, and all claims and demands against the company in respect of it, and
    (b) all other rights and liabilities incidental to the share as between the person whose share it was prior to the forfeiture and the company.

(2) Any share which is forfeited in accordance with the articles—
    (a) is deemed to have been forfeited when the directors decide that it is forfeited;
    (b) is deemed to be the property of the company; and
    (c) may be sold, re-allotted or otherwise disposed of as the directors think fit.

(3) If a person's shares have been forfeited—
    (a) the company must send that person notice that forfeiture has occurred and record it in the register of members;
    (b) that person ceases to be a member in respect of those shares;
    (c) that person must surrender the certificate for the shares forfeited to the company for cancellation;
    (d) that person remains liable to the company for all sums payable by that person under the articles at the date of forfeiture in respect of those shares, including any interest (whether accrued before or after the date of forfeiture); and
    (e) the directors may waive payment of such sums wholly or in part or enforce payment without any allowance for the value of the shares at the time of forfeiture or for any consideration received on their disposal.

(4) At any time before the company disposes of a forfeited share, the directors may decide to cancel the forfeiture on payment of all calls and interest due in respect of it and on such other terms as they think fit.

Procedure following forfeiture

61.— (1) If a forfeited share is to be disposed of by being transferred, the company may receive the consideration for the transfer and the directors may authorise any person to execute the instrument of transfer.

(2) A statutory declaration by a director or the company secretary that the declarant is a director or the company secretary and that a share has been forfeited on a specified date—
    (a) is conclusive evidence of the facts stated in it as against all persons claiming to be entitled to the share, and
    (b) subject to compliance with any other formalities of transfer required by the articles or by law, constitutes a good title to the share.

(3) A person to whom a forfeited share is transferred is not bound to see to the application of the consideration (if any) nor is that person's title to the share affected by any irregularity in or invalidity of the process leading to the forfeiture or transfer of the share.

(4) If the company sells a forfeited share, the person who held it prior to its forfeiture is entitled to receive from the company the proceeds of such sale, net of any commission, and excluding any amount which—
    (a) was, or would have become, payable, and

(b) had not, when that share was forfeited, been paid by that person in respect of that share, but no interest is payable to such a person in respect of such proceeds and the company is not required to account for any money earned on them.

Surrender of shares

62.—(1) A member may surrender any share—
    (a) in respect of which the directors may issue a notice of intended forfeiture;
    (b) which the directors may forfeit; or
    (c) which has been forfeited.
(2) The directors may accept the surrender of any such share.
(3) The effect of surrender on a share is the same as the effect of forfeiture on that share.
(4) A share which has been surrendered may be dealt with in the same way as a share which has been forfeited.

TRANSFER AND TRANSMISSION OF SHARES

Transfers of certificated shares

63.—(1) Certificated shares may be transferred by means of an instrument of transfer in any usual form or any other form approved by the directors, which is executed by or on behalf of—
    (a) the transferor, and
    (b) (if any of the shares is partly paid) the transferee.
(2) No fee may be charged for registering any instrument of transfer or other document relating to or affecting the title to any share.
(3) The company may retain any instrument of transfer which is registered.
(4) The transferor remains the holder of a certificated share until the transferee's name is entered in the register of members as holder of it.
(5) The directors may refuse to register the transfer of a certificated share if—
    (a) the share is not fully paid;
    (b) the transfer is not lodged at the company's registered office or such other place as the directors have appointed;
    (c) the transfer is not accompanied by the certificate for the shares to which it relates, or such other evidence as the directors may reasonably require to show the transferor's right to make the transfer, or evidence of the right of someone other than the transferor to make the transfer on the transferor's behalf;
    (d) the transfer is in respect of more than one class of share; or
    (e) the transfer is in favour of more than four transferees.
(6) If the directors refuse to register the transfer of a share, the instrument of transfer must be returned to the transferee with the notice of refusal unless they suspect that the proposed transfer may be fraudulent.

Transfer of uncertificated shares

64. A transfer of an uncertificated share must not be registered if it is in favour of more than four transferees.

Transmission of shares

65.—(1) If title to a share passes to a transmittee, the company may only recognise the transmittee as having any title to that share.

(2) Nothing in these articles releases the estate of a deceased member from any liability in respect of a share solely or jointly held by that member.

Transmittees' rights

66.—(1) A transmittee who produces such evidence of entitlement to shares as the directors may properly require—
   (a) may, subject to the articles, choose either to become the holder of those shares or to have them transferred to another person, and
   (b) subject to the articles, and pending any transfer of the shares to another person, has the same rights as the holder had.

(2) But transmittees do not have the right to attend or vote at a general meeting in respect of shares to which they are entitled, by reason of the holder's death or bankruptcy or otherwise, unless they become the holders of those shares

Exercise of transmittees' rights

67.—(1) Transmittees who wish to become the holders of shares to which they have become entitled must notify the company in writing of that wish.

(2) If the share is a certificated share and a transmittee wishes to have it transferred to another person, the transmittee must execute an instrument of transfer in respect of it.

(3) If the share is an uncertificated share and the transmittee wishes to have it transferred to another person, the transmittee must—
   (a) procure that all appropriate instructions are given to effect the transfer, or
   (b) procure that the uncertificated share is changed into certificated form and then execute an instrument of transfer in respect of it.

(4) Any transfer made or executed under this article is to be treated as if it were made or executed by the person from whom the transmittee has derived rights in respect of the share, and as if the event which gave rise to the transmission had not occurred.

Transmittees bound by prior notices

68. If a notice is given to a member in respect of shares and a transmittee is entitled to those shares, the transmittee is bound by the notice if it was given to the member before the transmittee's name has been entered in the register of members.

CONSOLIDATION OF SHARES

Procedure for disposing of fractions of shares

69.—(1) This article applies where—
   (a) there has been a consolidation or division of shares, and
   (b) as a result, members are entitled to fractions of shares.

(2) The directors may—
   (a) sell the shares representing the fractions to any person including the company for the best price reasonably obtainable;

(b) in the case of a certificated share, authorise any person to execute an instrument of transfer of the shares to the purchaser or a person nominated by the purchaser; and

(c) distribute the net proceeds of sale in due proportion among the holders of the shares.

(3) Where any holder's entitlement to a portion of the proceeds of sale amounts to less than a minimum figure determined by the directors, that member's portion may be distributed to an organisation which is a charity for the purposes of the law of England and Wales, Scotland or Northern Ireland.

(4) The person to whom the shares are transferred is not obliged to ensure that any purchase money is received by the person entitled to the relevant fractions.

(5) The transferee's title to the shares is not affected by any irregularity in or invalidity of the process leading to their sale.

DISTRIBUTIONS

Procedure for declaring dividends

70.—(1) The company may by ordinary resolution declare dividends, and the directors may decide to pay interim dividends.

(2) A dividend must not be declared unless the directors have made a recommendation as to its amount. Such a dividend must not exceed the amount recommended by the directors.

(3) No dividend may be declared or paid unless it is in accordance with members' respective rights.

(4) Unless the members' resolution to declare or directors' decision to pay a dividend, or the terms on which shares are issued, specify otherwise, it must be paid by reference to each member's holding of shares on the date of the resolution or decision to declare or pay it.

(5) If the company's share capital is divided into different classes, no interim dividend may be paid on shares carrying deferred or non-preferred rights if, at the time of payment, any preferential dividend is in arrear.

(6) The directors may pay at intervals any dividend payable at a fixed rate if it appears to them that the profits available for distribution justify the payment.

(7) If the directors act in good faith, they do not incur any liability to the holders of shares conferring preferred rights for any loss they may suffer by the lawful payment of an interim dividend on shares with deferred or non-preferred rights.

Calculation of dividends

71.—(1) Except as otherwise provided by the articles or the rights attached to shares, all dividends must be—
(a) declared and paid according to the amounts paid up on the shares on which the dividend is paid, and
(b) apportioned and paid proportionately to the amounts paid up on the shares during any portion or portions of the period in respect of which the dividend is paid.

(2) If any share is issued on terms providing that it ranks for dividend as from a particular date, that share ranks for dividend accordingly.

(3) For the purposes of calculating dividends, no account is to be taken of any amount which has been paid up on a share in advance of the due date for payment of that amount.

Payment of dividends and other distributions
72.— (1) Where a dividend or other sum which is a distribution is payable in respect of a share, it must be paid by one or more of the following means—
   (a) transfer to a bank or building society account specified by the distribution recipient either in writing or as the directors may otherwise decide;
   (b) sending a cheque made payable to the distribution recipient by post to the distribution recipient at the distribution recipient's registered address (if the distribution recipient is a holder of the share), or (in any other case) to an address specified by the distribution recipient either in writing or as the directors may otherwise decide;
   (c) sending a cheque made payable to such person by post to such person at such address as the distribution recipient has specified either in writing or as the directors may otherwise decide; or
   (d) any other means of payment as the directors agree with the distribution recipient either in writing or by such other means as the directors decide.
(2) In the articles, "the distribution recipient" means, in respect of a share in respect of which a dividend or other sum is payable—
   (a) the holder of the share; or
   (b) if the share has two or more joint holders, whichever of them is named first in the register of members; or
   (c) if the holder is no longer entitled to the share by reason of death or bankruptcy, or otherwise by operation of law, the transmittee.

Deductions from distributions in respect of sums owed to the company
73.— (1) If—
   (a) a share is subject to the company's lien, and
   (b) the directors are entitled to issue a lien enforcement notice in respect of it,
   they may, instead of issuing a lien enforcement notice, deduct from any dividend or other sum payable in respect of the share any sum of money which is payable to the company in respect of that share to the extent that they are entitled to require payment under a lien enforcement notice.
(2) Money so deducted must be used to pay any of the sums payable in respect of that share.
(3) The company must notify the distribution recipient in writing of—
   (a) the fact and amount of any such deduction;
   (b) any non-payment of a dividend or other sum payable in respect of a share resulting from any such deduction; and
   (c) how the money deducted has been applied.

No interest on distributions
74. The company may not pay interest on any dividend or other sum payable in respect of a share unless otherwise provided by—
   (a) the terms on which the share was issued, or

(b) the provisions of another agreement between the holder of that share and the company.

Unclaimed distributions

75.—(1) All dividends or other sums which are—
  (a) payable in respect of shares, and
  (b) unclaimed after having been declared or become payable, may be invested or otherwise made use of by the directors for the benefit of the company until claimed.
 (2) The payment of any such dividend or other sum into a separate account does not make the company a trustee in respect of it.
 (3) If—
  (a) twelve years have passed from the date on which a dividend or other sum became due for payment, and
  (b) the distribution recipient has not claimed it, the distribution recipient is no longer entitled to that dividend or other sum and it ceases to remain owing by the company.

Non-cash distributions

76.—(1) Subject to the terms of issue of the share in question, the company may, by ordinary resolution on the recommendation of the directors, decide to pay all or part of a dividend or other distribution payable in respect of a share by transferring non-cash assets of equivalent value (including, without limitation, shares or other securities in any company).
 (2) If the shares in respect of which such a non-cash distribution is paid are uncertificated, any shares in the company which are issued as a non-cash distribution in respect of them must be uncertificated.
 (3) For the purposes of paying a non-cash distribution, the directors may make whatever arrangements they think fit, including, where any difficulty arises regarding the distribution—
  (a) fixing the value of any assets;
  (b) paying cash to any distribution recipient on the basis of that value in order to adjust the rights of recipients; and
  (c) vesting any assets in trustees.

Waiver of distributions

77. Distribution recipients may waive their entitlement to a dividend or other distribution payable in respect of a share by giving the company notice in writing to that effect, but if—
  (a) the share has more than one holder, or
  (b) more than one person is entitled to the share, whether by reason of the death or bankruptcy of one or more joint holders, or otherwise, the notice is not effective unless it is expressed to be given, and signed, by all the holders or persons otherwise entitled to the share.

CAPITALISATION OF PROFITS

Authority to capitalise and appropriation of capitalised sums
78.— (1) Subject to the articles, the directors may, if they are so authorised by an ordinary resolution—
    (a) decide to capitalise any profits of the company (whether or not they are available for distribution) which are not required for paying a preferential dividend, or any sum standing to the credit of the company's share premium account or capital redemption reserve; and
    (b) appropriate any sum which they so decide to capitalise (a "capitalised sum") to the persons who would have been entitled to it if it were distributed by way of dividend (the "persons entitled") and in the same proportions.
(2) Capitalised sums must be applied—
    (a) on behalf of the persons entitled, and
    (b) in the same proportions as a dividend would have been distributed to them.
(3) Any capitalised sum may be applied in paying up new shares of a nominal amount equal to the capitalised sum which are then allotted credited as fully paid to the persons entitled or as they may direct.
(4) A capitalised sum which was appropriated from profits available for distribution may be applied—
    (a) in or towards paying up any amounts unpaid on existing shares held by the persons entitled, or
    (b) in paying up new debentures of the company which are then allotted credited as fully paid to the persons entitled or as they may direct.
(5) Subject to the articles the directors may—
    (a) apply capitalised sums in accordance with paragraphs (3) and (4) partly in one way and partly in another;
    (b) make such arrangements as they think fit to deal with shares or debentures becoming distributable in fractions under this article (including the issuing of fractional certificates or the making of cash payments); and
    (c) authorise any person to enter into an agreement with the company on behalf of all the persons entitled which is binding on them in respect of the allotment of shares and debentures to them under this article.

PART 5
MISCELLANEOUS PROVISIONS
COMMUNICATIONS

Means of communication to be used
79.— (1) Subject to the articles, anything sent or supplied by or to the company under the articles may be sent or supplied in any way in which CA2006 provides for documents or information which are authorised or required by any provision of that Act to be sent or supplied by or to the company.
(2) Subject to the articles, any notice or document to be sent or supplied to a director in connection with the taking of decisions by directors may also be sent or supplied by the means by which that director has asked to be sent or supplied with such notices or documents for the time being.

(3) A director may agree with the company that notices or documents sent to that director in a particular way are to be deemed to have been received within a specified time of their being sent, and for the specified time to be less than 48 hours.

Failure to notify contact details

80.— (1) If—
- (a) the company sends two consecutive documents to a member over a period of at least 12 months, and
- (b) each of those documents is returned undelivered, or the company receives notification that it has not been delivered, that member ceases to be entitled to receive notices from the company.

(2) A member who has ceased to be entitled to receive notices from the company becomes entitled to receive such notices again by sending the company—
- (a) a new address to be recorded in the register of members, or
- (b) if the member has agreed that the company should use a means of communication other than sending things to such an address, the information that the company needs to use that means of communication effectively.

ADMINISTRATIVE ARRANGEMENTS

Company seals

81.— (1) Any common seal may only be used by the authority of the directors.

(2) The directors may decide by what means and in what form any common seal or securities seal is to be used.

(3) Unless otherwise decided by the directors, if the company has a common seal and it is affixed to a document, the document must also be signed by at least one authorised person in the presence of a witness who attests the signature.

(4) For the purposes of this article, an authorised person is—
- (a) any director of the company;
- (b) the company secretary; or
- (c) any person authorised by the directors for the purpose of signing documents to which the common seal is applied.

(5) If the company has an official seal for use abroad, it may only be affixed to a document if its use on that document, or documents of a class to which it belongs, has been authorised by a decision of the directors.

(6) If the company has a securities seal, it may only be affixed to securities by the company secretary or a person authorised to apply it to securities by the company secretary.

(7) For the purposes of the articles, references to the securities seal being affixed to any document include the reproduction of the image of that seal on or in a document by any mechanical or electronic means which has been approved by the directors in relation to that document or documents of a class to which it belongs.

Destruction of documents

82.—(1) The company is entitled to destroy—
  (a) all instruments of transfer of shares which have been registered, and all other documents on the basis of which any entries are made in the register of members, from six years after the date of registration;
  (b) all dividend mandates, variations or cancellations of dividend mandates, and notifications of change of address, from two years after they have been recorded;
  (c) all share certificates which have been cancelled from one year after the date of the cancellation;
  (d) all paid dividend warrants and cheques from one year after the date of actual payment; and
  (e) all proxy notices from one year after the end of the meeting to which the proxy notice relates.

(2) If the company destroys a document in good faith, in accordance with the articles, and without notice of any claim to which that document may be relevant, it is conclusively presumed in favour of the company that—
  (a) entries in the register purporting to have been made on the basis of an instrument of transfer or other document so destroyed were duly and properly made;
  (b) any instrument of transfer so destroyed was a valid and effective instrument duly and properly registered;
  (c) any share certificate so destroyed was a valid and effective certificate duly and properly cancelled; and
  (d) any other document so destroyed was a valid and effective document in accordance with its recorded particulars in the books or records of the company.

(3) This article does not impose on the company any liability which it would not otherwise have if it destroys any document before the time at which this article permits it to do so.

(4) In this article, references to the destruction of any document include a reference to its being disposed of in any manner.

No right to inspect accounts and other records

83. Except as provided by law or authorised by the directors or an ordinary resolution of the company, no person is entitled to inspect any of the company's accounting or other records or documents merely by virtue of being a member.

Provision for employees on cessation of business

84. The directors may decide to make provision for the benefit of persons employed or formerly employed by the company or any of its subsidiaries (other than a director or former director or shadow director) in connection with the cessation or transfer to any person of the whole or part of the undertaking of the company or that subsidiary.

DIRECTORS' INDEMNITY AND INSURANCE

Indemnity

85.—(1) Subject to paragraph (2), a relevant director of the company or an associated company may be indemnified out of the company's assets against—

(a) any liability incurred by that director in connection with any negligence, default, breach of duty or breach of trust in relation to the company or an associated company,
(b) any liability incurred by that director in connection with the activities of the company or an associated company in its capacity as a trustee of an occupational pension scheme (as defined in section 235(6) of CA2006),
(c) any other liability incurred by that director as an officer of the company or an associated company.

(2) This article does not authorise any indemnity which would be prohibited or rendered void by any provision of the Companies Acts or by any other provision of law.

(3) In this article—
(a) companies are associated if one is a subsidiary of the other or both are subsidiaries of the same body corporate, and
(b) a "relevant director" means any director or former director of the company or an associated company.

Insurance

86.— (1) The directors may decide to purchase and maintain insurance, at the expense of the company, for the benefit of any relevant director in respect of any relevant loss.

(2) In this article—
(a) a "relevant director" means any director or former director of the company or an associated company,
(b) a "relevant loss" means any loss or liability which has been or may be incurred by a relevant director in connection with that director's duties or powers in relation to the company, any associated company or any pension fund or employees' share scheme of the company or associated company, and
(c) companies are associated if one is a subsidiary of the other or both are subsidiaries of the same body corporate.

Index

Aberdeen Rail Co v Blaikie Brothers
  [1843–60] 7.3.7.4
Accounts
  legislation supplementary to CA2006
    1.2.2.4
  provisions of CA2006 1.2.2.3
Adams v Cape Industries plc [1990]
  3.4.1.5, 3.4.1.6, 3.4.2
Agent's authority to bind the company
  3.7.9
Allen v Gold Reefs of West Africa, Ltd
  [1900] 1.2.3.3, 4.4.1.2
Annual return, provisions of CA2006
  1.2.2.3
Application to register a company *see*
  Companies House Form IN01
Armagas Ltd v Mundogas SA [1986]
  3.7.9.9, 3.7.9.11
Articles of association 2.2.5, 4.1
  altering articles 1.2.3.3
  amending the articles 4.4
    filing requirements 4.4.2
    the substantive law 4.4.1
  CA2006 provisions 1.2.2.3, 2.2.5, 4.2.1,
    4.3.1 to 4.3.4
  Companies House Form IN01, 2.2.7.22
    to 2.2.7.26
  contents of articles 4.3
  decision-making by shareholders 4.3.6.1
    to 4.3.6.3
  enforcing the articles 4.5
    direct enforcement 4.5.1, 4.5.2
    directors' rights 4.5.2.1
    indirect enforcement 4.5.3
    shareholders' rights 4.5.2.2 to 4.5.2.7
  entrenched provisions 2.2.7.24 to
    2.2.7.26

legal framework 4.2
model articles 1.2.2.4, 1.2.4.5, 2.2.5,
  4.2.2, 4.3.5, 4.3.6
restricted company articles 2.2.7.24 to
  2.2.7.26
sources of guidance on 1.2.4
Ashbury Railway Carriage and Iron
  Company (Ltd) v Riche [1875] 3.6.3
Audit, provisions of CA2006 1.2.2.3
Auditors 2.4.1.3
Authority, types of 3.7.9
Automatic Self-Cleaning Filter Syndicate
  Company, Ltd v Cuninghame
  [1906] 8.2.4
Aveling Barford Ltd v Perion Ltd [1989]
  9.3.4.3

Beckett Investment Management Group
  Ltd v Hall [2007] 3.4.2.7
Bhullar v Bhullar [2003] 7.3.7.8
Birch v Cropper, Re The Bridgewater
  Navigation Co Ltd [1889] 9.2.5.3
Board decisions 6.1.2 to 6.1.4
  resolutions 6.2.1
Board meetings 6.1.2 to 6.1.4, 6.4
  initial board meeting 2.4.1
  minutes 6.4.2
  procedure 6.4.1
Boardman v Phipps [1967] 7.3.7.5,
  7.3.7.9
Bonham-Carter v Situ Ventures Ltd [2012]
  5.4.2.2, 8.3.6.4, 8.3.8.5
Braymist Ltd v Wise Finance Co Ltd [2002]
  3.8.1.3
British and American Trustee and Finance
  Corporation, Ltd v Couper [1894]
  9.3.6.5

INDEX

Browne v La Trinidad [1887] 4.3.5.13
Brumder v Motornet Service and Repairs Ltd [2013] 7.3.6.5
Bushell v Faith [1970] 1.2.3.3, 5.4.2.4
Business name, provisions of CA2006 1.2.2.3, 2.2.7.1 to 2.2.7.21
Byng v London Life Association Ltd [1990] 4.3.6.3

CA1985 (Companies Act 1985) 1.2.2.1, 5.6.3.6, 8.3.4.3, 8.3.5.5
　transition to CA2006 1.2.2.5
CA2006 (Companies Act 2006) 1.2.2
　definition of terms used in the Act 1.2.2.3
　main areas covered by 1.2.2.3
　progress to Royal Assent 1.2.2.2
　scope of 1.2.2.3
　secondary legislation 1.2.2.4
　size of 1.2.2.1, 1.2.2.3
　sources of guidance on 1.2.2.3
　staggered implementation 1.2.2.5
　transition from CA1985 1.2.2.5
　see also specific areas of provisions
Capital
　meanings of 9.2.7
　reduction by a company 9.3.1, 9.3.3.5, 9.3.6
Capital maintenance doctrine 9.2.7, 9.3.3, 9.3.5.2, 9.3.5.8
Case law 1.2.3
Certificate of incorporation 2.3
Chandler v Cape plc [2012] 3.4.2.19 to 3.4.2.22
Charges, provisions of CA2006 1.2.2.3
Charterbridge Corporation Ltd v Lloyds Bank Ltd [1970] 7.3.4.7
Chief executive officer 5.6.5.1
Citico Banking Corporation NV v Pusser's Ltd [2007] 4.4.1.2
Colin Gwyer & Associates Ltd v London Wharf (Limehouse) Ltd [2002] 7.3.4.21
Commercial director 5.6.5.1
Common law, pre-incorporation contracts 3.8.2
Communications by/to company, provisions of CA2006 1.2.2.3

Companies (Disclosure of Address) Regulations 2009 2.7.31
Companies (Model Articles) Regulations 2008 1.2.2.4, 1.2.4.5, 2.2.5.2
Companies (Model Articles) Regulations 2009 4.2.2
Companies (Registration) Regulations 2008 2.2.4.3
Companies (Shares and Share Capital) Order 2009 2.2.7.36
Companies Act 1985 *see* CA1985
Companies Act 2006 *see* CA2006
Companies House
　Form IN01 (Application to register a company) 2.2.6, 2.2.7
　　ancillary matters 2.2.7.41
　　articles of association 2.2.5.3, 2.2.7.22 to 2.2.7.26
　　choice of the company's name 2.2.7.1 to 2.2.7.21
　　corporate directors 2.2.7.33, 2.2.7.34
　　corporate secretaries 2.2.7.27, 2.2.7.28
　　details of share capital 2.2.7.35
　　directors' addresses 2.2.7.29 to 2.2.7.32
　　initial shareholdings 2.2.7.39
　　prescribed particulars of rights attached to shares 2.2.7.36 to 2.2.7.38
　　statement of compliance 2.2.7.40
　Web Incorporation Service 2.2.2, 2.2.7.37, 2.2.7.38
　website
　　prescribed particulars section of Form IN01 2.2.7.37
　　WebCHeck service 2.2.7.14, 2.2.7.21
Company
　as a legal entity 1.3.5.2
　essential features of 1.3.5.2
　governance structure 1.3.5.2
　limited liability 1.3.5.2, 1.3.5.3, 1.3.5.4
Company as a separate entity 3.1
　agent's authority to bind the company 3.7.9
　entering into contracts 3.7
　fraudulent trading 3.5.1, 3.5.3, 3.5.4

legal basis 3.2.1
lifting the corporate veil 3.4
limits on 3.4
objects clauses and a company's capacity 3.6
provisions of CA2006 3.2.1.2
practical implications 3.2.2
pre-incorporation contracts 3.8
shareholders' limited liability 3.3
wrongful trading 3.5.1, 3.5.2, 3.5.4
Company Directors Disqualification Act 1986 1.2.2.6, 3.5.2.3, 5.3.2, 5.6.4.2, 5.6.4.4
Company failure *see* Failure of a company
Company formation *see* Forming a company
Company law 1.1
　achieving the aim of the regime 1.3.5
　aim of the regime 1.3.4
　articles of association 1.2.4
　balancing the interests of parties involved 1.3
　case law 1.2.3
　getting to grips with 1.3.1 to 1.3.3
　impact of shareholders' limited liability 3.3.3
　making sense of 1.3.6
　parties affected by 1.3.5.5
　reasons for the complex regime 1.3.6
　sources of 1.2
　transparency measures 3.3.3.5, 3.3.3.6
　see also CA2006; Company Directors Disqualification Act 1986; Insolvency Act 1986 *and other specific legislation*
Company Law Review Steering Group 2.2.7.21
Company limited by guarantee, definition 3.3.1.6
Company limited by shares, definition 3.3.1.5, 3.3.1.6
Company, Limited Liability Partnership and Business (Names and Trading Disclosures) Regulations 2015 1.2.2.4, 2.2.7.2 to 2.2.7.5, 2.2.7.13, 2.2.7.14
Company, Limited Liability Partnership and Business Names (Sensitive Words and Expressions) Regulations 2014 2.2.7.2, 2.2.7.5
Company name, provisions of CA2006 1.2.2.3, 2.2.7.1 to 2.2.7.21
Company Names Adjudicator Rules 2008 2.2.7.18
Company Names Tribunal 2.2.7.18
Company secretaries, provisions of CA2006 1.2.2.3 *see also* Corporate secretaries
Contracts
　agent's authority to bind the company 3.7.9
　company as a separate entity 3.7
　practical implications of the law 3.7.10
　pre-incorporation contracts 3.8
　residual relevance of the common law 3.8.2
Contracts (Rights of Third Parties) Act 1999 4.5.3.3
Cook v Deeks [1916] 7.3.7.8, 7.4.3.6
Corporate Governance Code (UK) 5.6.6.2
Corporate secretaries, Companies House Form IN01, 2.2.7.27, 2.2.7.28 *see also* Company secretaries
Corporate veil, lifting *see* Lifting the corporate veil
Cotronic (UK) Ltd v Dezonie [1991] 3.8.2.1, 3.8.2.2
Creditors
　and the capital maintenance doctrine 9.3.3, 9.3.5.2, 9.3.5.8
　effects of limited liability 1.3.5.4
　impacts of company failure 3.3
　phoenix trading problem 2.2.7.21
　position when a company fails 3.5.1, 3.5.2
　risk of company failure 3.3.3
　transparency measures 3.3.3.5, 3.3.3.6
Criterion Properties plc v Stratford UK Properties LLC [2004] 3.7.9.11
Cumbrian Newspapers Group Ltd v Cumberland & Westmoreland Herald Newspaper & Printing Co Ltd [1987] 9.2.5.9

Derivative claims 8.4.8
DHN Food Distributors Ltd v Tower

INDEX

Hamlets London Borough Council [1976] 3.4.2.6
Directive 2009/101/EC 2.2.7.28, 2.2.7.34
Directors
  appointment 5.4.1
  CA2006 provisions 1.2.2.3
  chief executive officer 5.6.5.1
  commercial director 5.6.5.1
  definition of director 7.3.1.2
  disclosure of details (Form IN01) 2.2.7.33, 2.2.7.34
  de facto directors 3.5.2.3, 5.6.1, 5.6.3
  de jure directors 3.5.2.3, 5.6.1, 5.6.2
  disclosure of addresses 2.2.7.29 to 2.2.7.32
  executive directors 5.6.1, 5.6.5
  finance director 5.6.5.1
  general authority 5.5.3 to 5.5.7
  initial board meeting 2.4.1
  law governing 5.1
  managing director 5.6.5
  minimum number 5.2
  non-executive directors 5.6.1, 5.6.6
  power to allot new shares 9.2.4
  removal of 5.4.2
  remuneration 9.3.1
  restrictions on who may be a director 5.3
  role and responsibilities 1.3.5.2, 2.4.1, 5.5 *see also* Directors' duties
  shadow directors 3.5.2.3, 5.6.1, 5.6.4
  terminology relating to 5.6
Directors' decision-making 6.1
  board meetings 6.1.2 to 6.1.4, 6.4
  directors' written resolutions 6.3.3 to 6.3.5, 6.5
  framework 6.3
  full board decisions 6.1.2 to 6.1.4
  impact of directors' duties on 6.6
  individual decisions 6.1.1, 6.1.2
  minutes of board meetings 6.4.2
  model articles approach 6.3
  recording of decisions taken 6.1.1, 6.1.3, 6.4.2
  resolutions 6.2.1
  terminology 6.2
Directors' duties
  background to statutory duties 7.1.1, 7.1.2, 7.2

  common law considerations 7.1.2, 7.2
  consequences of breaching the duties 1.2.3.3, 7.3.1.3 to 7.3.1.6, 7.4
  definition of director 7.3.1.2
  description of the duties 7.3
  excusing a breach of duties 7.3.1.4, 7.4.3
  impact on directors' decision-making 6.6
  interrelationship of duties 7.3.1.5, 7.3.1.6
  not to accept benefits from third parties 7.3.8
  pursuing a director for breach of duty 7.3.1.4, 7.4.2
  to act in accordance with the company's constitution 7.3.2
  to avoid conflicts of interest 7.3.7
  to declare personal interests in transactions with the company 7.3.9
  to exercise independent judgment 7.3.5
  to exercise powers only for the purposes for which they are conferred 7.3.3
  to exercise reasonable care, skill and diligence 7.3.6
  to promote the success of the company 7.3.4
  when a company is failing 3.5.1.4 to 3.5.1.7, 3.5.2
  planned reform of the law 3.5.4
Directors' written resolutions 6.3.3 to 6.3.5, 6.5
Disguised distributions 9.3.4.3
Distributions 9.3.4
Dividends 1.3.5.2, 2.2.7.35, 2.2.7.37, 9.3.1, 9.3.4
Duomatic principle (unanimous consent rule) 1.2.3.3, 8.3.8

Earp v Stevenson, Re Kudos Business Solutions (in liquidation) [2011] 3.5.2.3
Eclairs Group Ltd v JKX Oil & Gas plc [2013] 6.6.5
Eclairs Group Ltd v JKZ Oil & Gas plc [2014] 7.3.3.3, 7.3.3.4, 7.3.3.7

Eley v The Positive Government Security Life Assurance Company, Ltd [1875–76] 4.5.2.1
Entrenched provisions 2.2.7.24 to 2.2.7.26
Execution of documents 1.2.2.3
Executive directors 5.6.1, 5.6.5
Extrasure Travel Insurances Ltd v Scattergood [2003] 7.3.3.2

Failure of a company
  duties of directors 3.5.1.4 to 3.5.1.7, 3.5.2
  impacts on creditors 3.3
  impacts on shareholders 3.3
  Insolvency Act 1986 2.2.7.2, 2.2.7.21
  position of creditors 3.5.1, 3.5.2
  risk to creditors 3.3.3
Finance director 5.6.5.1
First Company Law Directive (68/151/ EEC) 2.2.7.28, 2.2.7.34
Forming a company 2.1
  articles of association 2.2.5
  CA2006 provisions 1.2.2.3
  certificate of incorporation 2.3
  Companies House Form IN01 (Application to register a company) 2.2.5.3, 2.2.6, 2.2.7
  Companies House website 2.2.2
  costs involved 2.2.1, 2.2.2
  documents to be submitted 2.2.3
  electronic submission 2.2.2
  first board meeting 2.4.1
  hard copy submission 2.2.2
  incorporation 2.3
  incorporation process 2.2
  memorandum of association 2.2.4
  post incorporation 2.4
  stages of 2.1.1
Foss v Harbottle [1843] 8.4.8.1 to 8.4.8.6
Fraudulent trading 3.5.1, 3.5.3
  planned reform of the law 3.5.4
Freeman & Lockyer v Buckhurst Park Properties (Mangal) Ltd [1964] 3.7.9.8, 3.7.9.11, 3.7.9.12

Gamlestaden Fastigheter AB v Baltic Partners Ltd [2007] 8.4.7.4

Gazette website 9.3.5.8, 9.3.5.12
Gencor ACP Ltd v Dalby [2000] 3.4.2.10
General filing requirement, provisions of CA2006 1.2.2.3
General meetings of shareholders 8.3.4.2, 8.3.7
Geneva Conventions Act 1957
Gilford Motor Company Ltd v Horne [1933] 3.4.2.9, 3.4.2.11
Governance structure of a company 1.3.5.2
Gross v Rackind, Re City Branch Group Ltd [2004] 3.4.2.5

Hawkes v Cuddy [2009] 7.3.5.3
Hely-Hutchinson v Brayhead Ltd (1968) 3.7.9.4 to 3.7.9.6, 3.7.9.11
Hickman v Kent or Romney March Sheep-Breeders' Association [1915] 4.5.2.4, 4.5.2.5
Hilder v Dexter [1902] 9.2.7.4
Holland v Commissioners for Her Majesty's Revenue and Customs [2010] 5.6.3.1, 5.6.3.2, 9.3.4.3
Hopkins v TL Dallas Group Ltd [2005] 3.7.9.11
Howard Smith Ltd v Ampol Petroleum Ltd [1974] 7.3.3.2, 7.3.3.7

Iesini v Westrip Holdings Ltd [2009] 8.4.8.8
In Plus Group Ltd v Pyke [2002] 7.3.7.8
Incorporation 2.3
  post-incorporation procedures 2.4
  process leading to 2.2
Initial shareholdings 2.2.7.39
Insolvency Act 1986 1.2.2.6
  fraudulent trading 3.5.1.6, 3.5.3
  minority shareholder protection 8.4.6.2
  payment of creditors 9.3.3.3
  shadow directors 5.6.4.2, 5.6.4.5
  shareholders' claim on assets 3.3.2.3
  shareholders' limited liability 3.3.1.4 to 3.3.1.7, 4.3.5.3
  use of the name of a failed company 2.2.7.2, 2.2.7.21

wrongful trading 3.3.3.4, 3.5.1.6, 3.5.2, 5.6.3.7
Intellectual Property Office website 2.2.7.21
Interpretation Act 1978 3.2.1.3
Investors, role in the company 1.3.5
It's a Wrap (UK) Ltd (in liquidation) v Gula [2006] 9.3.4.3

Killen v Horseworld Ltd [2012] 7.3.7.13
Kleanthous v Paphitis [2011] 7.4.2.2, 8.4.8.11

Large and Medium-sized Companies and Groups (Accounts and Reports) Regulations 2008 1.2.2.4
Law of Property Act 1925 3.2.1.3
Legal status of a company 1.3.5.2
Lexi Holdings plc (in administration) v Luqman [2009] 5.6.6.3, 7.3.6.5
Lifting the corporate veil
  existence of a trust relationship 3.4.2.15 to 3.4.2.17
  existence of an agency relationship 3.4.2.12 to 3.4.2.14
  grounds for lifting the veil 3.4.2
  interpretation of a contract 3.4.2.7
  interpretation of a statute 3.4.2.5, 3.4.2.6
  limits on the company's separate identity 3.4
  practical implications of the law for shareholders 3.4.3
  prevention of the misuse of a company in connection with wrongdoing 3.4.2.8 to 3.4.2.11
  shareholder responsibility for employees' welfare 3.4.2.18 to 3.4.2.22
Limited company, definition 3.3.1.6
Limited liability of shareholders 3.3
  scope of the limitation 3.3.2
Limited liability of the company 1.3.5.2, 1.3.5.3, 1.3.5.4
Liquidator of West Mercia Safetywear Ltd v Dodd [1988] 7.4.3.6
LNOC Ltd v Watford Association Football Club Ltd [2013] 3.7.8

Loch v John Blackwood, Ltd [1924] 8.4.6.2
London and Mashonaland Exploration Co Ltd v New Mashonaland Exploration Co Ltd [1891] 7.3.7.8

Macaura v Northern Assurance Company Ltd [1925] 3.2.2.3
MacDougall v Gardiner [1875] 4.5.2.7
Madoff Securities International Ltd v Raven [2011] 7.4.3.6
Managing director 5.6.5
McKillen v Misland (Cyprus) Investments Ltd, Re Coroin Ltd [2012] 7.3.4.4
Medicines Act 1968 2.2.7.8
Memorandum of association 2.2.4
  objects clause 3.6
Mental Health (Discrimination) Act 2013 4.3.5.21
Ministers of the Crown Act 1975 5.6.4.1
Minority shareholder protection 8.4

Name choice/change of, provisions of CA2006 1.2.2.3, 2.2.7.1 to 2.2.7.21
Non-executive directors 5.6.1, 5.6.6

O'Neill v Phillips [1999] 1.2.3.2, 4.5.3.4, 8.4.7.4
Objects clauses
  and a company's capacity 3.6
  current law 3.6.6
  practical implications of the law 3.6.7
Ordinary resolutions 6.2.1

Panorama Developments (Guildford) Ltd v Fidelis Furnishing Fabrics Ltd [1971] 3.7.9.11
Parker v McKenna [1874] 7.3.7.10
Parry v Bartlett [2011] 7.3.4.17, 8.4.8.10
Pender v Lushington [1877] 4.5.2.7
Phoenix trading problem 2.2.7.21
Phonogram Ltd v Lane [1982] 1.2.3.2, 3.8.2.2
Piercing the corporate veil 3.4.1.2
Precision Dippings Ltd v Precision Dippings Marketing Ltd [1986] 9.3.4.3
Pre-incorporation contracts 3.8
Prest v Petrodel Resources Ltd [2013]

3.2.1, 3.4.1.2, 3.4.1.5, 3.4.1.6, 3.4.2, 7.4.3.6
Profinance Trust SA v Gladstone [2011] 8.4.7.4
Progress Property Company Ltd v Moorgarth Group Ltd [2010] 9.3.4.3
Pulbrook v Richmond Consolidated Mining Company [1878] 4.5.2.5
Punt v Symons & Co, Ltd [1903] 7.3.3.6

Quin & Axtens, Ltd v Salmon [1909] 4.5.2.5

R (on the Application of People and Planet) v HM Treasury [2009] 7.3.4.11
Re a Company (No. 002567 of 1982) [1983] 8.4.6.2
Re a Company (No. 00370 of 1987), ex parte Glossop [1988] 9.3.4.3
Re Barings plc (No 5) [1999] 7.3.6.5
Re Barings plc (No 5) [2000] 7.3.6.5
Re City Branch Group Ltd [2004] 8.4.7.4
Re Coroin Ltd [2013] 8.4.7.4
Re Duomatic Ltd [1969] 1.2.3.3, 8.3.8.3, 8.3.8.4
Re Exchange Banking Co, Flitcroft's Case [1882] 9.3.3.4, 9.3.4.3
Re Halt Garage (1964) Ltd [1982] 9.3.4.3
Re Hill & Tyler Ltd (in administration) [2004] 9.2.8.5
Re HLC Environmental Projects Ltd (in liquidation) [2013] 7.3.4.7
Re Homer District Consolidated Gold Mines, ex parte Smith [1888] 4.3.5.13
Re Hydrodam (Corby) Ltd [1994] 3.5.2.3, 5.6.3.7
Re Kitson & Co Ltd [1946] 8.4.6.2
Re Kudos Business Solutions Ltd (in liquidation) [2011] 7.3.6.5
Re Lo-Line Electric Motors Ltd [1988] 5.6.3.6
Re McCarthy Surfacing Ltd [2008] 9.3.4.3
Re New British Iron Company, ex parte Beckwith [1898] 4.5.3.3
Re Oxted Motor Co, Ltd [1921] 8.3.8.4
Re Patrick and Lyon Ltd [1933] 3.5.3.3

Re Produce Marketing Consortium Ltd [1989] 3.5.2.3, 7.3.6.5
Re Smith and Fawcett, Ltd [1942] 7.3.3.2
Re Tobian Properties Ltd [2012] 8.4.7.1, 8.4.7.4
Re Uniq plc [2011] 9.2.8.3
Re Westmid Packing Services Ltd [1998] 7.3.6.5
Re Wragg, Ltd [1897] 9.2.6.5
Re Yenidje Tobacco Co, Ltd [1916] 8.4.6.2
Reckitt & Colman Products Ltd v Borden Inc [1990] 2.2.7.21
Redeemable shares 9.3.1, 9.3.5.2 to 9.3.5.8
Regal (Hastings) Ltd v Gulliver [1967] 7.4.3.6
Regentcrest plc (in liquidation) v Cohen [2001] 7.3.4.4, 7.3.4.5
Register of members 1.2.2.3
Registered office 1.2.2.3
Resolutions 6.2.1
  by shareholders 8.3.4, 8.3.5
  directors' written resolutions 6.3.3 to 6.3.5, 6.5
  extraordinary resolutions 8.3.4.3
  ordinary resolutions 8.3.4.1, 8.3.4.2
  shareholders' written resolutions 8.3.4.2, 8.3.5
  special resolutions 8.3.4.1, 8.3.4.2
Risk of company failure, limiting liability 3.3.3
Roberts v Frohlich [2011] 3.5.2.3
Royal British Bank v Turquand [1856] 3.7.9.11
Rule in Foss v Harbottle [1843] 8.4.8.1 to 8.4.8.6
Runciman v Walter Runciman plc [1992] 6.5.3

Salmon v Quin & Axtens, Ltd [1909] 4.5.2.5
Saloman v A Saloman & Co Ltd [1897] 3.3.3.6, 3.4.2.3, 3.2.1.4
Schofield v Schofield [2011] 8.3.8.4, 8.3.8.5
Scottish Co-operative Wholesale Society Ltd v Meyer [1959] 7.3.5.3
Scottish Insurance Corporation, Ltd v

Wilsons & Clyde Coal Company Ltd [1949] 9.3.6.5
Secretary of State for Trade and Industry v Deverell [2001] 3.5.2.3, 5.6.4.4
Service of documents on company, directors etc., provisions of CA2006 1.2.2.3
Share capital 2.2.7.35
Share certificates 2.4.1.3
Share premium 2.2.7.35
Shareholders, 8.1
　authorisation to issue further shares 9.2.4.5
　capital reduction by a company 9.3.1, 9.3.3.5, 9.3.6
　decision-making by 1.2.2.3, 1.2.3.3, 6.2.1, 8.3
　decisions by sole shareholders 8.3.6
　derivative claims 8.4.8
　directors' remuneration 9.3.1
　disguised distributions 9.3.4.3
　distributions 9.3.4
　dividends 1.3.5.2, 2.2.7.35, 2.2.7.37, 9.3.1, 9.3.4
　extraordinary resolutions 8.3.4.3
　general meetings 8.3.4.2, 8.3.7
　impacts of company failure 3.3
　implications of rules on lifting the corporate veil 3.4.3
　minority shareholder protection 8.4
　ordinary resolutions 6.2.1, 8.3.4.1, 8.3.4.2
　powers of 8.2.3 to 8.2.6
　resolutions 1.2.2.3, 1.2.3.3, 6.2.1, 8.3.4, 8.3.5
　role of 1.3.5, 8.2
　special resolutions 1.2.3.3, 6.2.1, 8.3.4.1, 8.3.4.2
　statutory pre-emption right 9.2.4.6 to 9.2.4.9
　supervisory function 8.2.3, 8.2.4
　unanimous consent rule (Duomatic principle) 1.2.3.3, 8.3.8
　unfair prejudice remedy 1.2.2.3, 1.2.3.2, 8.4.7
　voting rights 1.2.3.3
　ways of extracting money from a company 9.3
　written resolutions 8.3.4.2, 8.3.5
Shareholders' limited liability
　impact on the company law regime 3.3.3
　legal basis 3.3.1
　scope of the limitation 3.3.2
Shares 1.3.5.2, 1.3.5.3, 9.1
　acquisition by a company of its own shares 9.3.1, 9.3.5
　allotment 'at par' 9.2.7.4
　allotting shares 9.2.4
　buy-backs 9.3.1, 9.3.5.2 to 9.3.5.6, 9.3.5.9 to 9.3.5.12
　CA2006 provisions 1.2.2.3, 9.1.1
　capital maintenance doctrine 9.2.7, 9.3.3, 9.3.5.2, 9.3.5.8
　capital reduction by a company 9.3.1, 9.3.3.5, 9.3.6
　denomination 2.2.7.35
　disguised distributions 9.3.4.3
　distributions 9.3.4
　dividends 1.3.5.2, 2.2.7.35, 2.2.7.37, 9.3.1, 9.3.4
　financial assistance prohibition 9.2.8
　initial shareholdings 2.2.7.39
　meanings of 'capital' 9.2.7
　nominal value (par value) 2.2.7.35, 9.2.7.4
　non-cash consideration 9.2.6
　ordinary shares 9.2.5.7 to 9.2.5.9
　par value (nominal value) 2.2.7.35, 9.2.7.4
　partly paid 2.2.7.35, 3.3.2.2, 9.2.7.4
　payment for 9.2.6
　preference shares 9.2.5.7 to 9.2.5.9
　premium 9.2.7.4
　prescribed particulars of rights attached to 2.2.7.36 to 2.2.7.38
　putting money into a company 9.2
　redeemable shares 9.3.1, 9.3.5.2 to 9.3.5.8
　rights attached to 2.2.7.35, 9.2.5
　shareholder authorisation to issue further shares 9.2.4.5
　statutory pre-emption right of shareholders 9.2.4.6 to 9.2.4.9
　taking money out of a company 9.3

Shuttleworth v Cox Brothers and Company (Maidenhead), Ltd [1927] 4.4.1.2
Small Business, Enterprise and Employment Act 1986 3.5.2.3
Small Business, Enterprise and Employment Act 2015 3.5.4.2 to 3.5.4.4, 5.3.2, 5.6.4.1, 5.6.4.2, 5.6.4.6, 7.3.1.2
Small Companies and Groups (Accounts and Directors' Report) Regulations 2008 1.2.2.4
Smith v Butler [2012] 3.7.9.11, 4.3.5.9, 5.6.5.6
Smithton Ltd v Naggar [2014] 5.6.3.1, 5.6.3.3
Special resolutions 6.2.1
Striking off, provisions of CA2006 1.2.2.3

Thanakharn Kasikorn Thai Chamkat (Mahachon) v Akai Holdings Ltd (in liquidation) [2010] 3.7.9.11
The Gramophone and Typewriter Ltd v Stanley [1908] 3.4.2.13

Thompson v The Renwick Group plc [2014] 3.4.2.21
Tort of passing off 2.2.7.2, 2.2.7.21
Trade Marks Act 1994 2.2.7.2, 2.2.7.21
Trade marks database, Intellectual Property Office website 2.2.7.21
Trading disclosure rules, legislation supplementary to CA2006 1.2.2.4
Transparency measures, protection for creditors 3.3.3.5, 3.3.3.6
Trevor v Whitworth [1887] 9.3.3.4

UK Corporate Governance Code 5.6.6.2
Unanimous consent rule (Duomatic principle) 1.2.3.3, 8.3.8
Unfair prejudice remedy 1.2.2.3, 1.2.3.2, 8.4.7

Weavering Capital (UK) Ltd (in liquidation) v Dabhia [2012] 7.3.6.5
White v Bristol Aeroplane Co Ltd [1953] 9.2.5.9
Wrongful trading 3.5.1, 3.5.2
  planned reform of the law 3.5.4